The Revels Plays
COMPANION
LIBRARY

E. A. J. HONIGMANN former editor
J. R. MULRYNE, ROBERT SMALLWOOD, PETER CORBIN, SUSAN BROCK and
SUSAN CERASANO general editors

For over forty years *The Revels Plays* have offered the most authoritative editions of
Elizabethan and Jacobean plays by authors other than Shakespeare. The *Companion
Library* provides a fuller background to the main series by publishing important
dramatic and non-dramatic material that will be essential for the serious student of
the period.

Drama of the English Republic, 1649–60   CLARE
'Art made tongue-tied by authority'   CLARE
Three Jacobean witchcraft plays   eds CORBIN, SEDGE
Beyond The Spanish Tragedy: *A study of the works of Thomas Kyd*   ERNE
John Ford's political theatre   HOPKINS
The works of Richard Edwards   KING
*Marlowe and the popular tradition: Innovation in the English drama
before 1595*   LUNNEY
Banquets set forth: Banqueting in English Renaissance drama   MEADS
Thomas Heywood: Three marriage plays   ed. MERCHANT
Three Renaissance travel plays   ed. PARR
John Lyly   PINCOMBE
A textual companion to Doctor Faustus   RASMUSSEN
Documents of the Rose Playhouse   RUTTER
John Lyly: Euphues: The Anatomy of Wit *and* Euphues and His England
ed. SCRAGG
Richard Brome: Place and politics on the Caroline stage   STEGGLE

The Stukeley Plays

MANCHESTER
1824

Manchester University Press

for Andrew Gurr

THE REVELS PLAYS COMPANION LIBRARY

The Stukeley Plays

The Battle of Alcazar by George Peele

The Famous History of the Life and Death of Captain Thomas Stukeley

edited by Charles Edelman

Manchester University Press

Manchester and New York

distributed exclusively in the USA by Palgrave

The right of Charles Edelman to be identified as the author of this work has been
asserted by him in accordance with the Copyright, Designs and Patents Act 1988.

Published by Manchester University Press
Oxford Road, Manchester M13 9NR, UK
and Room 400, 175 Fifth Avenue, New York, NY 10010, USA
www.manchesteruniversitypress.co.uk

Distributed exclusively in the USA by
Palgrave, 175 Fifth Avenue, New York, NY 10010, USA

Distributed exclusively in Canada by
UBC Press, University of British Columbia, 2029 West Mall, Vancouver, BC,
Canada V6T 1Z2

British Library Cataloguing-in-Publication Data
A catalogue record for this book is available from the British Library

Library of Congress Cataloging-in-Publication Data applied for

ISBN 0 7190 6234 9 *hardback*
EAN 978 0 7190 6234 6

First published 2005

14 13 12 11 10 09 08 07 06 05   10 9 8 7 6 5 4 3 2 1

Typeset in Sabon
by SNP Best-set Typesetter Ltd., Hong Kong

Printed in Great Britain
by CPI, Bath

CONTENTS

ILLUSTRATIONS

Illustrations from the quartos are reproduced by permission of the Folger Shakespeare Library.

GENERAL EDITORS' PREFACE

Since the late 1950s the series known as The Revels Plays has provided for students of the English Renaissance drama carefully edited texts of the major Elizabethan and Jacobean plays. The series includes some of the best-known drama of the period and has continued to expand, both within its original field and, to a lesser extent, beyond it, to include some important plays from the earlier Tudor and from the Restoration periods. The Revels Plays Companion Library is intended to further this expansion and to allow for new developments.

The aim of the Companion Library is to provide students of the Elizabethan and Jacobean drama with a fuller sense of its background and context. The series includes volumes of a variety of kinds. Small collections of plays, by a single author or concerned with a single theme and edited in accordance with the principles of textual modernisation of The Revels Plays, offer a wider range of drama than the main series can include. Together with editions of masques, pageants and the non-dramatic work of Elizabethan and Jacobean playwrights, these volumes make it possible, within the overall Revels enterprise, to examine the achievements of the major dramatists from a broader perspective. Other volumes provide a fuller context for the plays of the period by offering new collections of documentary evidence on Elizabethan theatrical conditions and on the performance of plays during that period and later. A third aim of the series is to offer modern critical interpretation, in the form of collections of essays or of monographs, of the dramatic achievement of the English Renaissance.

So wide a range of material necessarily precludes the standard format and uniform general editorial control which is possible in the original series of Revels Plays. To a considerable extent, therefore, treatment and approach are determined by the needs and intentions of individual volume editors. Within this rather ampler area, however, we hope that the Companion Library maintains the standards of scholarship that have for so long characterised The Revels Plays, and that it offers a useful enlargement of the work of the series in preserving, illuminating and celebrating the drama of Elizabethan and Jacobean England.

J. R. MULRYNE
ROBERT SMALLWOOD
PETER CORBIN
SUSAN BROCK
SUSAN CERASANO

ACKNOWLEDGEMENTS

This project would never have been begun, no less completed, without the advice and encouragement of general editor Robert Smallwood and of Andrew Gurr. I have also benefited greatly from the interest that many distinguished colleagues have shown in my work, and for their willingness to share their knowledge. Jonathan Bate, David Bevington, Dympna Callaghan, Kent Cartwright, David Elder, R. A. Foakes, Werner Habicht, Peter Holland, David Scott Kastan, Roslyn Lander Knutson, Barbara Kreps, Christopher Kyle, William Leadbetter, Patricia Parker, Carol Chillington Rutter, William Sherman, Stuart Sillars, Herbert Weil, Judith Weil and Paul Werstine are all contributors to this book. Special thanks go to Martin Wiggins for giving me pre-publication access to his stimulating articles on both *The Battle of Alcazar* and *Captain Thomas Stukeley*.

The Folger Shakespeare Library's generosity in awarding me a fellowship ensured that my research was conducted under the best possible circumstances. Barbara Mowat, Gail Kern Paster, Heather Wolfe and Georgianna Ziegler were unendingly patient and always willing to share their inexhaustible expertise, as were Betsy Walsh and the brilliant staff in reader services: Harold Batie, LuEllen DeHaven, Rosalind Larry, Leigh Anne Palmer, and Camille Seerattan. Thanks also to Carol Brobeck and Colin Bayly of the Folger for the welcome and the assistance they so cheerfully provided.

Edith Cowan University's provision of academic study leave is much appreciated.

As always, Lesley, Jacob and David Edelman provided support in innumerable ways.

ABBREVIATIONS AND REFERENCES

EDITIONS COLLATED, THE BATTLE OF ALCAZAR

Q   W. W. Greg, ed., *The Battle of Alcazar*, London, 1594, Malone Society Reprint, 1907.

Dyce[1]   Alexander Dyce, ed., *The Works of George Peele*, v. 2, London, 1828.

Dyce[2]   Alexander Dyce, ed., *The Dramatic and Poetical Works of Robert Greene and George Peele*, London, 1861.

Bullen   A. H. Bullen, ed., *The Works of George Peele*, v. 1, London, 1888.

Yoklavich   John Yoklavich, ed., in *The Life and Works of George Peele*, gen. ed. Charles Tyler Prouty, v. 2, New Haven, 1961.

EDITIONS COLLATED, CAPTAIN THOMAS STUKELEY

Q   Judith C. Levinson, ed., *The Famous History of Captain Thomas Stukeley*, London, 1605, Malone Society Reprint, 1975.

Simpson   Richard Simpson, ed., *The School of Shakspere*, v. 1, London, 1878.

EDITIONS OF DRAMATIC WORKS CITED IN COMMENTARY

Alcazar and *Stukeley*   Refers to the two plays in this edition.

Beaumont   *The Knight of the Burning Pestle*, ed. Sheldon P. Zitner, Manchester, 1984.

Chapman   *The Plays of George Chapman*, ed. Thomas Marc Parrott, New York, 1961.

Dekker   *The Dramatic Works of Thomas Dekker*, ed. Fredson Bowers, Cambridge, 1953–61.

Fletcher   *The Dramatic Works in the Beaumont and Fletcher Canon*, gen. ed. Fredson Bowers, Cambridge, 1966–96.

Jonson   *The Alchemist*, ed. F. H. Mares, Manchester, 1997.
Volpone, ed. R. B. Parker, Manchester, 1999.
Other works from *Ben Jonson*, ed. C. H. Herford and Percy and Evelyn Simpson, Oxford, 1925–52.

Kyd   *The Spanish Tragedy*, ed. Philip Edwards, London, 1959.

Marlowe   *Doctor Faustus*, ed. John D. Jump, London, 1962.
The Jew of Malta, ed. N. W. Bawcutt, Manchester, 1978.
Tamburlaine the Great, ed. J. S. Cunningham, Manchester, 1981.

Marston   *The Works of John Marston*, ed. A. H. Bullen, London, 1887.

Middleton   *The Works of Thomas Middleton*, ed. A. H. Bullen, London, 1885–6.

Massinger   *The Plays and Poems of Philip Massinger*, ed. Philip Edwards and Colin Gibson, Oxford, 1976.

Peele	*The Life and Works of George Peele*, gen. ed. C. T. Prouty, 3 v., New Haven, 1952–70.
Shakespeare	*The Complete Oxford Shakespeare*, gen. ed. Stanley Wells and Gary Taylor, Oxford, 1987.
Webster	*The Complete Works of John Webster*, ed. F. L. Lucas, London, 1927.

As no complete edition with act/scene/line numbers of the plays of Thomas Heywood exists, the earliest quarto editions are cited. All other plays are cited in the earliest quarto edition.

PRIMARY WORKS CITED IN COMMENTARY

Aeneid	Virgil, *The Aeneid*, trans. John Dryden, reprt ed., New York, 1909 [cited by book/line number].
APC	*Acts of the Privy Council of England*, 42 v., Nendeln, 1974.
Brown	Robert Brown, ed., *The History and Description of Africa: and of the notable things therein contained. Written by al-Hassan ibn Mohammed al-Wezaz, al-Fasi, a Moor, baptized as Giovanni Leone, but better known as Leo Africanus; done into English in the year 1600 by John Pory*, London, 1896.
Camden	William Camden, *The Historie of the Life and Reigne of the Most Renowmed and Victorious Princesse Elizabeth, late Queene of England*, London, 1630.
Campion	Edmund Campion, *Historie of Ireland*, in *Two Histories of Ireland, the one by Edmund Campion, the other by Meredith Hamner, Dr of Divinity*, Dublin, 1633.
Castries	H. de Castries, ed. *Les Sources Inédites de L'Histoire du Maroc: Archives et Bibliothèques d'Angleterre*, 2 v., Paris, 1918–25.
CSP Dom.	*Calendar of State Papers, Domestic Series, of the Reign of Elizabeth*, Nendeln, 1967.
CSP For.	*Calendar of State Papers, Foreign Series, of the Reign of Elizabeth*, Nendeln, 1966.
CSP Ire.	*Calendar of State Papers Relating to Ireland of the Reigns of Henry VIII, Edward VI, Mary, and Elizabeth* (1509–73), Nendeln, 1974.
CSP Rom.	*Calendar of State Papers, Relating to English Affairs. Preserved Principally at Rome, in the Vatican Archives and Library*, London, 1916.
CSP Spn.	*Calendar of State Papers Relating to English Affairs [of the reign of Elizabeth] Preserved Principally in the Archives of Simancas*, Nendeln, 1971.
Dell'unione	Ieronomo de Franchi Conestaggio [attrib.], *Dell'unione del regno di Portogallo alla corona di Castiglia*, Genoa, 1585.
Dolorous Discourse	*A Dolorous Discourse of a most terrible and bloudy Battel, fought in Barbarie*, London, 1579.
Dymmok	John Dymmok, *A Treatice of Ireland*, ed. Rev. Richard Butler, Dublin, 1842.
Explanation	*The Explanation of the true and lawful right and tytle of the Most Excellent Prince Anthonie*, London, 1585.

Gull's Hornbook	Dekker, *The Gull's Hornbook*, ed. E. D. Pendry, *Stratford-upon-Avon Library 4*, London, 1967.
Hakluyt	Richard Hakluyt, *The Principal Navigations, Voyages, Traffiques, and Discoveries of the English Nation*, 12 v., Glasgow, 1903.
Holinshed	Raphael Holinshed, *Chronicles of Englande, Scotlande, and Irelande*, 6 v., London, 1807–8.
Metamorphoses	Ovid, *Metamorphoses*, trans. A. D. Melville, Oxford, 1986 [cited by book/line number, e.g. 4.23 is Book 4, line 23].
Moryson	Fynes Moryson, *An Itinerary written by Fynes Moryson Gent. First in the Latine tongue, and then translated by him into English*, London, 1617.
Polemon	John Polemon, *The Second part of the booke of Battailes, fought in our age: taken out of the best authors and writers in sundrie languages*, London, 1587.
SP Dom. Eliz.	Public Records Office, *State Papers Domestic, Elizabeth I 1558–1603*.
SP Dom. Mary	Public Records Office, *State Papers Domestic, Mary 1553–58*.
SP For.	Public Records Office, *State Papers Foreign, Elizabeth I 1558–77*.
SP Ire.	Public Records Office, *State Papers Ireland, Elizabeth I to George III 1558–1782*.
Statutes	*Statutes at Large Passed in the Parliaments Held in Ireland*, v. 1, Dublin, 1786.
Uniting	Gerolamo Franchi di Conestaggio [attrib.], *The Historie of the Uniting of the Kingdome of Portugall to the Crown of Castill*, London, 1600.

SECONDARY WORKS CITED IN COMMENTARY

Abbott	Edwin Abbott, *A Shakespearian Grammar*, London, 1883.
Adams	Joseph Quincy Adams, 'Captaine Thomas Stukeley', *Journal of English and Germanic Philology* 15 (1916): 107–29.
Bartley	J. O. Bartley, *Teague, Shenkin and Sawney: Being an Historical Account of the Earliest Irish, Welsh, and Scottish Characters in English Plays*, Cork, 1954.
Bovill	E. W. Bovill, *The Battle of Alcazar*, London, 1952.
Bradley	David Bradley, *From Text to Performance in the Elizabethan Theatre: Preparing the Play for the Stage*, Cambridge, 1992.
Brady	Ciaran Brady, 'The Killing of Shane O'Neill: Some New Evidence', *Irish Sword* 5 (1982–83): 116–23.
Connolly	S. J. Connolly, ed., *Oxford Companion to Irish History*, Oxford, 1998.
Cook	Weston F. Cook Jr, *The Hundred Years War for Morocco: Gunpowder and the Military Revoluton in the Early Modern Muslim World*, Boulder, 1994.
Edelman, *Military*	Charles Edelman, *Shakespeare's Military Language: A Dictionary*, London, 2000.
Greg	W. W. Greg, *Two Elizabethan Stage Abridgements: The Battle of Alcazar & Orlando Furioso*, London, 1922.

Harvey	Paul Harvey, *Oxford Companion to Classical Literature*, Oxford, 1937.
Hattaway	Michael Hattaway, ed., *The Second Part of Henry VI*, Cambridge, 1991.
Hill	George Hill, *An Historical Account of the Macdonnells of Antrim*, Belfast, 1873.
Horne	David H. Horne, *The Life and Minor Works of George Peele*, New Haven, 1952.
Levinson	Judith C. Levinson, introd. and ed., *The Famous History of Captain Thomas Stukeley*, London, 1975.
O'Hart	John O'Hart, *Irish Pedigrees: or The Origin and Stem of the Irish Nation*, 5th ed., 2 v., Dublin, 1892, 1: 311–12.
Rice	W. G. Rice, 'A Principal Source of *The Battle of Alcazar*', *Modern Language Notes* 58 (1943): 428–31.
Ronart, *East*	Stephan and Nandy Ronart, *Concise Encyclopaedia of Arabic Civilization: The Arab East*, Amsterdam, 1959.
Ronart, *West*	Stephan and Nandy Ronart, *Concise Encyclopaedia of Arabic Civilization: The Arab West*, Amsterdam, 1966.
Sugden	Edward H. Sugden, *A Topographical Dictionary to the Works of Shakespeare and his Fellow Dramatists*, Manchester, 1925.
Swinburne	A. C. Swinburne, *Contemporaries of Shakespeare*, ed. E. Gosse and T. J. Wise, London, 1919.
Tilley	Morris Palmer Tilley, *A Dictionary of the Proverbs in England in the Sixteenth and Seventeenth Centuries*, Ann Arbor, 1950.
Wiggins, 'Choice'	Martin Wiggins, 'A Choice of Impossible Things: Dating the Revival of *The Battle of Alcazar*', in *Shakespeare & Ses Contemporains: Actes de colloque 2002 de la Société Française Shakespeare*, ed. Patricia Dorval, Montpellier, 2002, 185–202.
Wiggins, 'Things'	Martin Wiggins, 'Things that go Bump in the Text: *Captain Thomas Stukely*', *Papers of the Bibliographical Society of America* 98 (2004): 5–20.
Yahya	Dahiru Yahya, *Morocco in the Sixteenth Century: Problems and Patterns in African Foreign Policy*, Harlow, 1981.

OTHER ABBREVIATIONS: TEXTUAL COLLATIONS, NOTES

conj.	conjectured by
F	First Folio of Shakespeare's Plays (1623)
MLR	*Modern Language Review*
N&Q	*Notes and Queries*
OED	*Oxford English Dictionary*
OSD	opening stage direction [at start of scene]
Plot	The playhouse Plot of *The Battle of Alcazar*
Q	quarto
SD	stage direction
SH	speech heading
SQ	*Shakespeare Quarterly*
subst.	substantially
TLS	*Times Literary Supplement*

INTRODUCTION

SIR THOMAS STUKELEY

Thomas Stukely, an Englishman, a Ruffian, and a ryetous spender, and a notable boaster of himselfe.

William Camden[1]

Mrs Porter whose husband kept an oylshop at the end of Glocester Street near Queens square, whose maiden name was Stukeley of the Devonshire branch told me there was an original picture of him there that when she was a girl, she prickt the eyes of it with pins.

Dr William Stukeley (1687–1765)[2]

'The town of Affton', writes Thomas Westcote in his *View of Devonshire* (1630), is 'now the seat of a worshipful family of Stukely ... Of this family was Thomas Stukely,[3] called commonly the lusty Stukely whose high spirit was of so high a strain that it villified subjection (though in the highest and chiefest degree) as contemptible, aiming (as high as the moon) at no less than sovereignty'.[4]

Thomas, the third son of Sir Hugh Stukeley, was born in about 1525.[5] Nothing is known of his childhood; he first attracted public notice in his twenties, as a follower of Edward Seymour, the Duke of Somerset, and, in view of his later career, we should not be surprised that the earliest document of any substance with Stukeley's name on it is an arrest warrant. In November of 1551, soon after the Protector was deposed and accused of treason, the Privy Council sent 'a lettre to the Sherif of Devon to serche for ... Stukleye, servaunt to the Duke of Somerset, and to apprehend hym and send hym salfely hither'.[6] The summons was never carried out – Stukeley escaped to France, and served King Henry II in his war against the Habsburgs, attaining the office of 'the King's standard-bearer to the men of arms or horsemen at Boulogne'.[7]

The grateful Henry wrote to Edward VI 'recommending to his favour an Englishman, Sir Thomas Stukeley, who had served the French King gallantly in his wars, and now returns to England, which he had left without having obtained previous permission to do so'.[8] Stukeley then began what was to become his usual game: he played both sides at once, telling the English authorities that Henry had instructed him to gather intelligence for an attack on Calais. King Edward wrote in his journal:

Stucley being latly arrived out of Fraunce, declared how that the French king, being holly perswaded that he wold never retorne againe into Englaund, bicause he came away without leave, uppon th'apprehension of the duke of Somerset his old master, declared to him his entent, that apon a peax made with th'emperour, he ment to besieg Cales, and thought surely to winne it by the way of the Sandhilles, for having Ricebank, both to famish the toune and also to beat the market place; and asked Stucleis opinion.[9]

Rightly suspicious of Stukeley's story, Edward sought a report from his ambassador to France, William Pickering. He learned 'how that Stucley had not declared to him [Pickering] al the while of his being in Fraunce, no one word touching the communication afore specified and declared, and also how mr. Pikeringe thought and certainly advertised, that Stucley never hard the French king speake no soch worde'. Stukeley, 'for that he untruly slaunderid the king our good brother, as other such runnagates doe dayly the same',[10] was sent to prison, where he remained until the end of Edward's reign.

Upon his release,[11] Stukeley returned to the continent. Since he had betrayed Henry II, his opportunity lay with the other side, and he joined the Duke of Savoy in Flanders. When the Duke decided on a state visit to England, he asked Stukeley to accompany him, so Stukeley wrote to Queen Mary, asking remission of all the debts he claimed to have incurred in the service of her late father and brother.[12]

Soon after his arrival, Stukeley married Anne Curtis. Whether she was the niece or the granddaughter of Thomas Curtis, the wealthy alderman of London, is not clear – more importantly, she was his sole heir. Stukeley's married life is almost completely undocumented, and the only available evidence that a wedding did indeed take place is, yes, an arrest warrant, this time for counterfeiting.[13] Stukeley having decided on another continental holiday, the Privy Council sent 'a letter to the Shirief of the countie of Devon to cause all the goodes of Thomas Stukeley, being fled for counterfeyting of the King and Quenes Majesties' coyne, to be praysed [appraised] openly and delyvered to the wiefe of the said Stukeley, taking first sufficient bandes [bonds] of her to aunswere the same of the valour therof as it is prised to thier Majesties' use, whenne the same shalbe demaunded'.[14]

Within a year Stukeley was back in England. Although the circumstances are obscure, he seems to have been involved in an altercation with the former Master of the Mint, Sir John York: Privy Council papers for 2 April 1556 note a recognisance (bond) of £500, providing Stukeley would 'kepe the peace and be of good abearing towards Sir John Yorke, knight, and neither by himself or eny other by his procurement go about to do any bodely hurte to the saide Sir John'.[15]

By the summer of 1558 he was in trouble again: charged with piracy against some Spanish ships, he was required to appear before the Lord High Admiral, Edward Clinton. Fortunately, Clinton informed the Privy Council 'he dothe not fynde matter sufficient to charge Stewkely w[th]all'.[16] His fortunes (in both senses of the word) took another turn for the better in the following year. A document of unknown authorship preserved in the State Papers Foreign states, 'The Alderman Curtes is ded, and by this tyme is busy Stukley in the myddst of his cofurs, having marryed his daughter or neyse'.[17] Between 1560 and 1563, with money to spend, he was the typical soldier and courtier: George North's translation of Sebastian Münster's Cosmographia was published in 1561 with a dedication 'to the ryght woorshypfull good Mayster Thomas Steuckley, hys obedient servaunt George North whysheth prosperous health, wyth entreate of muche worship'. North goes on to praise his benefactor,

whose large and ample benefices I have not seldome tymes receyved, with your favorable goodnes, not onely to me, but also to everye one, whose nede you knew to want your reliefe . . . Besydes these your liberalities, your own travel in foreyne & straunge nacions wyth the perfect understandyng & almost natural speakyng of theyr languages importeth you to be as trym a courtier as you are knowen to be a worthy soldiour.[18]

The 'good Mayster Thomas' also became associated with Robert Dudley, the Earl of Leicester, as we know by a letter from Sir Hugh Poulet, the military governor of Jersey, asking Dudley 'to continue his friendship with his nephew, Thomas Stewcley'.[19]

A high point of this time, one to have major implications for Stukeley's future, was the visit of the powerful Ulster chieftain Shane O'Neill to make formal submission to the Queen. As William Camden records in his Historie:

Now was Shan O-Neal come out of Ireland, to performe what hee had promised a yeere before, with a guard of ax-bearing galloglasses, bareheaded, with curled haire hanging downe, yellow surplices dyed with saffron, or mans stale [urine], long sleeves, short coates, and hairy mantles; whom the English people gazed at with no lesse admiration then now a dayes they doe them of China and America. He being received with all kindnesse, and falling downe at the Queenes feete, confessed his crime and rebellion with howling, and obtained pardon.[20]

A few of the items on O'Neill's social calendar are noted in the diary of Henry Machyn: Stukeley may or may not have been present at Cheapside when 'the wyld Yrysman . . . dynyd at the Sant John' or when he 'dyd rune at the rynge . . . beyond sant James in the field',[21] but, as subsequent events show, O'Neill and Stukeley met and became friends at this time.

Machyn does note that, soon after O'Neill's return to Ireland, Stukeley had the honour of entertaining the Queen by staging a mock sea-battle on the Thames: 'The xiiii day of June [1563] the Quen['s] grace removyd from Whythall by water toward Grenwyche, and abowt Ratclyff and Lymhowse capten Stukely dyd shuwe here grace the pleysur that cold be on the water with shuttyng of gones after like warle [and] with plahhyng of drumes and trum[pets]'.[22]

At the same time, planning for Stukeley's next adventure was under way. Bishop Alvaro de Quadra, the Spanish ambassador to London, wrote to his King on 1 May 1563:

> Five vessels are being fitted out here by private individuals, the principal of whom is a young gentleman called Thomas Stukeley who is going in command. The talk is that they are going on a voyage of discovery to Florida, where a certain Captain Jean Ribault of Dieppe went to some months ago, who now accompanies Stukeley . . . Some days since Stukeley sent to me to say that these people were sending him on a bad and knavish business, but that he would be with me and would show me how to play them a trick that would make a noise in the world.[23]

Although Robert Seall's ballad, *A Comendation of the adventerus viage of the wurthy Captain. M. Thomas Stutely Esquyer and others, towards the land called Terra florida*,[24] exhorted

> Now Stutely, hoice thy sail
> Thy wished land to finde
> And never doo regard vain talke
> For wurds they are but winde

there was little doubt in De Quadra's mind that Elizabeth had dispatched Stukeley to 'attack [Spanish] ships on their voyage from the Indies'[25] and seize their goods. Which party in this business, if any, was telling the truth will never be known; Stukeley, as usual, professed loyalty to both sides. Within a month De Quadra reported that Stukeley was ready to defect:

> He recently came and spoke with me just as he was sailing, and told me that he was leaving the country discontentedly and almost desperately. He had embarked in the six ships all that remained of his property, more with the intention of going to serve your Majesty than with the idea of any profit he could gain in the discovery on which he was bound . . . my own opinion is that Stukeley is bent rather on committing some great robbery than discovering new lands.[26]

When De Quadra confronted Queen Elizabeth about the purpose of Stukeley's voyage, 'her answer was that she was informed that this voyage was in no way injurious to any friendly princes',[27] an interesting reply in that Elizabeth had already written to the Earl of Sussex, Lord Deputy of Ireland:

> Because it may so happen that for lack of favourable wynds [Stukeley] may be dyverted from his direct voyadge . . . We doo will, and require yow, that if he shall happen to come to any port of [Ireland], that ye cause hym and his company to be well used . . . *And if he shall also bryng or send into any port ther any manner of French shipps which he shall arrest to our use*, we wold that the same might be receyved and the Goods and Ladyngs therin put in Inventory, and layd upp in savety.[28]

While the Spanish worried about their shipping and Queen Elizabeth worried about her share of booty taken from the French, Stukeley made no distinction at all: he stole from everyone, taking two French ships out of Galicia carrying Spanish goods worth 30,000 ducats, then attacking a Portuguese vessel in the harbour of Bayonne, killing three and wounding some others while seizing 15,000 ducats' worth of merchandise. Another Portuguese ship was taken, then one from Biscay, then a wine-laden vessel from Pontevedra, followed by yet more robberies.[29] Protests to the Queen grew so furious that her ambassador to Madrid, Sir Thomas Chaloner, noted in a letter, he 'hangs his head for shame' and begged that Stukeley be restrained.[30] Succumbing to the pressure, Elizabeth ordered Stukeley's arrest, and once again our hero found himself enjoying Her Majesty's hospitality, although not in the way he would have chosen. Luckily, the political situation worked in Stukeley's favour: he asked Shane O'Neill to intercede at the precise moment that England was backing him in his campaign against the Scottish lords of Ulster. O'Neill requested that Stukeley be pardoned, adding that his friend's advice could be of help against the Scots.[31]

Whether Elizabeth believed O'Neill's astonishing assertion that he doubted 'such a prudent man as Stukeley would do anything against the Queen or her laws',[32] or simply saw a convenient way to rid herself of a problem by the time-honoured means of sending it to Ireland, she agreed, and informed Lord Deputy Sir Henry Sidney that Stukeley was at his disposal.[33]

Stukeley responded, of course, by contacting the new Spanish ambassador, Guzman de Silva, and again offering to defect. De Silva wrote to Philip II, 'He again gave me to understand the ardent desire he had to serve your Majesty . . . he says Sidney is very anxious to take him to Ireland in consequence of his great friendship with John O'Neil, by means of which he thinks for certain that, in case your Majesty were so pleased, he could effect something in that island'.[34]

Although Stukeley's meetings with O'Neill came to nothing, his arrival in Ireland at the beginning of 1566 marks a new phase in his career, starting with his second marriage. When Anne died is not clear: she survived at least until c. 1562, when her and Stukeley's son William was born.[35] Stukeley's second wife was Elizabeth, the widow of the recently deceased Walter Peppard, a wealthy gentleman who had been granted mining leases by Queen Mary.[36] As Elizabeth married Walter in 1539,[37] she must have been somewhat older than Stukeley; information is so lacking that only Izon, amongst Stukeley's biographers, mentions her, but several documents show that she and Stukeley were indeed married. A dispatch of September 1570, from Raimond de Fourquevaux, the Spanish ambassador to Madrid, gives news of the arrival there of a *'gentillome anglois nommé Richard Stuely [sic] maryé à un riche dame en Hirlande'*, a message sent to Lord Burghley from Spain in 1573 reports, 'Mrs Stukeley has sent certain letters from Ireland to her husband', and a 1583 document deals with the reversion of a lease to 'Elizabeth Stukeley, widow', and her son 'Anthony Peppard'.[38]

Presumably using his wife's money and the proceeds from his stint as a pirate, Stukeley purchased the estate adjoining O'Neill's land from Sir Nicholas Bagenal, and Bagenal's title of Marshal of Ireland along with it. The Queen, understandably believing that no good could come of this, forbade the transaction; Guzman de Silva wrote from London, 'the reason they give is that they cannot trust him as he is a friend of O'Neil, and might make common cause with him. The real reason probably is that they consider him a Catholic.'[39]

Undeterred, Stukeley bought the important office of Seneschal of Wexford, a post with military, civil and judicial duties, from Sir Nicholas Heron, and at the same time infuriated the Queen by buying 'hydes and skyns, brought from the Inds' that a Southampton pirate, Edward Cooke, had taken from a Dutch ship. 'Surely we marvell', she wrote to Sidney, that 'Stewkley wold have such boldnes as to deale with pyrates or with their prises',[40] and ordered Heron to resume his post. Heron avoided having to return to work by dying, so Elizabeth appointed Nicholas White, 'a bookish attorney' with little military experience.[41]

Antagonism between White and Stukeley soon developed into open war: the Seneschal was convinced that Stukeley was behind civil disturbances that broke out in June of 1569, and, at a meeting of the Council of Fernes, Constable Thomas Masterson added treason to the growing list of crimes with which Stukeley had been charged. While Stukeley waited in jail, the Council took testimony from his associates, including one Richard Stafford, who revealed that when his companion, William

Hore, asked if Stukeley's anger was due to his failure to gain the office of Seneschal, Stukeley replied, 'I sett not a farte for her, Hore, nor yet for her offyce'.[42] (Even three years later, after Stukeley had left Ireland for Spain, his hatred of White had not abated: James Rigsby, who had sailed with Stukeley, testified upon his return to England that Stukeley said he would 'teache hyr [Elizabeth] to displace a soldior & to put in one with a pen & inckehorne at hys gyrdel'.[43])

Stukeley was indicted and sent to Dublin Castle, but possibly owing to the influence of Sidney, who always supported him, the case never came to trial. During this time Stukeley maintained and extended his contacts with Irish dissidents and Spanish agents; after his release he made a short trip to London, returned to Ireland, and on 17 April 1570, with son William alongside, Stukeley sailed from Waterford, landing at Vivero in Galicia on the 24th. He was never to see England or Ireland again.

Whatever Stukeley's true religious convictions, if any, may have been, once in Spain he took on the persona of a zealous Catholic exile. Giovanni Battista Castagna, papal nuncio in Madrid (and later Pope Urban VII), informed Rome of 'an English gentleman resident in Ireland, who gives himself out as sent by those gentlemen who are in arms for the Catholic religion in the kingdom of Ireland, to crave aid of the Catholic King . . . at present he lives here as a Catholic, going to mass, and observing the fasts and other Catholic usages'.[44] None of this impressed Maurice Gibbon Fitzgibbon, Archbishop of Cashel, who considered himself chief representative of Irish Catholics in Spain. He and Stukeley soon became fierce rivals, denouncing each other to both King Philip and the Pope: as discussed in Appendix II, Cashel is one of several possible inspirations for the Irish Bishop in *The Battle of Alcazar*.

One might surmise that Stukeley's arrival in Spain only months after Pope Pius V issued his bull excommunicating Queen Elizabeth, *Regnans in Excelsis*, was propitious, but Philip II had no interest in war with England and was horrified by what he considered the Pope's recklessness. Nevertheless, Philip could use Stukeley to distract the Queen with fear of an invasion, and in this he was highly successful: diplomatic correspondence preserved in the *State Papers* reveals increasing alarm as the King of Spain made a show of honouring Stukeley, creating him Marquess of Ireland and awarding him with both a stipend and a residence (see p. 9; *Alcazar*, 2.2.79). But Stukeley knew that Philip II had no real intention of embarking on such a venture at that time.[45]

For the next eight years, in both Madrid and Rome, Stukeley sought every means of gaining men and money for an invasion of Ireland, to be led, of course, by himself. He approached Cardinal Michael Bonelli, papal legate in Madrid, saying he wanted to 'lay himself at his Holiness' feet, to crave of him his holy blessing, tell him the condition of that realm [of

Ireland], and implore his counsel and aid';[46] Bonelli's lengthy 'Narrative of Thomas Stucley's Negotiation' includes the information that Stukeley had spent all the wealth of 'the sole heiress of the richest gentleman there has been for a great while in London' on 'the enterprise so long ago initiated for the salvation of so many souls and the service and augmentation of our holy Mother the Roman Catholic church, and the honour and glory of Christ our Saviour'.[47]

Philip was pleased to send Stukeley to Rome, giving money, passports and licence for the two horses Stukeley was to take along.[48] A letter from Secretary of State Gabriel de Zayas to Don Guerau de Spes, who had replaced Guzman de Silva as ambassador to London in 1568, reveals why: Stukeley's 'talent, intelligence, and weight were insufficient for the purpose in hand, and for this reason, and in order not to stir up feeling prematurely, an honest excuse was found to divert him'.[49]

The State Papers Rome show no record of Stukeley being in the city until December of 1571;[50] the main contributor to this delay must have been his service as a galley captain in the fleet of Don John of Austria at the battle of Lepanto.[51] Whatever chance Stukeley may have had to gain support in recognition of his Lepanto service was forestalled, however, by the discovery of the Ridolfi plot: the papal nuncio Castagna told Rome that it had caused Philip II 'infinite mortification . . . [and] an attempt upon Ireland, or to try to burn the English fleet . . . would at least hasten the death of the Duke of Norfolk, and of all the other nobles that are prisoners, if they are not by this time dead'.[52]

The years 1573 and 1574 were spent in Spain, and for at least some of 1575 Stukeley was in Rome, hoping that Gregory XIII, who succeeded Pius in 1572, would be more forthcoming than his predecessor;[53] in February of 1577 Thomas Wilson, ambassador to the Low Countries, reported to Lord Burghley that Stukeley and 'the other rabble of rebels' were seen in Brussels with Don John.[54] From there, Stukeley crossed Europe on what was to be his final trip to Rome; Henry Cheek, one of Burghley's agents, wrote from Florence:

> The 21st of this month [March 1577] Mr Stuckley departed from Siena towards Rome, where he is in great favour with the Pope . . . He is full of money, and mayntayneth his old manner of spending. The night before his going from Siena, he invited all English gentlemen of the towne, saving myself, to supper, but they refused to go unto him.[55]

At last, on 14 January 1578, Ptolomeo Galli, Pope Gregory's secretary, was able to inform Robert Fontana, Collector Apostolic in Portugal, that

> Sir Thomas Stucley, an English gentleman, has been despatched by his Holiness with 600 soldiers and some munitions of war on a voyage to

Ireland for the defence of the poor Catholics of that island against such oppression by the heretics, a duty most pleasing to God and very appropriate to the charge which his Holiness has of Vicar of Christ on earth.[56]

The mission was doomed to failure before it started. Stukeley's ships were unseaworthy, his equipment inadequate, his troops undisciplined and racked with internal dissension. When he reached Porto Palomos, Stukeley wrote to Rome that five of his officers, 'infamous and ill-conditioned men', had deserted;[57] one of Stukeley's Italian captains, Hercole del Mastro da Pisa, hated him and did everything he could to undermine him (see Appendix I). Aware that his ships were incapable of sailing to Ireland, Stukeley put into Lisbon, his arrival observed by an English merchant, William Pillen, whose deposition, taken in England in June of 1578, reads:

He [Pillen] saith that at his being in Lushborne, abowte the xiii[th] of the same moneth, wherein was Stukley and abowte vii[c] sowldiers, as Stukley gave himself owte. And this examinate sawe them and thowght they were soe manie in nomber. And they were mustred before the Kinge of Portingall, and as yt was geven owte, there were lxxx of them vearie expert sowldiers, and well liked of the King of Portingall . . . He saith that the vessell wherein Stukley and his companie came was olde and worne, and that this examinat sawe the same there broken.[58]

Pillen also told of

two certeine times of his being with Stukley, and att one time more when he mett him in the streate, he ever talked with this examinate of his state and of England, in which talke, as nigh as this examinat could call to remembrance, he told this examinat as followeth: 'Pillen, I was proffred of the King of Spaine great titles of honor, and I refused the same. The title which the Pope gave me to be Marques of Lymster, and a Baron or Errle of Washford (as this examinat remembreth) I could nott refuse. They saie in Ingland that I am goinge to Ireland; noe, noe, I am not appointed for it. I knowe Ireland as well as the best; there is nothinge to be gotten but hunger and lice. They saie I am a traitor to the Quenes Ma[tie]; noe, they are traitors that saie soe. I will ever accept her as my quene. Yt ys trewe that there is in Ingland my cruell enemie Cecill, the Treasorer, whome I care nott for. I have had of the Pope a [hundred] thowsand ducats, and I have, a thowsand ducattes a moneth, and am to serve the King of Portingall in Aphrica aganst the Mores'.[59]

In his protestations to Pillen that he was pleased to abort the Irish invasion and join King Sebastian of Portugal's expedition bound for Africa, Stukeley may have been saving face. The same month, Thomas Wilson, who had returned from Brussels to become Secretary of the Privy Council, reported, 'I have receaved letters this daie of the 11th and 12th of Maye from Lysbone, wherby I understande Stewkely's purposed voyage to Ireland is altered, to serve the Kyng of Portugale agaynste Africa, much agaynst his wyll, but the King wyll have it so'.[60]

Whatever dream of power or riches Stukeley may have had, as Westcote wrote more than fifty years later, 'God, not approving his cause, dashed it, yet gave him the fortune to die honourably ... and so Alcacarquibar, called commonly Alcazar, was made famous 4th August, 1578, for three kings in re and one in spe there slain that day'.[61]

THE BATTLE OF THE THREE KINGS

Great battles are often fought in obscure places: who would otherwise remember Waterloo or Gettysburg? Compared with the great north African cities of Fez and Marrakesh, Alcazar (as the Portuguese called El-Ksar El-Kebir)[62] was a sixteenth-century backwater. Leo Africanus writes:

> In this towne are practised divers manuarie artes and trades of merchandize: also it hath many temples, one college of students, and a stately hospitall. They have neither springs nor wels, but onely cesternes in stead thereof. The inhabitants are liberall honest people, though not so wittie as some others.[63]

Yet this was, according to Richard Johnson's ballad,

> Where sixscore thousand fighting men was slaine,
> three kings within this battaile died,
> With forty Dukes and Earles beside,
> the like will never more be fought againe.[64]

To rely on the speeches of the Presenter and Abdelmelec in Peele's *The Battle of Alcazar* (1.Prol.7–53; 1.1.63–96) to comprehend the events that led to this battle is to invite only confusion. Therefore, to quote John Polemon's *Second Booke of Battailes* (1587), 'that ye may the better understand what the principall persons that were present & fought at this battaile were, & also to know the quarel and cause thereof, I have thought good to insert ... as it wer [a] pleasant and profitable preamble of the foundation and familie of these mightie kings'.[65] My preamble, however, will be neither 'pleasant' nor 'profitable' unless I account for the bemusement that Peele has given to every reader of his play, including this one, by the inconsistent and sometimes wildly inaccurate names given to the 'principall persons' of Morocco. In this introduction, 'historical' names are used, with Peele's version or versions given in parentheses at the first occurrence; further details and explanation are given in the genealogy chart and accompanying notes (fig. 1).

I THE SAADIAN DYNASTY

(only persons mentioned in the plays are listed)

Muhammad al-Qaim
Alcazar: Muly[1] Sharif

Muly Muhammad al-Shaykh
Alcazar: Muly Mahamet Sheikh

Muly Abdallah al-Ghalib *Alcazar*: Muly Abdallas	Abd al-Mumin *Alcazar*: Abdelmunin	Abd al-Malek *Alcazar & Stukeley*: Abdelmelec / Muly Molocco[2]	Muly Ahmed al-Monsour 'The Victorious' *Alcazar*: Muly Mahamet Seth *Stukeley*: Muly Hamet

Muly Muhammad al-Maslukh, 'The Moor'
Alcazar & Stukeley: Muly Mahamet / The Moor

NOTES

[1] The honorific 'Muly' (or 'Muley') is not a corruption, as might be assumed, of 'Mullah', a religious leader, but is an early transliteration of *Mulay*, or *Maulay*, i.e. 'My Lord', commonly used in Morocco since the fourteenth century as a title for the king or other high-ranking nobility (Ronart, *Arab West*, p. 275).

[2] 'Abdelmelec' is Polemon's (and hence Peele's) transliteration of *Abd al-Malek*. Strictly speaking, he should be referred to as *Muly Abdelmelec* (Mulay Abd al-Malek), as is consistently done in Thomas Hogan's report of his trade mission to Morocco in 1577 (see p. 14). 'Muly Molocco' derives from combining the honorific 'Muly' with the shortened name, 'Malek'; the *Dolorous Discourse* (see p. 12) uses 'Mulla Maluca'. Both 'Abdelmelec' and 'Muly Molocco', with many variants, are common in early modern texts.

Polemon's 'familie of mightie kings' was the Saadian dynasty, founded in the early sixteenth century when Muhammad al-Qaim, 'the true Arabian Muly Sharif' (*Alcazar* 1.1.50), left his native Arabia for Morocco, taking with him great 'store of gold and treasure' (1.1.66). In 1554, after thirteen years of fighting his neighbours and driving the Portuguese from some of their coastal garrisons, Muhammad al-Qaim's son, Muly Muhammad al-Shaykh (Muly Mahamet Sheikh) claimed the city of Fez and became the first ruler of what might be called a united Morocco.[66] The dynasty he began proved to be almost exactly contemporaneous with the reign of England's Queen Elizabeth, beginning in 1554, four years before her accession, and ending in the same year of 1603. Just as Elizabeth worked to establish England as a major European power alongside France and Spain, Morocco was forced to resist the expansionist aims of Spain and the Turks: while Constantinople sought to extend its empire westwards, Philip II knew that Turkish control of Morocco would place a major threat on his very doorstep.

Muly Muhammad al-Shaykh's reign, marked by increased ties with Spain as a means of resisting the Ottomans,[67] was to last only three years. In 1557, as later told in the first English account of the battle of Alcazar, *A Dolorous Discourse of a most terrible and bloudy Battel, fought in Barbarie* (1579), 'the King passing on a tyme from Moroccus, the chiefe city of his countrey, towards another countrey of his, called Sus, was in the mydway, at a place called Bibon, murdred by his owne men'.[68] He was succeeded by Muly Abdallah al-Ghalib (Muly Abdallas), eldest of 'divers sons by sundry his wives and concubines, for there they may have as manye wives as they wyll'. This 'proud Abdallas' (*Alcazar*, 1.Prol.9) broke the tradition of having the crown pass to each of the King's brothers in succession before going on to the next generation, and 'caused the throtes of eleven of [his] brethren to be cutte in one morning'.[69]

Two brothers, Abd al-Malek (Abdelmelec/Muly Molocco)[70] and Muly Ahmed (Muly Mahamet Seth in *Alcazar*, Muly Hamet in *Stukeley*), later given the surname al-Monsour 'the victorious', escaped and grew up among the Turks.[71] Abd al-Malek made his way to Algiers and offered his services to Philip II, promising friendly relations with Spain in return for support in regaining his right to the Moroccan throne. He is next heard of fighting for the Ottomans at Lepanto – the first of two times he was to be on the other side of a battle from Stukeley. King Philip, his navy having taken Abd al-Malek captive, put him under protection and then allowed him to go to Constantinople, with the understanding that he would provide Spain with intelligence on Turkish affairs; by May of 1572 Abd al-Malek was back in Algiers with a new governor.[72]

Muly Abdallah al-Ghalib died in 1574, and Abd al-Malek was powerless to intervene when his nephew, Muly Muhammad, claimed the throne. As the son of 'a bondwoman, that was a blacke Negro',[73] he gained the surname 'al-Maslukh', or 'the Moor' – he was not, at least by the standards of the time, the bloodthirsty tyrant called both 'Muly Mahamet' and 'the Moor' in *Alcazar*, but was considered by some chroniclers to be both just and sagacious.[74]

Like Stukeley, Abd al-Malek was not hesitant to play both sides at once, purportedly working for Spain and Constantinople and promising concessions to both should he come to rule Morocco.[75] After he took part in the successful Ottoman assaults on La Goulette and Tunis in August to September of 1574 (*Alcazar*, 1.1.26), the Turks were prepared to intervene in Morocco, and Abd al-Malek seized the opportunity, leaving Algiers with an Ottoman force sent by Sultan Murad III, and marching towards Fez[76] 'to whip that tyrant traitor king from hence' (*Alcazar*, 1.1.55). After Abd al-Malek's victory at the battle of ar-Rukn (*Alcazar*, 1.2), 'the Moor' fled, first to the Atlas mountains (*Alcazar*, 2.1) and then to Spain; when Philip showed no interest in helping, 'thus deprived of his kingdome, [he] fled for succour to Sebastian then king of Portugall'.[77]

Whatever possessed the young King of Portugal to lead a military expedition to Africa will never be fully understood. According to Polemon, Sebastian 'sought for no other pleasure than by martiall matters, which had caused him in former yeeres to passe over to Tangar, to thentent to conquer Barbarie, but with vain endeavour . . . he was very glad that a most wished occasion whereby he might fill his long lust and longing, was offered unto him, who was desirous of praise, and studious to enlarge his empire and religion'.[78] The military historian Weston F. Cook describes the army Sebastian put together as something from 'a cartoon'. The King

> set Counter-Reformation militancy aside to assemble about 2,000 Germans, staffed with Lutheran pastors. He also asked William of Orange for a loan, a request the Calvinist lord declined to offer; but William did send several hundred Walloons, many of them Catholic prisoners.[79]

Sebastian's own Portuguese were 'the largest and least professional units; at the core of this army were four *tercios* of Portuguese infantry, about 3,000 men each under young nobles distinguished by inexperience'.[80] In January 1577, Sebastian met with his uncle Philip II at Guadalupe (*Alcazar*, 3.Prol.17), but received only token support of 'ships, food, and about 3000 Castilian hires'.[81] Once Stukeley arrived with his Italians, Sebastian's force was complete, including an astounding number of noncombatants, from priests to musicians to 'horse-boys, laundresses and courtesans' (*Alcazar*, 4.1.11).

England was not idle while all this was going on. In May 1577, Edmund Hogan arrived in Barbary on a mission from Queen Elizabeth, seeking the precious commodity of saltpetre, the main ingredient of gunpowder. Hogan's fascinating story of his time in Morocco is found in Hakluyt's *Principal Navigations*;[82] after lengthy negotiations he struck a deal with Abd al-Malek to exchange saltpetre for cannon and shot, which the Moroccan king would soon put to good use.

The fleet left Lisbon in June of 1578. After disembarking at the north African port of Arzila, Sebastian was faced with a crucial decision: how to proceed to the first objective, the port of Larache. The choice was between a safe twenty-mile voyage down the coast or a dangerous and difficult march of thirty-five miles in high summer; by choosing the latter, Sebastian effectively sealed his fate.[83] This extraordinary march began on 29 July; after two days, the column had advanced all of six miles, and with food and water running short, the condition and discipline of the troops rapidly deteriorated from its already frightful state.[84] By Sunday 3 August they had reached the Mekhazen river near the city of El-Ksar El-Kebir, and were, amazingly, within two days' relatively easy march of Larache (*Alcazar*, 4.2), when an advance guard caught sight of a troop of Moroccan horse. While the mortally ill Abd al-Malek's armies waited nearby, the Portuguese camped at the confluence of two rivers, with the Wad Warur at their front, and the Mekhazen behind them (*Stukeley*, 23.2). The next day,

> the fourth daie of August, which was mundaie, in the yeere of our salvation 1578, the battaile was begun between the two kings about twelve of the clocke, and the Moores did first begin to shoote off their great ordenance against the Christians . . . [and] the Christians answered them with theirs. And straight waie the harquebuziers on foote on both sides discharged as thick as haile, with such an horible, furious, and terrible tempest, that the cracking and roaring of the gunnes did make the earth so to tremble, as though it woulde have sunke downe to hell, and the element seemed to burne with the fire, flames, lightning, and thunder of the gunnes.[85]

Only the briefest description of the fight can be given here.[86] Abd al-Malek, who had numerical superiority but little faith in the reliability of his troops, attacked with his cavalry on the Portuguese flanks, while his artillery and harquebusiers advanced in the centre. The combination of firepower and skilful horsemanship threw the Portuguese into some disarray, but a strong counter-attack had its expected effect on Moroccan morale: in Cook's analysis, 'as it became apparent the Christian army would not collapse immediately, pieces of [Abd al-Malek's] army began to desert the field'.[87] At this point the dying Abd al-Malek somehow rallied his men and ordered another charge; the Portuguese broke and fled, and the battle of Alcazar was won. It was

> a great and terrible battaile, wherein the said yong king Sebastian was not onelye overcome but also slaine in the field together with Mulei Mahumet whose part he tooke, at what tyme neyther did Mulei Maluco the king that fought against them escape. For he, in the time of the battaile being sicke and wearye of sitting his horse, was removed into his horselitter and there dyed during the battaile.[88]

Amongst the 'ten or fifteen at the most' Italians to survive the battle[89] was the aforementioned Captain Hercole da Pisa. He provided information on Stukeley's fate when he wrote to Bastiano San Giuseppe, the Pope's commissary and paymaster in Lisbon, to ask for help in arranging his ransom. As San Giuseppe then reported to Rome, 'being in the field at the front with the Italians, as [Stukeley] marked the first assault of the enemy, he hastily retired, and deserting the Italian troops plunged into a squadron of Castilians, and then there came a piece of artillery that took off both his legs; and so he ended his days, behaving in a manner quite contrary to that of the poor Italians, who thrice repulsed the furious onset of the foe'.[90]

How devastating the outcome of this battle was for Portugal would be impossible to overestimate. According to *The Historie of the Uniting* (1600), 'some noble families were there whollie extinct', and the losses extended far further than the nobility:

> There was none in Lisbone but had some interest in this warre, who so had not his sonne there, had his father; the one her husbande, the other her brother; the traders and handie-crafts men who had not their kinsemen there (and yet many of them had) did venture their wealth in it, some of them for the desire of gaine, and others for that they could not call in that which they had lent to gentlemen, and soldiours: by reason whereof all were in heavines, everie one seemed to foretell the losse of such friends, and goods he had in Affrick: and although they stoode yet doubtfull, yet might you understand their secret sighes.[91]

King Sebastian's death had grave implications for the rest of Europe: as an agent of the German commercial family, the Fuggers, wrote to his employers from Lisbon, 'what is even more terrible is that this kingdom must now fall under Spanish rule'.[92] The Portuguese succession fell to Sebastian's great-uncle, the senile Cardinal Henry,[93] who soon died; Don Antonio, Prior of Crato and Sebastian's (illegitimate) cousin, having made an extraordinary escape after being captured at Alcazar (*Stukeley*, Sc. 26), returned to claim the crown. Although he enjoyed popular support, Antonio was no match for another of Sebastian's uncles, Philip II:[94] as the Fugger agent predicted, Spanish troops, led by the Duke of Alva and Sancho de Avila, swept through the country and drove Antonio into exile, first in France, then England.

Controlling all Iberia, including Portugal's fleet and the income from its spice trade, Philip would have been able to move against England immediately, if not for the more pressing situation he faced in the Low Countries, and the fear of French intervention. Reluctance to wage open war did not stop him, however, from promoting assassination attempts against his former sister-in-law: from 1584 to 1587 there were no fewer then four serious murder plots.[95] Once Elizabeth sent troops to the Low Countries in late 1585, Spaniards and Englishmen were in combat against one another, and, with the execution of Mary Queen of Scots on 8 February 1587, England knew that the launching of the Invincible Armada had become a matter of when, not if.

THE BATTLE OF ALCAZAR

Authorship and date

The Battle of Alcazar does not appear in the Stationers' Register, and the first unambiguous notice of the play's existence is the quarto, printed 'by Edwarde Allde for Richard Bankworth' in 1594: *The Battell of Alcazar, Fought in Barbarie, betweene Sebastian king of Portugall, and Abdelmelec king of Marocco. With the death of Captaine Stukeley. As it was sundrie times plaid by the Lord high Admiral his Servants.*

The title page (fig. 2) names no author. That collaboration at this time was common is known (an important topic to be taken up with regard to *Stukeley*), but the uniform style of the verse and the overall coherence of dramatic structure – even when the many textual difficulties are taken into account – point to a single dramatist. Edmond Malone was the first to suggest Peele, in a handwritten note on his copy of the quarto, but without adding any reason, and no unimpeachable external evidence to confirm this conjecture has been found. Robert Allott names Peele as the author of six lines from *Alcazar* (2.2.42–7) in *England's Parnassus* (1600),[96] but Allott is wrong about his authors elsewhere. We are left, then, with matters such as verbal echoes and the similarity of rhetorical style to works known to be by Peele: such 'internal evidence', no matter how persuasive, does not exclude other candidates, but, since no alternative comes to mind, Peele's authorship, perhaps by default, remains undisputed.

THE
BATTELL
OF ALCAZAR, FOVGHT
in Barbarie, betweene Sebaſtian king
of Portugall, and Abdelmelec king
of Marocco. With the
death of Captaine
Stukeley.

As it was ſundrie times plaid by the Lord high Admirall his ſeruants.

Imprinted at London by Edward Allde for Richard
Bankworth, and are to be ſolde at his ſhoppe in
Pouls Churchyard at the ſigne of the
Sunne. 1 5 9 4.

2 *The Battell of Alcazar* (1594), title page

Very tenuous as evidence for authorship, but still significant, is Peele's *A Farewell Entitled to the Famous and Fortunate Generals of our English Forces: Sir John Norris and Sir Francis Drake*. This poem was registered on 23 February 1589, the same day Queen Elizabeth gave Norris and Drake her instructions for an expedition to destroy what was left of Spain's fleet after the Armada, and at the same time restore the pretender Don Antonio to the Portuguese throne.[97] The 'Generals'[98] are exhorted to

> Bid Theaters and proude Tragaedians,
> Bid Mahomets Poo, and Mightie Tamburlaine,
> King Charlemaine, Tom Stukeley, and the rest
> Adiewe: To Armes, to Armes, to glorious armes
>
> (20–3)[99]

No other play with Stukeley is known to have existed at this time, and it seems only logical that Peele would advertise at least one of his own characters in a list of dramatic heroes.[100]

If the *Farewell* does indeed refer to *The Battle of Alcazar*, then, even if Peele was not the author, an upward limit of February 1589 for the play's date is established. The *terminus a quo* is 1587, the year Polemon's *Second Booke of Battailes* was published.[101] That the play must have been written after the Armada of August 1588, as argued by Yoklavich,[102] is less certain. The many 'fortress England' speeches in plays of this period are often pointed to as evidence of post-Armada patriotism, a prime example being Sebastian's warning to anyone who would attack England:

> To invade the island where her highness reigns,
> 'Twere all in vain, for heavens and destinies
> Attend and wait upon her majesty . . .
> . . . The wallowing ocean hems her round about,
> Whose raging floods do swallow up her foes,
> And on the rocks their ships in pieces split
>
> (2.4.106–19)

Such sentiments, however, did not suddenly appear late in 1588; they are just as likely to be a call to arms written under the threat of invasion, not a victory boast. Nor was the Armada defeated by raging floods and rocks; the main contributors were the superior range and firepower of England's guns and the ability to replenish supplies of ammunition after the first day's battle. As I have written elsewhere, there are actually very few explicit references to the Armada of 1588 in plays of this period, probably because the new wave of national confidence after the battle never really happened; England knew that, just as the Ottomans had recovered quickly from Lepanto, Spain was far from beaten.[103]

Obviously, I do not argue that the play *was* written before August of 1588, only that it could have been – with all factors taken into account, late in 1588 seems the most likely date of composition.

Text

There are, in a sense, two early texts of *The Battle of Alcazar*: the 1595 quarto, and a nearly complete playhouse Plot, made for a revival some years after *Q* was printed. The Plot (capitalised to avoid confusion with 'plot', as in 'narrative') will be taken up separately below; for now, we will stay with *Q*.

In his study of the *Alcazar* quarto,[104] W. W. Greg sprinkles his commentary with words such as 'corrupt' and 'mutilated', implying a text whose condition is far worse than it actually is. There are some glaring inconsistencies in speech headings, including two English captains suddenly transformed to two Italians,[105] but plays with equally serious 'continuity' problems, such as Shakespeare's *Henry V*,[106] have not been condemned out of hand as completely garbled. A number of passages are spectacularly incoherent, but the majority of these can be explained by a compositor omitting one or a few lines.[107]

That *Alcazar* is deficient when compared with many or even most other dramatic texts of the 1590s is undeniable, but *theatrically* it is both coherent and well-structured, neatly divided into five acts, each introduced by the Presenter. What sets it apart is its length, or more precisely, the lack of it: a mere 1591 lines in Greg's edition, leading him to conclude that the quarto does not represent the play as it was first performed in a London theatre:

> When critically examined the text of *Alcazar* printed in 1594 proves to be a version drastically cut down by the omission and reduction of speeches, by the elimination and doubling of parts, and by the suppression of spectacular shows, for representation in a limited time, by a comparatively small cast, with the minimum of theatrical paraphernalia.[108]

There can be little doubt that the quarto is an abbreviated text, but Greg's argument that it is 'drastically cut', and his speculations about the means and purpose of the cuts, are questionable. After first stating his uncertainty on the matter, he notes that the London theatre companies often toured, and then infers, rather confidently, that *Q* was prepared for 'acting in the provinces'.[109] But as David Bradley observes in his magisterial study, to which this edition is much indebted, the belief 'that the major London companies were reduced in personnel when travelling in the provinces is probably an unshakeable myth of theatrical history', even though there is 'no convincing evidence for the belief . . . and much that points in the opposite direction'.[110] Given this refutation, each of Greg's suppositions will be taken up (albeit in a different order), starting with the cutting of the play 'for representation in a limited time'.

The average length of an Elizabethan performance, in London or the provinces, is a complex and controversial subject. Whatever one's views on the wider topic, Andrew Gurr makes the important observation that

> the playing time for plays in provincial towns was generally the same as for London. Some local authorities did lay down a limit on how far into the night playing might go, but that was infrequent, and did not restrict the length of time available for the plays.[111]

I would add that such restrictions do not arise from a vacuum, since authorities have no need to forbid something that no one is doing. If a 'curfew' on playing was ordered, it must have been because performances were too long, not too short, and Bradley offers examples of complaints being made for that reason.[112]

As any theatrical promoter knows, touring incurs extra expenses such as transport and accommodation, so Greg's inference about 'eliminating and doubling of parts' seems plausible. Elizabethan actors often doubled and even tripled roles (as the Plot of *Alcazar* shows), but the amount of doubling is a matter of conjecture – that companies always put the minimum number of players on stage is open to the greatest doubt. In any case, Greg offers no evidence for *increased* doubling (with the same number of characters) when on tour, as no such evidence exists. Cutting *characters*, and hence actors, is another matter, but there is no sign of this having occurred: *Alcazar* offers several counterparts to 'Innogen' of *Much Ado About Nothing*, characters given entry directions who never speak, but Greg concedes, 'we are bound to assume that all those whose names still stand in the stage directions did actually appear'.[113]

Along with wanting to save on wages, our supposed touring company was keen to reduce the amount of 'theatrical paraphernalia' it had to carry. It is indeed true that, if the dumb shows preceding Acts 3 and 4 (not in Q but described in the Plot) are omitted, then some costumes and props, such as a few 'dead men's heads in dishes' (4.Prol.7 SD), could be left behind. But Greg more than eliminates any savings by suggesting that, to cut down on actors, the bodies of Sebastian and Muly Mahamet were played by dummies, the soon-to-be stuffed Muly Mahamet (5.1.219–55) 'already dissected' – hence 'the Mores lymes' in Henslowe's inventory.[114] Meanwhile, the one truly cumbersome prop, Muly Mahamet's chariot, was brought along.

I have saved the most important of Greg's points for last, for he is undoubtedly correct in noting that Q bears evidence of the 'omission and reduction of speeches'. The majority of such excisions, however, bear no resemblance to any systematic editing as would have been done for production: they are, as Greg himself concedes, 'clumsy'.[115] I count sixteen instances, each marked by '[. . .]' in this edition, of incomprehensibility that is apparently due to the omission of some text; nearly all occur in mid-speech, and nearly all appear to be, as Bradley writes, 'the accidental omissions of a careless compositor'.[116]

Some deletions may have been more substantial: in Stukeley's argument with the Irish Bishop (2.2), characters appear to respond to things others do not say, and in 4.2, where King Sebastian and his lords are obviously meant to debate whether to fight or withdraw, one side of the argument (the better one, for withdrawal) is almost completely absent.[117]

These omissions do not account for what might have been the skilful work of a playhouse professional, whose cuts would not be noticeable without knowledge of the 'full text', nor is there any point in arguing that Q is 'complete and unabridged'; the unusual number of mute characters shows that this play, as first performed, must have been longer than the published version. How much longer is another matter: we need to remember that The Battle of Alcazar is not, in fact, all that short. As Alfred Hart notes, the plays of Shakespeare and especially Jonson are lengthier than most others of the period; when Jonson is removed, the average play from 1587 to 1616 'does not much exceed 2400 lines'.[118] Bradley, when limiting the period from 1576, the year Burbage's Theatre opened, to 1594, arrives at an average of only 1623 lines, all of 30 lines longer than The Battle of Alcazar.[119] Two other Peele plays, The Old Wives Tale and The Arraignment of Paris, are actually shorter than Alcazar, as is The Troublesome Reign of King John, Part Two. Greene's Orlando Furioso is the about same length, and the first part of The Troublesome Reign is only slightly longer.

We now turn to the 'other text', the Plot.

The Plot

Perhaps because none exists for any play by a 'canonical' author, the few surviving playhouse Plots have not received the attention they deserve; they are amongst our most valuable artefacts from the Elizabethan theatre. A Plot is, in Greg's clear and concise description,

> a schematic analysis of the entries and exits of the characters, with addition of the actors who filled the various roles and of the properties required . . . each consists, or presumably once consisted, of a thin board with a sheet of stout paper pasted on either side. Each one that is sufficiently preserved shows a hole cut near the top for suspension on a peg.[120]

The Plott of the Battell of Alcazar was acquired by the British Museum in 1836 and repaired by an unknown member of its staff. The left column, relating to Acts 1–2 and the beginning of the Act 3 Prologue, is nearly complete, but the right column is badly damaged: most of the remainder of the Act 3 Prologue, 3.1 and 3.4 are missing, and a mere trace of Act 4 has survived. The second column ends there; all of Act 5, written on the back or on a second sheet, is lost. Greg's reconstruction of the right column must rank as one of his greatest achievements: even if this were all he did, every student of the Elizabethan theatre would still be in his debt. Bradley, although he is critical of Greg's understanding of the Plot's *purpose*, offers his own reconstruction that differs from Greg's in only minor respects.

This Plot is particularly important in that it is the only one for which we have a text, such as it is, of the play for which it was made, therefore each 'text' can help elucidate the other, although this advantage has been somewhat compromised by misperceptions about what a Plot was for. To Greg, its object 'was evidently to remind actors and prompter of the sequence, dispositions, and requirements of the various scenes, doubtless a necessary precaution in a repertory theatre: we may suppose they were suspended in rehearsal and performance in a convenient place in the play-house'.[121] Essentially, Greg is describing a 'call-sheet', which indeed could have been one of the Plot's functions – why else the peg-hole? – but that this was the primary purpose is questionable.

The word 'plot' meant 'ground-plan' (*OED sb* 3a); although a theatrical plot was not a builder's plot, its main function was likely to have been as a 'planning' document. By comparing the *Alcazar* Plot with seven other extant examples (some fragmentary, some nearly intact), Bradley shows that it must have been 'made up before the Book was complete'.[122] More than a reminder to the actors of what costume to wear or what prop to carry on, it was a 'working document', composed during the process of *deciding* the actors' doubling patterns, the availability of supernumeraries, technical requirements, music cues and other elements of production. It also would have been essential in organising the distribution of the actors' scrolls.[123]

The actors' names show that this Plot was for a later production, which in Greg's view was not the shortened touring version represented in Q but a 'full text' performance, making use of the larger cast and better facilities available in London. Bradley shows, however, that Q requires the same number of actors, and makes the same technical demands, as set out by the Plotter. The details of Bradley's study, presented in a lively and readable fashion, cannot (and need not) be reproduced here: his conclusion is that, 'errors . . . in the transmission aside', the 1595 quarto represents Peele's play as it was performed at the Rose, and perhaps other London playhouses, 'with reasonable accuracy'.[124]

The play in performance

The *Q* title page advertises that the text is 'as it was sundrie times plaid by the Lord high Admirall his servants', but what evidence there is suggests that *Alcazar* came into the Admiral's possession second-hand. The first *recorded* performance was almost definitely given at the Rose by Lord Strange's Men on 20 February 1592, as noted in Henslowe's *Diary*; it was followed by thirteen more, the last on 20 January 1593.[125] This is a matter of debate, since Henslowe's play is *Mulammulluco*, to choose one of his thirteen spellings,[126] not *The Battle of Alcazar*: *Mulammulluco*, of course, is *Muly Molocco*, the alternative name for Abdelmelec.

In his introduction to the Yale edition, John Yoklavich summarises past thinking on the matter of whether or not *Muly Molocco* and *Alcazar* are the same play:

> Malone, apparently, first suggested that these entries in Henslowe's *Diary* might refer to Peele's play. Later scholars . . . accepted the theory, but [E. K.] Chambers hesitated to identify 'mulammulluco' with *Alcazar*, and Greg argued against the theory with convincing reasons.[127]

Amongst the 'convincing reasons' are that Abdelmelec is called Muly Molocco only twice in the play and that he is not the main character. Yoklavich also cites other contemporary literature, such as Montaigne's *Essays* and Munday's *The Strangest Adventure that Ever Happened* (see pp. 31, 37), in observing that 'the name 'Muly Molocco' must have been far more familiar than 'Abdelmelec''; he and Greg also make the obvious and valid point that that both *Q* and the Plot are entitled *The Battle of Alcazar*, and 'there is no evidence that the play was known by a nickname'.[128]

Yoklavich's citing of Montaigne and Munday seems more an argument *for* Henslowe thinking of his play as *Muly Molocco* than one against it, and, as Bradley notes, while Muly Molocco is the fourth largest part, it is still a major part. More importantly, by whatever title, this was an Edward Alleyn play (see pp. 25–6), and Alleyn, although 'he retained his livery as the Lord Admiral's man', was with Strange's Men when *Muly Molocco* was performed at the Rose in 1592–93.[129]

Yoklavich is correct in stating that there is no written record of Peele's play ever being referred to by another name, but on the other hand, there is no record that it was not. Henslowe refers to *The Spanish Tragedy*, another Lord Strange's success of the same 1592–93 season, as *Jeronymo*, and, as discussed below, he also could have misnamed Heywood's *Four*

Prentices of London (see pp. 41–2). *Alcazar*'s not appearing in the Stationers' Register may be important: if it had, an alternative title could very well have been entered – the Register for 22 July 1598 shows 'a booke of the Merchaunt of Venyce otherwise called the Jewe of Venyce'.

The design of *Alcazar* is consistent with its being known at some point as *Muly Molocco*. Even though he does not have the most lines, the king whom the Presenter calls 'this brave Barbarian lord Muly Molocco' (1.Prol.12) is indeed the play's central character: the action follows his fortunes, beginning with his return to Morocco and ending with his death and a eulogy in his honour. As to why he is 'Muly Molocco' only twice, and 'Abdelmelec' many times, one important reason is that Abdelmelec, one of those splendidly exotic, polysyllabic names so loved by Marlowe and his imitators, scans; the two lines that have 'Muly Molocco' (1.Prol.12, 2.1.52) are unmetrical.

The hint of another connection between *Alcazar* and *Muly Molocco* is given by some stage directions for the firing of the playhouse cannon:[130]

The trumpets sound, the chambers are discharged (3.4 OSD)

Alarums within, let the chambers be discharged, then enter to the battle, and the Moors fly (5.1 OSD)

Explosions are ubiquitous in Elizabethan plays, but the only other extant texts from 1592 until 1613 that ask for 'chambers' to be 'discharged' are the quartos of Shakespeare's 2 and 3 *Henry VI*, popularly known as the *Contention* plays:[131]

Alarmes within, and the chambers be discharged, like as it were a fight at sea (2H6, sig. F1v)

Alarmes to the battel, Yorke flies, then the chambers be discharged (3H6, sig. E4r).

The performance history of these plays, like their titles, is 'contentious', but, as Michael Hattaway notes, they were likely to have been composed at the time Shakespeare was associated with Strange's Men.[132] The distinctive wording of the directions implies that they were written into their respective texts by the same person, who was connected with Strange's company at the time they were performing *Muly Molocco* at the Rose.[133]

Finally, Greg's point that Muly Molocco was a famous person argues *for* the two plays being one, not against it: there is no need to create a 'lost' play of *Muly Molocco* when *The Battle of Alcazar* is suitable in every respect except its published title.

The date of the Plot

The names of the actors in the Plot show that it was prepared for a performance by the Admiral's Men, but the date of the 'Plotter's production', like everything else about this play, is difficult to determine. The upward limit is November 1601, when Edward Alleyn's elder brother Richard, who played the Presenter, died; the earliest possible date is 1597, when Robert Shaa and William Kendall, both of whom played a variety of roles, were hired.[134] Greg proposed a more precise date, basing his deduction on the status of the actor Dick Jubie, to whom the Plotter assigns the parts of the Portuguese Lord, Christophero de Tavora, and the Queen of Morocco, Abdil Rayes. Not much else of Dick Jubie is known, other than that he took several roles in the lost play *1 Tamar Cham* in 1602, the year his son was baptised, but this is enough to establish him as an adult actor (of uncertain age) and not a boy. Greg, assuming that Abdil Rayes *had* to be played by a boy, disqualified this Dick Jubie and went searching for another, finding him in an actor known only as 'Dick' in the fragmentary Plots of *Frederick and Basilia* and *The Second Part of Fortune's Tennis* (both 1597–98). Since apprentices were usually identified by given name only, Greg, noting that several members of the Jubie family were associated with the Admiral's Men, proposed that this 'Dick' could be another Dick Jubie. Greg's surmise is not very plausible – although re-use of a name if a child died was common, two living children with the same name would be most unusal[135] – nevertheless, he concluded that the Plotter's production would not have been later than 1598–99, when 'Dick' was around as a boy actor.

However, this creates problems elsewhere, for Edward Alleyn temporarily retired from acting in late 1597, and did not return until 1600 – there is no record of his breaking that retirement.[136] Furthermore, the assumption that, where male and female roles are doubled, casting a boy as the woman takes automatic precedence over casting the adult male is not backed by any evidence. So, as Martin Wiggins notes, we must choose either 1600–1, when Alleyn was performing several of his famous roles, but with an adult Jubie as the Queen, or 1598–99, with a boy actor as the Queen, but requiring Alleyn's coming out of retirement.[137]

To solve this puzzle, we need to go beyond generalisations about male and female roles, and look at the individual parts Dick Jubie played in *Alcazar*. Abdil Rayes, as Abdelmelec's Queen, may be assumed to be an older woman; while it is hard to imagine Juliet being played by a grown man, that men never played mature females is open to question, and like everything else about the Elizabethan theatre, scholars have come to no consensus on this point. Jubie's male role, Christophero de Tavora, is the twenty-four-year-old King Sebastian's 'good Hephaestion' and 'bedfellow' (2.4.76), implying a younger actor. Interestingly, and maddeningly, the Plotter does not double the part of Sebastian, and omits the name of the actor who played him.[138] We may assume that in Elizabethan times, just as today, actors often played roles for which they were, in terms of the realistic theatre, far too old, but, even so, an unidentified sharer playing Sebastian is unlikely, and, while it is dangerous to infer too much from this, things do point in the direction of the Plotter casting two young men as 'King and best friend'; for the latter to double as Abdil Rayes would not represent too difficult a task. Overall, the date of 1600–1 for the Plotter's production, as proposed by Wiggins and R. A. Foakes,[139] is the most likely.

Sources

In the approximately ten years between the battle of El-Ksar El-Kebir and the writing of the play, several treatises describing both the conflict and the reasons it was fought were published. The *Dolorous Discourse* appeared in 1579, but there is no clear indication that Peele saw it or used it directly; his main source of historical information, as Warner G. Rice first noted in 1943,[140] was *The Battaile of Alcazar, fought in Barbarie, betwene Sebastian, King of Portugall, and Abdelmelec the King of Marocco, the fourth of August 1578*, one of twelve accounts '*taken out of the best authors and writers in sundrie languages*' by John Polemon, and collected in his *Second Booke of Battailes*. This version, which Polemon credits to a 'nameless Portugall auctor',[141] was originally written by the Portuguese Frey Luis Nieto, translated anonymously into French in 1579 and then from French into Latin by Thomas Freigius the following year.[142] Peele follows a number of passages very closely, at times nearly verbatim.[143]

    Not everything, however, can be accredited to Polemon. Peele also went to two works whose primary subject was not the battle but its aftermath, specifically Philip II's succession to the Portuguese throne. *The Explanation of the true and lawful right and tytle of the Most Excellent Prince Anthonie* (1585)[144] justifies Don Antonio's claim, in part, by blaming the Portuguese defeat on Philip's treachery in encouraging Sebastian, but then reneging on promised aid (3.Prol., 3.1, 3.3).[145] While the *Explanation* is the 'original' source, Peele may have consulted George Whetstone's short adaptation comprising Chapter 13 of *The English Myrror* (1586).[146]

    The other account is as pro-Spanish as the *Explanation* is pro-Portuguese: *Dell'unione del regno di Portogallo alla corona di Castiglia*, published in Genoa in 1585. The title page names '*Ieronomo de Franchi*

Conestaggio, gentilhomo Genovese' as the author, but most historians agree that the book is by Juan de Silva,[147] Spain's ambassador to the Portuguese court, who accompanied the troops to Africa, was captured, and later released by Muly Ahmed al-Monsour as a personal favour to Philip.[148] An English translation, *The Historie of the Uniting of the Kingdome of Portugall to the Crown of Castill,*[149] also attributed to Conestaggio, did not appear until 1600, but some passages in *Alcazar* are almost certainly drawn from it, so Peele must have known it in the original Italian. (To cite 'Conestaggio' would be inaccurate and 'De Silva' confusing, so references in the commentary are to the *Uniting*; readers should keep in mind that Peele did not see the English version.)

Beyond these documentary sources, there was a world of 'common knowledge' to draw on. *The Battle of Alcazar* is usually considered to be an early example of the Elizabethan history play, but the events depicted took place only a decade before it was written, and a major character, Muly Mahamet Seth, was alive and well and King of Morocco: 'current affairs play' is not exactly elegant, but perhaps more accurate.

The play

> Where art thou, boy? where is Calipolis?
> Fight earth-quakes, in the entrailes of the earth,
> And easterne whirle-windes in the hellish shades
> > Jonson, *The Poetaster* (3.4.346–8)

> to split the ears of the groundlings, who for the most part are capable of nothing but inexplicable dumb shows and noise
> > Shakespeare, *Hamlet* (3.2.10–13)

To the extent that it is known at all, *The Battle of Alcazar* is notorious for the ridicule it receives from Jonson, Dekker, Marston and especially Shakespeare, whose Ancient Pistol delightfully parodies roles made famous by Edward Alleyn, including Muly Mahamet: 'Then feed and be fat, my fair Calipolis' (*2H4*, 2.4.176).[150] But to know this play primarily from a parody is hardly fair, since most scholars regard *1 & 2 Tamburlaine*, another Pistol target, as the repository of 'Marlowe's mighty line' rather than wild rhetorical excess, even though Marlowe provides a fair measure of the latter.

The association with Marlowe is stronger than Alleyn having played Muly Mahamet, Tamburlaine and Barabas: *The Battle of Alcazar* belongs to a family of plays that are all, in G. K. Hunter's apt expression, 'sons of Tamburlaine'.[151] If we apply Alvin B. Kernan's brilliant analysis of Marlowe's prosodic style to *The Battle of Alcazar*, it is easy to see how intent Peele was to emulate what Kernan calls 'the steady, heavy beat of

"Marlowe's mighty line", carrying authority, determination and steady onward movement'. One need not look hard for the 'persistence of the rhetorical figure Hyperbole, conveying a constant striving for a condition beyond any known in this world', nor for the 'frequent use of ringing proper names and exotic geographical places to realise the sensed wideness, brightness, and richness of the world'.[152]

Marlowe's love for words with the privative suffix 'less', as in Zenocrate's 'With ceaselesse and disconsolate conceits/Which dies my lookes so lifelesse as they are' (*1 Tamb.*, 3.2.14–15) is echoed in the Presenter's 'rage and ruthless reign' (2.Prol.1) of war, and Muly Mahamet's 'He on whose glory all thy joy should stay/Is soulless, gloryless, and desperate' (2.3.32–3); the Presenter's Act 1 prologue also makes ample use of parataxis, 'the joining of several phrases by "and" to create a sense of endless ongoing, of constant reaching'.[153]

Peele's success in 'out-Tamburlaining *Tamburlaine*'[154] may have made for popular theatre, but not great poetry: imitating Marlowe is easy, matching him is next to impossible. Swinburne writes of the 'heavy tumidity' of the verse in *Alcazar*; to David H. Horne 'it is jerky and monotonous, with little attempt to utilize such devices as feminine endings, run-on lines, and variation of the caesural pause'.[155] One can easily imagine why the part of Muly Mahamet would have appealed to Edward Alleyn – one can also imagine Alleyn taking the writer aside and saying 'George, you're no Kit Marlowe'.

Where Peele learned from Marlowe, and surpassed him in a positive way, is in his command of the visual resources of the Elizabethan stage. *The Battle of Alcazar*, with its chariot entrance (borrowed from *Tamburlaine*), its blazing star, men placing their hands in fire to prove their loyalty, dead men's heads in dishes and murders replete with on-stage disembowelling, has a series of spectacular effects worthy of Cecil B. DeMille.[156] The use of the Presenter and dumb show is innovative and effective: as A. C. Braunmuller notes, Peele was the first to take the Presenter, 'familiar from civic shows like [his own] *Descensus Astraeae*', and place him on the playhouse stage.[157] Peele also transformed the dumb show, a convention going back to Seneca and put to elaborate use in *Gorboduc* and other early modern plays, by making it part of the Prologue; departing from the classical model, he introduces characters from the main play to act alongside the traditional Fates, Furies and other mythological figures.[158]

Ironically, this is what makes the play seem clumsy and old-fashioned to modern readers, who are understandably suspicious of any device that Shakespeare (the gold standard) not only eschews, albeit with some notable exceptions, but also denigrates, as in *Hamlet*. Like the Chorus of Greek tragedy, the dumb show is a convention that for all our trying, we cannot appreciate in the way its original audience did – while mute actors pantomime the words of the Presenter, one's memory of having played Queen Elizabeth, George Washington, or an ear of corn in a school pageant instantly arises. But dumb shows were the big 'production numbers' of the time and must have appealed to spectators then as a Broadway musical does today; as Dieter Mehl shows, they remained popular throughout the Elizabethan and Jacobean periods, and were employed by thoroughly professional dramatists such as Heywood well into the 1630s.[159]

'Mislike me not for my complexion'

> Mislike me not for my complexion,
> The shadowed livery of the burnished sun
> Shakespeare, The Merchant of Venice

Along with showing an advance in the ability of dramatic authors to exploit the physical resources of the Elizabethan stage, Peele's play would have been stunningly new and different to its audience in a way that has had far-reaching implications: The Battle of Alcazar represents the starting point for the complex and fascinating representation of the Moor in early modern drama.

'Moor' could be defined in a number of ways. As Jonathan Bate notes:

> The primary usage of the term 'Moor' in early modern English was as a religious, not a racial, identification: Moor meant 'Mohamedan', that is Muslim. The word was frequently used as a general term for 'not one of us', non-Christian . . . [The second sense] was racial and geographical; it referred to a native or inhabitant of Mauretania, a region of North Africa corresponding to parts of present-day Morocco and Algeria.[160]

Although Polemon describes the Saadian dynasty as being of 'the Mahometicall superstition . . . descended of the bloud & line of the damned and cursed false prophet Mahomet',[161] Alcazar is without any clear reference to Islam; Muly Mahamet is 'unbelieving' and a 'hapless heathen prince' (1.Prol.32, 4.Prol.1), but any mention of 'god' or 'gods' by him or other Moroccans either is vaguely pagan or alludes specifically to Greek or Roman deities. The importance of Alcazar lies in its multi-faceted approach to Bate's second definition, racial difference.

Before the play is a minute old, the Presenter brings Muly Mahamet to the stage with words that emphasise his colour: 'black in his look and bloody in his deeds', and his entrance for the first dumb show, 'in his shirt, stained with a cloud of gore' (1.Prol.16–17), must have been an impressive piece of theatre. The actor's face would have been made up with burnt cork and oil;[162] his hands could have been similarly painted or he might have worn black gloves. One of the most striking aspects of Henry Peacham's drawing of *Titus Andronicus*, if it does represent what the artist actually saw rather than what he imagined the appearance of the characters to be,[163] is how very 'coal-black' (3.2.77) Aaron the Moor is – as with Laurence Olivier's Othello, the 'exposed' legs (here probably covered with black hose rather than make-up) tend to grab one's attention, but the 'negro Moor' (2.Prol.3) Muly Mahamet and the other Moroccans of *Alcazar* would not be wearing chitons.

With his 'bloody deeds', accompanied by his flamboyant rhetoric, Muly Mahamet is the earliest known example of one 'type' of Moor in Elizabethan drama, but this characterization is far from the only one. Eldred Jones's assertion that the title 'Moor' is never used in reference to a particular character except for Muly Mahamet[164] is not quite accurate: the entering stage direction of 1.1 reads 'enter Abdelmelec with Calsepius Bashaw and his guard, and Zareo, a Moor, with soldiers' (1.1 OSD). True, the audience does not hear these words, but that is irrelevant, since Zareo and the others are there to be seen. This is an important point, because Jones's assumption that Abdelmelec and his followers 'were no doubt portrayed with very light makeup as white or tawny Moors, while the villain and his henchmen were more heavily made up as black Moors'[165] is open to *every* doubt.

To distinguish degrees of Moorishness by shades of skin colour would require technology that could hardly have existed in the sixteenth century, and the play, unlike the sources, has no direct allusion to Muly Mahamet's having inherited his colour from his mother. The word 'tawny' is never used, but, even if it were, 'black' and 'tawny' were not consistently applied in early modern drama: a person's colour could change at will, usually as required by the metre: Aaron's 'blackamoor child' (4.2.51.SD) is a 'black slave' (4.2.119), but he quietens the infant with 'peace, tawny slave, half me and half thy dam' (5.1.27). Eleazer of *Lust's Dominion* remarks 'Although my flesh be tawny, in my veines/Runs blood as red, and royal as the best', and follows with 'When thou in Crimson jollitie shalt Bath/Thy limbs as black as mine, in springs of blood' (1.1.154–5; 5.3.52–3).

A common trend in recent scholarship is to designate any Elizabethan who was not English and male as the essential 'other'. Moors may or may not have been more 'other' than Jews, Catholics, women, homosexuals, Turks, Irish, Welsh or any other such other, but the concept is particularly reductive if applied to *Alcazar*: unlike *Titus Andronicus*, *Othello* or *Lust's Dominion*, this play is set in Africa, and most of the major char-

acters, villainous or virtuous, are Africans, the most virtuous being the
'courteous and honourable Abdelmelec' (1.1.99).

Peele's 'brave Barbarian lord Muly Molocco' (1.Prol.12) is seemingly
interchangeable with 'Moly Moluch, King of Fez', the main subject of
Montaigne's essay 'Against Idleness, or Doing Nothing':

> Never did man more stoutly or more vigorously make use of an undanted
> [*sic*] courage than he. He found himselfe very weake to endure the cere-
> monious pompe which the Kings of that country, at their entrance into the
> camp are presented withall, which according to their fashion is full of all
> magnificence and state, and charged with all manner of action; and there-
> fore he resigned that honour to his brother, yet resigned he nothing but
> the office of the chiefe Captaine. Himselfe most gloriously executed and
> most exactly perfourmed all other necessary duties and profitable offices:
> holding his body laid along his cowch, but his minde upright and courage
> constant, even to his last gasp and in some sort after.

Montaigne's 'some sort after' is, of course, the story of Abd al-Malek's
death on the battlefield:

> ... then was he laid on his bed: but comming to himselfe again, starting
> up as out of a swown, each other faculty failing him, he gave them warning
> to conceale his death (which was the necessariest commandement he could
> give his servants, lest the souldiers, hearing of his death, might fall into
> despaire) and so yeelded the Ghost, holding his fore-fingers upon his
> mouth, an ordinary signall to impose silence. What man ever lived so long
> and so neere death? Who ever died so upright and undaunted? The
> extreamest degree, and most naturall, courageously to manage death, is to
> see or front the same, not onely without amazement, but without care; the
> course of life continuing free even in death.[166]

'Brave' and 'thrice noble' (5.1.31), Abdelmelec is the opposite of his
'accursed' (1.Prol.40) nephew; just as some of Muly Mahamet was
'absorbed' into the far more complex and interesting Aaron (who
may belong to Peele as much as he does to Shakespeare),[167] we see in
'thrice puissant and renowned Abdelmelec' (1.1.99) the ancestor of
Shakespeare's noble 'Prince of Morocco, a tawny Moor all in white' (*MV*
2.1 OSD), often, but wrongly, played as a buffoon, and indeed Othello.

Abdelmelec's 'younger brother Muly Mahamet Seth' (1.2.22) was,
according to Polemon, a far less admirable figure:

> he was acknowledged for king but with unwilling heartes, and in a manner
> repining threat: neither in deede was hee received with the same cheere-
> fullnesse and joye, that they used to receive other kings: and the cause
> thereof was, for that there was not mettall in this newe king [Muly] Hamet,

an artlesse man, not caring for martiall matters, nor such an one as was
fit for to upholde the dignitie of a king, but contrariwise effeminate, nice,
given to delicacies, delyghtes and pleasures, and lurking at home in the
pallace.[168]

These unglamorous attributes do not find their way into *The Battle of
Alcazar*; Peele obviously wanted to end on a positive note for Morocco.
In fact, Muly Ahmed al-Monsour was, at the time of the play's composition, a powerful reigning monarch, and England's political, commercial
and military relationship with Morocco was a vital element of Elizabethan
foreign policy. As has been noted, Abd al-Malek's victory at Alcazar was
due, in part, to the artillery he imported from England, and the 1580s
saw a continuation and intensification of diplomatic and commercial
traffic between the two countries. Morocco was not only a major sugar
exporter; its military importance to England was at its highest at the time
of the Spanish Armada and its aftermath.

Just as Abd al-Malek made a career of bolstering internal security by
promising to favour both Spain and the Ottoman Empire against each
other, depending on whom he was with at the time, Muly Ahmed al-
Monsour treated Spain and England in precisely the same fashion,
and for the same reasons. Early in 1589, he sent a message to Queen
Elizabeth offering

> unto your Ma[tie] not only to imploye in her assystaunce men, money, vyc-
> tualls, and the use of his poortes, but also his owne person, if your Ma[tie]
> should be pleased to require it: and to desyre, for the better withstanding
> of ther common enemy the Kinge of Spayne, here might [be] a sownde and
> perfect leage of amytie betwen them.[169]

The Moroccan King wanted

> to let her understande that for the better furtheraunce of her prynsely
> purpose to restore D. Antonio to the kingdome of Portugall, he thought
> it a good coorse, that the armye by sea that she shoold send with him
> [Antonio], shoold enter into the Straytes, and thear to shippe soche assys-
> taunce as he should send: wherby the King of Spayne, for the defense of
> those partes of Spayne within the Straytes, that coast uppon Barbarye,
> shoold be constraned to withdraw his forces owt of Portugall: whereby
> D. Antonio, fyndinge the contrey unfurnished of forreyn forces, may be
> better able to recover his contrey.[170]

Lastly, if all this went ahead, 'he woold delyver unto her Ma[tie] 150,000
ducats'.[171] In return, Muly Ahmed al-Monsour asked, 'in case of warre
falling out between him and anie princes his neighbors not being christians, to hire for his money certain shippes and mariners within this
realme, in such numbers and of such burden as shall have need to use',

and that he should be able to buy from England 'such provisione and commodityes as, from tyme to tyme, he shall have need of, being content that hir Matie shall doe the like for anie thing that may be had out of his dominiones for hir use'.[172] Knowing that Elizabeth could not possibly ally herself openly with a Moslem nation in a war against a Christian one, Sir Robert Cecil drafted a reply, saying that Muly Ahmed al-Monsour's offer of money was welcome, and should the King 'be assayled by any eathenique [heathenish] prince', England would be 'thankfull and readhye to requite', but 'touchinge his offer of men [the Queen] thinketh it not good, neyther for the seyd Kinge, nor for herself'.[173]

This is not to say that Peele was aware of all this and drew his portrait of the Moroccan king accordingly. Nevertheless, it is significant that one Moorish character was neither a historic villain like Muly Mahamet nor a historic hero like Abdelmelec, but a contemporary political figure whose importance would have been known to some members of the audience at the first performances, many more when the play was revived in 1592 and again in 1600 or 1601, perhaps the very time that a delegation of sixteen 'Barbarians',[174] headed by the King's emissary Abd el-Oahed ben Massaood, were visitors to the Elizabethan court. In 1600, still seeking 'an alliance to conquer Spain with a mixture of the English Navy and African troops',[175] the 'Barbarie Imbassador'[176] and his party achieved little except to make themselves very unpopular by running up huge expenses and then, instead of giving left-over provisions to the neighbouring poor as charity, 'reserved their fragments, & sold the same unto such poore as would give most for them'.[177]

The Battle of Alcazar also has Moorish women, but their parts are so small that little can be said about them – when editing the quarto for his Malone Society edition, Greg was unaware that Abdil Rayes was Abdelmelec's Queen, and listed her as one of his (male) 'followers': Q gives her only three speeches totalling thirteen lines, while Rubin Archis has four speeches for nineteen lines and a song. Calipolis's eighteen lines in the notorious scene where Muly Mahamet tells her to 'feed and faint no more' (2.3.70) show a firm resolve to bear misfortune patiently and a distinct lack of enthusiasm for a dinner of raw meat; she is mute in her two other scenes.

While Peele's presentation of the Moor in *Alcazar* represents a moment of genuine importance in the history of English drama, a key factor is missing. These Moors never reflect upon their own race, for they are in their own country; if the play has 'outsiders', they are the Europeans. Only when Aaron, the Prince of Morocco, and Othello reached the stage, each of them a single black man in a white man's world, would what Peele began come to fruition.

THE FAMOUS HISTORY OF THE LIFE AND DEATH OF
CAPTAIN THOMAS STUKELEY

'Tom Stukeley' may have been sufficiently prominent in *The Battle of Alcazar* to be included in Drake and Norris's farewell and to be mentioned by name on the title page of the quarto, but he is nevertheless a comparatively minor character whose speeches, in Bradley's nicely turned phrase, 'are mostly the padded out hyperboles of a wide-boy who has been reading his *Tamburlaine*'.[178] A play exploiting the entire Stukeley legend was still waiting to be written, and, some time before 11 August 1600, this challenge was taken up, as the Stationers' Register for that day records:

> Tho. Pavier Entred for his copies under the hande of mr vicars and the wardens these iii copies viz: Item ye history of the life & Deathe of Captaine Tho. Stucley, with the Mariage to ald. Curtis his daughter, & his valiant endinge of his life at the battell of Alcazar. xviii^d.

Five years later the play was published, the title page (fig. 3) showing *The Famous Historye of the life and death of Captaine Thomas Stukeley. With his marriage to Alderman Curteis Daughter, and valiant ending of his life at the Battaile of Alcazar. As it hath beene Acted.* The date of the Register entry does not tell us when the play was written, which could have been any number of years earlier, nor does 'As it hath beene acted' say who did the acting. No other known work, however, is a candidate for *Stewtley*, which first appears in Henslowe's note, 'lente more the 8 of desember 1596 for stewtleyes hosse iij^{li}'.[179] Henslowe recorded the first of ten performances at the Rose three days later, the last on 27 June 1597.[180] Here our problems begin: whether or not Q is anything like the play as acted in 1596 is a matter of great controversy.

It would be hard to find a text that is in a more 'disordered condition'[181] than *Captain Thomas Stukeley*. Scenes 1–6,[182] set in London, are reasonably coherent but for such minor inconsistencies as are found in many plays of this period, and very well written (see pp. 42–3). By comparison, Scenes 7–12, showing Stukeley's adventures in Ireland, are amateurish, and the first of them, written in blank verse, is inexplicably followed by a shorter, alternative version in 'stage-Irish' prose, with many Gaelic expressions (see Appendix III). Scenes 13–18, showing Stukeley in Spain, mark a return to the assurance of the London scenes, but then, as Richard Simpson comments in the introduction to his edition,[183] once Stukeley leaves for Rome, 'all is confusion'.[184] After Scene 19, set in Lisbon, the action does not go to Rome as promised, but to Morocco, where a Chorus reminds us that Stukeley, 'as you heard', was 'by the Pope created ... Marquess of Ireland' (20.11), even though we have neither

THE
Famous Hiſtorye of
the life and death of Captaine
Thomas Stukeley.

With his marriage to Alderman
Curteis Daughter, and valiant ending
of his life at the Battaile of
ALCAZAR.

As it hath beene Acted.

Printed for Thomas Pauyer, and are to be ſold at
his ſhop at the entrance into the
Exchange, 1605.

3 *The Famous Historye of the life and death of Captaine Thomas
Stukeley* (1605), title page

heard nor seen any such thing. Later, as Stukeley and his rival Vernon lie dying on the battlefield, Vernon (who goes wherever Stukley goes throughout the play) speaks of their meeting 'in Ireland, Spain, and at the last in Rome' (28.15). To this seemingly missing Roman sequence we add the Chorus's promise, after the capture of Don Antonio, that we will see 'all those mishaps that this poor prince attend' (27.13). Antonio never re-appears.[185]

   As a partial solution to these and other inconsistencies, Simpson proposed in the 1870s that whatever form the original *Stukeley* may have taken, the 1605 quarto is an amalgam of the original drama on Stukeley and two other plays. The scenes involving Don Antonio are 'taken from some play on the subject of [this prince] . . . a drama intended to recommend to the English the claims of Antonio to the crown'. Furthermore, 'there are interwoven, in the 5th act, fragments of another play upon the *battle of Alcazar*, or *Stucley*, or the Moor Mahamet and his wife Calipolis'.[186] Furthermore, 'amidst these fragments there are a few interpolations by the writer of the first three acts'.[187] E. H. C. Oliphant agreed in a 1905 essay: 'that this play . . . is a joint production is fairly evident'. After giving a detailed list of which putative author wrote which part, nominating Fletcher as the author of the early sequences, he closes with 'how or why the mixing up of the two plays was effected I do not pretend to be able to guess'.[188]

   The 'how or why' was supplied by Joseph Quincy Adams in 1916:

> The play as it has come down to us . . . had been crudely reworked and hurriedly patched up for a revival. The occasion for the revival was probably the rumour of King Sebastian's escape from the Battle of Alcazar, and the appearance of a pretender, who, boldly asserting that he was Sebastian, laid claim to the throne of Portugal.[189]

Adams's reviser wrote the new Irish version of Scene 7, changed the names of some characters in Scene 5 from their names in Scene 3,[190] and, as Simpson proposed, replaced the last scenes with material 'from another drama, an account of King Sebastian's disastrous campaign in Africa . . . the fourth act of *Stewtly*, located in Rome, was entirely discarded'.[191] Therefore, 'the play that has come down to us in the edition of 1605, with the title *Captaine Thomas Stukeley*, represents all that is extant of two older plays – the *Stewtley* of Henslowe's *Diary*, 1596, and another play, which in the absence of a title, we may refer to as *Sebastian and Antonio*'.[192]

   The powerful trio of Simpson, Oliphant and Adams standing in unanimity, their multi-play theory has become an orthodoxy. Levinson does not accept all its aspects, but concludes, 'it seems probable that the quarto comprises portions of at least two plays'.[193] The only difficulty here, as Wiggins writes in an incisive essay, is that no evidence that the Portuguese and African material comes from another play has been offered, nor is there any evidence 'that any separate play on Don Antonio ever existed'.[194]

Indeed, however bad the text of *Stukeley* may be, it is a model of dramatic coherence compared with *Sebastian and Antonio* as Adams describes it. First, this lost play is 'an account of King Sebastian's disastrous campaign in Africa', inserted 'to satisfy the demands of an audience intensely interested in the claims of the Portuguese Pretender'.[195] One page later, it

> would seem to have been devoted to the careers of King Sebastian and his cousin Antonio; apparently it celebrated primarily the life of Antonio. The play may have been inspired by the desperate efforts of Antonio to gain the throne of Portugal from the hands of the Spaniards who had seized the country after the death of Sebastian at the battle of Alcazar . . . It should be remembered that the cause of Antonio was stoutly championed by the English.[196]

Two pages on, Sebastian is forgotten: we have 'a drama celebrating the career of Antonio'.[197]

The cause of this dramaturgical mayhem is obvious. If Sebastian is still alive, then Don Antonio is not the rightful king of anything – a play 'celebrating the career of Antonio' is of immediate interest only if Sebastian is dead. Hence, Adams's assertion of topicality in 1598–99 will not withstand the slightest scrutiny: Don Antonio was important ten years earlier, when *The Battle of Alcazar* was written, just before he joined Drake and Norris's expedition to reclaim his crown. In 1590, after that project's disastrous failure, Antonio went to France; he died in Paris on 26 August 1595. It would have been wonderful if the new material inserted into *Stewtley* showed Sebastian's miraculous escape and his secret life in a Venetian monastery, as told in Munday's *The Strangest Adventure that Ever Happened* (1601); unfortunately the real miraculous escape was Antonio's.[198] To be sure, the original of *Stukeley* might have had something, as the Chorus promises, to show 'those mishaps that this poor prince attend' (27.13), but the words 'poor prince' imply an historical perspective that could well have been written in 1596, the year of Henslowe's *Stewtly* and a year after Antonio died.

Wiggins makes some trenchant observations on this subject: the author of the corrected drama, as Simpson calls him,[199] must have accounted himself very lucky to have two (or more) plays at hand on the same subject;[200] it is also strangely convenient that the parts of the plays

Adams's reviser did not use have disappeared without a trace. Indeed, if the company had two plays, *Stewtley* and *Sebastian and Antonio*, why would someone insert material from one into the other: 'Why not just revive *Sebastian and Antonio* in the first place?'[201]

To *prove* the multiple-play idea wrong is impossible; one can only submit an alternative. Although no imagined reconstruction of the 'original' *Stukeley* can satisfy all the anomalies of the text, the 1605 quarto is more likely to be the product of contemporaneous collaboration by two or more dramatists, rather than a later revision.

As Carol Chillington Rutter writes, collaboration was the standard means of production at the Rose in 1596: 'The working habits of playwrights are displayed in the pages of Henslowe's loan accounts with the Admiral's Men and Worcester's Men, where one discovers that the typical Rose play was a collaboration involving sometimes as many as five playwrights who frequently submitted their scripts piecemeal and who rarely occupied themselves on one play for longer than a month.'[202] Andrew Gurr agrees that playwriting at this time was usually a collective exercise, 'in 1598, 82 per cent of the plays bought for the [Admiral's] company were written in collaboration'.[203]

This system was not necessarily 'imposed' on a community of writers who would rather have worked alone, as in countless stories of gifted writers slaving under the Hollywood studio system of the 1930s and 1940s, endlessly re-writing each other's screenplays. Rutter considers it

> a fallacy to suppose that collaboration was unhealthy or was forced on the playwrights, when Henslowe's Diary shows that they could work as quickly and lucratively alone as in partnership. This must mean that collaboration was a chosen, even perhaps a preferred, method of writing. It may have been more efficient in permitting each playwright to do the job he liked best–kings or clowns, plotting or poetry or prose – in the play.[204]

Tasks may have been divided in other ways – Neil Carson cites evidence to show that at times the dramatists wrote separate parts of the text, but at other times they worked very closely together throughout.[205]

Authorship

If the premise of collaboration is accepted, some speculations might be made about who was part of the writing team; however unpersuasive Adams's idea of *Sebastian and Antonio* might be, I believe him to be precisely correct in attributing much of the first half of the play to Thomas Heywood.

Adams begins with thirteen 'general characteristics suggesting Heywood', noting 'the breezy spirit of adventure . . . the intimate and sympathetic picture of London middle-class life in the first act, and the flattering portrayal of English bourgeois character throughout the Stukeley parts', along with the 'strong note of patriotism'.[206] Since these characteristics are shared by any number of dramatists active in the 1590s, they do not necessarily point to Heywood, but Adams adds, 'in *Stukeley* the "humour" of the character of Alderman Curtis is the constant use of the tag "Bones a dod, man"', and notes that in Heywood's *The Second Part of If You Know Not Me, You Know Nobody*, the London haberdasher Hobson is fond of the expression, 'Bones a me'. Adams also observes that 'Curtis's other tag, "by yea and nay", and a third, "passion of me"', are also in the Heywood play.[207]

Curtis is hardly the only gruff city man in early modern drama, and one would expect such colourful expressions to be common: 'passion of me', while spoken by Hobson, is also found in plays by Middleton and Dekker. 'Bones a dod', however, is seemingly unique to *Stukeley*, and, in turning to 2 *If You Know Not Me*, we hear Hobson's very similar 'bones a God' four times and 'bones a me' over fifty times. The Chadwyck-Healey *English Drama* database[208] (admittedly not totally comprehensive) has these expressions appearing in no other play of the period; Curtis's description of Stukeley as a 'spend-good' (1.107), also echoed by Hobson, is found in no other text.

Even without these verbal clues, Heywood's 2 *If You Know Not Me* would still be important to us. As Sir Thomas Gresham, Hobson, the Lord Mayor and the Sheriff of London discuss the site for a new Royal Exchange, they see '*A blasing Starre*', and after the Sheriff remarks on this 'sight so wonderfull' (sig. E2v) Gresham's factor arrives with

> Unwelcome newes, sir, the King of Barbarie is slaine . . .
> . . . in that renowned Battell,
> Swift Fame desires to carry through the world:
> The Battle of Alcasar, wherein two Kings
> Besides this King of Barbarie was slaine,
> Kings of Moroco and of Portugale,
> With Stewkeley that renowned Englishman
> That had a spirit equall with a King,
> Mad fellow with these Kings in war-like strife,
> Honor'd his Countrey and concluded life.
>
> (sig. E3r)

After Gresham reflects on the implications for his investments in the Moroccan sugar trade, Hobson says:

> By the Marie-god it was a dangerous day,
> Three Kings beside yong Stewkeley slaine:

Ile tell you my Lord Maior what I have seene
When sword and bucklers were in question,
I have seene that Stewkeley beat a street before him,
He was so familliar growne in every[209] mouth,
That if it happened any fighting were,
The question straight was, was not Stewkely there.
Bones a me he would hew it.

(sig. E3v)

This sword-and-buckler man, 'yong Stewkely', as he is described here, is identical to 'that unthrifty boy, Tom Stukeley' (2.30) of our play, and nothing at all like the real Stukeley, who was in his fifties when he died at Alcazar, or Peele's comparatively colourless character. Admittedly, there could have been many a ballad about Stukeley, now lost, in circulation, and Heywood need not have written the earlier play to have borrowed from it, but there are yet more comparisons that may be drawn between parts of *Stukeley* and Heywood.

Versification

One of the most difficult of the problems facing the editor of this text is the manner in which Pavier's compositor set Scenes 1 to 6 and Scene 13. Apparently unable to decide if many passages were in verse or prose, he gave up, printing them as neither.

An easily overlooked feature of Elizabethan dramatic manuscripts is that the most recognisable indicator of verse, a capital at the beginning of each line, is hardly ever seen, and the 'justified right' that marks prose was (and is) possible only in print. Hence the compositor was the first editor of many an early modern play: often, he had just to *know* whether something was prose or verse, particularly when, owing to the size of the handwriting or narrowness of the paper, many verse lines went to the right edge.

Two Heywood manuscripts in the British Library, *The Captives* and *The Escapes of Jupiter*,[210] are perfect examples of what the unfortunate compositor (if he cared) had to deal with. Of course, it would be foolish to contend that Heywood's notoriously 'terrible' handwriting[211] somehow shows that he wrote *Stukeley*: others wrote as badly, there is no manuscript to examine, and we cannot tell for sure if the printer's copy was authorial, scribal, a playhouse book, or took some other form.[212] The handwriting of whoever prepared the manuscript is not the point; the dramatic style of the original author is.

Printers and editors must choose between prose or verse, but they are the only people who need always do so. From the mighty line of Marlowe to the subtle permutations of Shakespeare's late plays, blank verse is capable of almost infinite variation, and, English being heavily iambic, what sounds like verse can, as Stephen Orgel observes, 'be prose that has the rhythm of verse'.[213] No actor with the slightest amount of skill or sensitivity would say that verse and prose should be handled the same way, yet any good actor is aware that no hard and fast distinction exists – there is a middle ground with elements of both. Nobody knew this better than that master actor Winston Churchill, who set out his famous radio speeches in something very close to verse, called 'speech form' or 'psalm form' by his staff.[214]

Like his younger colleague Middleton, Heywood often provided his actors with dialogue, as Paul Merchant notes, for which 'it would probably be a vain pursuit to attempt a precise distinction between his loosely accented, colloquial verse and its twin, his casual conversational prose'.[215] *The Fair Maid of the Exchange*, *1 Fair Maid of the West*, *The Wise Woman of Hogsdon*, *2 If You Know Not Me*, *The Captives* and *The English Traveller*, all known to be by Heywood or reasonably attributable to him, show a fluid movement between prose and verse and have passages that could be set out as either. Again, these characteristics are not exclusive to Heywood amongst dramatists of the mid-1590s, but what we know of Heywood's circumstances in late 1596 also make him at least a very likely part-author of *Stukeley*.

Nearly forty years after the time that now concerns us, Heywood boasted of *The English Traveller*, 'this Tragi-Comedy [is] one reserved amongst two hundred and twenty in which I have had either an entire hand, or at the least a maine finger'.[216] Nothing is known for certain of his earliest theatre work until October of 1596, when Henslowe loaned thirty shillings to the Admiral's Men for the purchase of 'hawodes bocke',[217] but, as Vittorio Gabrieli and Giorgio Melchiori note, 'the fact that in 1596 a shrewd impresario like Henslowe' would make this payment 'shows that by that time [Heywood] enjoyed a fair reputation as a playwright'.[218] Two years later, Francis Meres accounted Heywood one of the dramatists 'best for comedy' in *Palladis Tamia*;[219] what might Heywood, who would have been in his twenties, have written during this time to deserve Henslowe's trust and Meres's praise?

One strong possibility is *The Four Prentices of London*. Like *The Battle of Alcazar*, this play does not appear in Henslowe's *Diary* under its published title, but could very well have been what Henslowe calls the '2 pte. of godfrey of bullen', marked as a 'ne' play on 19 July 1594.[220] It is also generally accepted that Heywood is 'Hand B', who supplied extra lines for the Clown in the additions to the manuscript of *Sir Thomas More*; Gabrieli and Melchiori argue persuasively that these additions were produced 'not later than 1594'.[221] Heywood's 'book'[222] was bought in October 1596, and *Stewtly* was played, marked 'ne', on 11 December. If we assume that the book was indeed performed later that year or early the following year, then only four other 'ne' plays, all lost, qualify: *Vortigern* (4 December), *Nebuchadnezzar* (19 December), *That Will Be Shall Be* (30 December) and *Alexander and Lodowick* (14 January).

What little one can tell of these plays' style or content by their titles says that Heywood could have had a hand in any or all of them, and none of this is sufficient to take before an 'authorship jury'. There is nothing to prove that one of *Stukeley*'s authors was borrowing from himself – he could easily have been an early Heywood imitator, or one who simply shared some characteristics with Heywood. As with all circumstantial evidence, none of the other 'usual suspects' is eliminated, but, of all writers thought to be around the Admiral's Men in late 1596, Heywood must be accounted the prime suspect.

Perhaps to the reader's great relief, I offer no opinion on who might have written the other parts of the play. The African scenes in particular share few characteristics with those set in London, except for one short speech (21.52–8) when Stukeley, a rather stodgy character in the latter part of the play, changes back to the 'wild, lewd, unthrift' (2.131) Stukeley of the beginning, implying that 'the party of the first part', as Groucho Marx says in *A Night at the Opera*, at least did some revising for 'the party of the second part'.

The play
However *Stukeley* was first put together, what ended up in Pavier's print shop must have been at least slightly different from what was performed, and there is no limit to collaboration or revision scenarios one could conjure up to explain the presence of the extra Irish scene, the mention of a Roman sequence that does not occur, and the play's other anomalies; to do so would be to create another *Sebastian and Antonio*. What most critics agree on, myself included, is that the first part of it is an excellent piece of work. Oliphant considers it 'amongst the best of the less-known plays of the so-called Elizabethan era . . . in the first three acts the character of Stukeley is magnificently conceived and excellently sustained, and the play contains some scenes that would do no discredit to any play of the period – notably the humorous third scene of the first act'.[223]

In his study of the Elizabethan history play, Irving Ribner says that *Stukeley* is written 'in the manner of the biographical drama',[224] but a better genre, at least for the early scenes, is supplied by the Chorus:

> Thus far through patience of your gentle ears
> Hath Stukeley's life in *comic history*
> Been new revived . . .

(20.1–3)

Here, 'historical' characters and incidents form the background to a purely fictional story: the hero is not the historical Stukeley but 'another person of the same name', and, in showing his youthful exploits, the emphasis is on the 'comic'. Indeed, the London scenes are a fine example of what came to be called city comedy, a form whose antecedents lay in the works of Menander, Terence and Plautus. Contrary to the known record, young Stukeley is a student at the Inns of Court, where, to the dismay of his father, he neglects his studies and spends his time drinking, brawling, playing tennis and running up debts. To the even greater dismay of his fictional friend and rival Vernon, Stukeley follows city comedy tradition in marrying the wealthy Nell (not Anne) Curtis for her father's money.

The transfer of the action to Ireland establishes the 'structural spine'[225] of the play: wherever Stukeley goes, Vernon will (unwittingly) go too. These scenes also provide good opportunities for Stukeley to be contemptuous of authority, but the pedestrian blank verse has little of the colour and wit that characterise the previous sequence, and the 'promise' of the London scenes is soon dissipated. Ironically, an historical record of Stukeley's affairs in the 1560s was available to the dramatist, and would have made for excellent theatre had he chosen to use it, but it is almost completely ignored. Stukeley's friendship with Shane O'Neill, the Florida venture and his life as a pirate are all absent; instead, Stukeley is merely a captain come to fight the Ulster rebels at Dundalk.

O'Neill is a pale imitation of his prototype, and there is only the merest hint of his violent death at the hands of the Macdonnells in Antrim (Sc. 12). His presence serves no purpose, a view apparently shared by the unknown author of *The Famous History of Stout Stukley* (1650). This prose pamphlet of twenty-four pages is an adaptation of the play, frequently quoting it verbatim: Stukeley and Vernon go from London to Ireland to Spain to Africa (as in *Q*, no trip to Rome). Chapter 6, headed *How Stukley met Vernon and Harbert in Ireland, and how he was shut out of the town by Herbert, Governor of the Town by the English*,[226] has no mention at all of O'Neill.

Stukeley's Spanish adventure (Scenes 13–18), including the quarrel with the Governor of Cadiz and Stukeley's victory through the traditional means of charming the Governor's wife, is both conventional and enjoyable. Scene 13 shows the same mix of prose and verse that marked Scenes 1–6, and is the last to do so, but when in Spain Stukeley is still 'lusty Tom Stukeley' (17.25): he speaks very respectfully to the King (Sc. 14), but is happy to tell his marshal, Valdes, 'foutre for [the King's] ducats' (18.19).

With the introduction of Philip II, the play moves into new territory. He and his famous generals, the Duke of Alva and Sancho de Avila, are depicted as scheming hypocrites who draw King Sebastian on with 'expectation of a strong supply' (14.105), so that 'Spain and Portingall shall be unite', and Philip shall be 'the sovereign ruler of them both' (14.96–7). This theme is developed further in Scene 16, where Philip sends Stukeley to Rome to gain the Pope's approval for the invasion of Africa, then gloats over using the Englishman in his plan to get rid of Sebastian, and in Scene 19, set in the Portuguese court, where Don Antonio, who is not in *Alcazar* at all, is introduced as a prominent character. The author or authors of these wildly unhistorical scenes give more emphasis to the anti-Spanish attitude found in the *Explanation* than does Peele,[227] having Sebastian declare his 'dearest cousin' Antonio successor 'unto the crown of Portingall', should he fall in Africa (19.65–7).

As with *The Battle of Alcazar*, critical response to *Captain Thomas Stukeley* has been strongly influenced by perception of what the original, 'uncorrupted' text was like. Since the quarto follows Stukeley and Vernon to four different places, with indication that a fifth location, Rome, was to be included, Simpson assumes 'it was manifestly intended . . . to be a biographical play, exhibiting in five acts distinct pictures of the hero's life, in different age and circumstances',[228] a logical but unlikely inference.

Wilfred T. Jewkes's analysis of the five-act structure in early modern drama shows that except for the 'University' dramatists, Marlowe, Kyd, Greene and Peele, it was the exception rather than the rule; for Heywood, Dekker and Shakespeare, act divisions are rarely shown in the early texts, nor are they structurally apparent. Furthermore, the quarto of *Stukeley* is already a long play of over 2800 lines without the extra Scene 7; this is particularly important because the 'missing' Roman sequence would have to make the play well over 3000 lines long. However, we have another possibility, one which I believe to be more probable: the Roman sequence is *not* missing, for it never existed in the first place.

I have argued that many of Q's inconsistencies are the result of collaboration. Most would have been ironed out in rehearsal, although the changes were not included in the printer's copy. It is important to remember that the two *major* textual cruxes in the play are caused by what the Chorus says, and to assume that a Roman sequence or, as will be seen, the further adventures of Don Antonio were once in the play is to give the Chorus far too much authority: why cannot his speeches have been slightly revised in the final putting together of the different dramatists' contributions? The *story*, of course, takes both Stukeley and Vernon to Rome, but the only indication that a visit to Rome was enacted, rather than occurring off-stage, is the Chorus's 'For by the Pope created *as you heard* / Marquess of Ireland' (20.10–11). One would be splitting hairs to say that 'as you heard' could refer to the audience's general knowledge rather than what it heard that day in the playhouse; one would not be splitting hairs to suggest that the writer of this part of the play assumed, or even was told, there would be a Roman scene, but that this idea was later abandoned. The rest of the Chorus's speech tells us to imagine all of the hero's adventures until he arrives in Africa with King Sebastian; changing only a few words would include Rome in these off-stage events.

The African sequence and the order of the final scenes
To use a Chorus and dumb show to introduce the African sequence should not be considered untidy, or a lapse in dramatic construction: as noted above (pp. 28–9), the device was very popular throughout the period, and, although it would be far too much of a stretch to cite this as evidence of authorship, in *The Four Prentices of London* (sig. C1r–C2r) and *The Fair Maid of the West, Part 2* (sig. G4r–v) Heywood uses a dumb show to fill in the narrative – in *Fair Maid*, as in *Stukeley*, it occurs late in the play.

The depiction of the battle of Alcazar owes much, including some inconsistencies,[229] to both Polemon and the *Explanation*. The author must also have used Peele as a 'source', since it is hard to see how else the character of Calipolis found her way into the play,[230] although the Moroccans, inhabiting only nine scenes rather than an entire play, obviously have less to do.

Adams's statement that Stukeley is 'almost lost sight of'[231] once the action gets to Africa is not quite accurate. His absence from Scene 22, the pre-battle parley in which the opposing sides state their defiance and hurl insults at one another, is indeed conspicuous, but unlike the comparable 4.2 of *Alcazar*, the scene in which Sebastian, Avero, Antonio and Stukeley decide 'in counsel together' (23 OSD) whether to attack or withdraw, Stukeley is chief spokesman for a prudent military strategy, counteracting Sebastian's recklessness (this is not necessarily inconsistent with the Stukeley of the early scenes: in *King John*, obviously a far more coherent play than this one, Shakespeare combines the same youthful bravado and *realpolitik* in the Bastard). Of course, Stukeley also has a seemingly interminable death scene.

We have arrived at the most vexing of the play's textual irregularities, starting with the capture of Don Antonio, followed by the Chorus:

> Thus of Alcazar's battle in one day
> Three kings at once did lose their hapless lives.
> Your gentle favour must we needs entreat,
> For rude presenting such a royal fight,
> Which more imagination must supply
> Than all our utmost strength can reach unto.
>
> (27.1–6)

So far, this is straightforward: of the 'three kings', Sebastian and
Abdelmelec have died on stage, and Muly Mahamet has fled and may be
presumed dead (we have heard or seen nothing of Stukeley since he went
off to fight at the end of Scene 23). But then the Chorus returns to the
subject of Antonio:

> Suppose the soldiers, who you saw surprised
> The poor dismayèd Prince Antonio,
> Have sold him to the wealthy Moor they talked of,
> And that such time as needs must be allowed,
> Already he hath passed in servitude.
> Sit now and see unto our story's end,
> All those mishaps that this poor prince attend.

(27.7–13)

'Sit now' as long we might, we see no such thing; Antonio neither appears
nor is he mentioned for the rest of the play.

There is no way of knowing how much additional action with Don
Antonio was written, or where it was placed, and, as with the 'Roman
scene', we might also ask if this Chorus speech may have been later
revised. Assuming for the moment there were indeed some 'further
mishaps' of Antonio shown, Wiggins's suggestion that the Chorus's 'sit
now and see' (27.12) could be introducing another dumb show,[232] just as
'regard this show' leads to one at 20.21, is apt.

But a massive complication follows: at the end of the Chorus speech,
the Q stage directions read 'After Antonio's going out / Enter Muly hamet
with victorie', even though (in one of many unmarked exits) Antonio and
his captors left the stage thirteen lines earlier – even if Antonio took part
in a dumb show, surely the Chorus would begin with a clear stage, as
earlier in this play, and in Alcazar.

These directions deserve our careful attention: the plural is used
because there are two different directions here, printed on two different
lines:[233] if they are treated as one, then another Antonio sequence must
have led directly to the entrance of the Moroccans 'with victorie'.

Of all elements that comprise this text, stage directions must be given
the least authority; Levinson counts five entrances and twenty-two exits
that are missing or incomplete,[234] and other directions are either mean-
ingless or preposterously misplaced. The printer's difficulty in deciding
what is prose and what is verse has been noted; the placement of stage
directions in Elizabethan dramatic manuscripts presented a similar
problem, as they were often written in the margins, boxed and put wherever there was room for them. Therefore they could be some distance
from the exact line or lines to which they related.

On sig. L3r of Q (see fig. 4), the compositor seems to have been

# of Tho. Stukely.

What haſt thou Sirra, that may ſaue thy life?

Anto. All that I haue my frends, ile giue ye fréely,
So it may pleaſe ye but to ſaue my life?
Which to deſtroy will do ye little good.

2. Soul. Come then be bréfe, lets ſée, what haſt thou?

Anto. This purſe containeth all the coine I haus,
Theſe Bracelets my dead Lord beſtowed on me,
That if I ſcapt, I might remember him,
In my deuotions and my daily praiers.

2. Soul. Whoſe prieſt waſt thou?

anto. Ferdinands, duke of Aueros.

2. Soul. Well liſten fellowes twil do vs little good
To kil him, when we may make benefit
By ſelling of him to be ſome mans ſlaue:
And now I call to mind the wealthy More,
amaleck that dwelles héer in the Feſſe, héele giue as much
as any man, how ſay ye ſhal it be ſo.

2 Soul. No better counſell can be.

anto. Thy will O God be done, what ere become of me

Chorus.

Thus of Alcazars battell in one day
thrée kings at once did loſe their haples liues.
Your gentle fauour muſt we néeds entreat,
For rude preſenting ſuch a royall fight,
Which more imaginatian muſt ſupply:
Then all our vtmoſt ſtrength can reach vnto.
Suppoſe the Soldiours, who you ſaw ſurprizd,
the poore diſmayed prince antonio:
Haue ſold him to the wealthy More they talkt off,
And that ſuch time as néeds muſt be allowed,
already he hath paſt in ſcruttude,
Sit now and ſée vnto our ſtories end,
all thoſe miſhaps that this poore Prince attend.

After antonio's going out
Enter Muly hamet with victorie.

L 3   ſoul.

---

4 The Famous Historye of the life and death of Captaine Thomas
Stukeley (1605), sig. L3r

struggling for space, and could well have missed a line or lines: the Second Soldier's last three lines are squeezed into two, and Antonio's final line, 'Thy will . . .' is a heptameter going to the right margin, the only one in the latter part of the play. In view of other misplaced directions, it is not surprising to see 'After antonio's going out' inserted at the bottom of the page, where it makes as much sense as does 'Oneale Flies, Alexander pursues him out' (see n. 12.69), which also starts at the bottom of a page (sig. F1r). If 'After Antonio's going out' was meant to relate to anything above it, the appropriate place would be near Antonio's last line; there is no *necessary* connection to 'Enter Muly hamet with victorie'.

The ensuing 'victory' scene on the next page in Q is only twenty-three lines, and is obviously deficient. It begins in the middle of a soldier's report of the names and number of enemy dead, a report no one has asked him for, while the entry direction strongly implies that the first speech must have been Muly Hamet's, in which he claims victory before hearing details of casualties. The soldier relates the deaths of several Portuguese lords, Stukeley and Muly Mahamet, with no mention of King Sebastian, so one wonders why Muly Hamet's first words are 'See that the body of Sebastian / Have Christian and kingly burial' (29.9–10). He then, as in *Alcazar*, gives instructions for the stuffing of Muly Mahamet, and the Moroccans exit, whereupon Stukeley, already reported dead, enters with Vernon to die all over again.

The inescapable inference is that Q has the final scenes of the play in the wrong order, and that Stukeley's death was to be shown before a report of it in the (fragmentary) victory scene, exactly as occurs in *The Battle of Alcazar*. There is nothing in the Stukeley–Vernon death scene that argues for its being the final episode – the eponymous heroes Richard III and Macbeth both die on the battlefield before their vanquishers end the play with a victory pronoucement – hence this edition reverses the order of quarto Scenes 28 and 29.[235]

CONCLUSION

The Battle of Alcazar and *The Famous History of the Life and Death of Captain Thomas Stukeley* are hardly the only Elizabthan plays whose appeal is drastically curtailed by their coming to us in such poor texts. For all his rhetorical excesses, Peele's reputation would be much higher than it is had printers served him better, and I suspect that, like other plays of the period long thought to be unperformable until someone proved otherwise, *Alcazar* could, in the hands of an inventive director and a cast of skilled actors, provide an exciting evening's theatre.

One point, nearly always overlooked, is that the elaborate verse of Marlowe, Kyd and Peele does *not* imply an elaborate, artificial style of acting. Indeed, the reverse might be true – the more seemingly histrionic the line, the simpler and more subtle its delivery should be. Unfortunately, in my experience, not many actors are aware of this, but *The Battle of Alcazar* is a much better play if approached in this manner. Modern theatre companies would do very well to look at *Captain Thomas Stukeley*. This play seems worse than it is because some textual inconsistencies announce, rather loudly, that part of it is missing. But if, as argued above, some of the 'missing' material never actually existed, then minor cuts to the Chorus's speeches remove the most glaring problems. If we then dispense with Scene 12 (Shane O'Neill's death), what remains is a coherent play, full of sprightly dialogue and interesting characters. The author of 'the book of the play', *The Famous History of Stout Stukley*, certainly knew this, for the hypothetical performance text as described here has precisely this narrative. The 'play of the book of the play' could be a very good play indeed.

NOTES

1 William Camden, *The Historie of the Life and Reigne of the Most Renowmed and Victorious Princesse Elizabeth, late Queene of England*, London, 1630, Bk 1, pp. 61–2.

2 Along with being a physician, William Stukeley was a noted antiquarian. This comment was written in his copy of *The Life and Death of Captain Thomas Stukeley*, a quarto now held at the Folger Shakespeare Library. Dr Stukeley also notes of his relative, 'It is said that he was one of the finest men of his time: of a daring, ambitious Spirit, a great spendthrift'.

3 As with most early modern names, there is a variety of spellings to choose from. The quarto of *The Battle of Alcazar* usually uses 'Stukley'; *The Famous Historye of the life and death of Captaine Thomas Stukeley* has 'Stukeley' on the title page, but 'Stukely', 'Stukly' and 'Stuklie' are also found in the text. As will be seen in quotations, other documents provide numerous variations. The *Dictionary of National Biography*, Richard Simpson's biographical essay and John Izon's book all use 'Stucley', but Juan E. Tazón's recent study has 'Stukeley'. After much vacillation, I have decided on 'Stukeley', so that the title of the second play in this volume is the same as in previous editions.
   The first Stukeley biography of any substance is Richard Simpson's essay, published posthumously, in *The School of Shakspere*, v. 1, London, 1878. Based on research in the *State Papers* and other documents, it is both thorough and readable, although there are conspicuous gaps, particularly concerning Elizabeth Peppard, the wealthy widow Stukeley married in Ireland (see p. 6). A. F. Pollard's essay in the *Dictionary of National Biography* is, by virtue of space limitations, cursory, and has some errors – Pollard has Stukeley travelling to 'Bivero (in Sicily)', when Bivero is simply an alternative spelling for the Spanish town of Vivero.

John Izon's *Sir Thomas Stucley, c. 1525–1578: Traitor Extraordinary*, London, 1956, deserves more respect than it has been given. The style is hilarious, full of invented private thoughts and conversations, such as this account of the Spanish ambassador's meeting with Stukeley: 'Warily he asked himself, could this Thomas Stucley be sincere in his protestations? Could he be trusted? He hardly knew what to make of him. Such a gentle Hercules, so mild, suave, soft spoken, took him completely by surprise. There was something astonishingly winning about the man . . .' (p. 60), and his characterisation of the Ulster rebel Shane O'Neill: 'this O'Neill lived like a Sultan, and his wine, like his horses and hounds and women, was vintage' (p. 68). Nevertheless, Izon's research is both careful and extensive, and his book is delightful to read.

Juan E. Tazón's *The Life and Times of Thomas Stukeley (c. 1525–78)*, London, 2003, gives large doses of historical background, in which Stukeley is not mentioned, that could be included in a biography of anyone who lived at the time. Some material, drawn from Spanish sources, is most interesting, but there are what I believe to be some errors regarding Stukeley's marriages (see p. 6). Tazón's first chapter covers the Stukeley legend in literature, and his reading of the two plays in this volume differs from mine in most respects.

4 Thomas Westcote, *A View of Devonshire in MDCXXX, with a Pedigree of Most of Its Gentry*, ed. George Oliver and Pitman Jones, Exeter, 1845, p. 271. Westcote was born in 1567, and would not have known Thomas Stukeley, although older members of his family surely would have done.

5 Simpson (p. 4) goes through some elaborate guesswork based on the probable age of Stukeley's brother when the brother's daughter was born, and concludes that Stukeley was born 'sometime before 1520'.

6 *APC* 3: 422 (21 Nov. 1551).

7 *Literary Remains of King Edward the Sixth*, ed. John Gough Nichols, London, 1857, p. 456.

8 *Calendar of State Papers, Foreign Series, of the Reign of Edward VI* (1547–53), London, 1861, p. 218 (3 Aug. 1552).

9 *Literary Remains*, pp. 455–6.

10 *Literary Remains*, pp. 462–3.

11 *APC* 4: 312 (6 Aug. 1553).

12 *Calendar of State Papers, Foreign Series, of the Reign of Mary*, Nendeln, 1967, p. 126 (9 Oct. 1554).

13 *APC* 5: 131–2 (22 May 1555). Judging by the number of cases listed in the Privy Council papers, 'coining' was akin to a national sport at the time.

14 *APC* 5: 152 (24 June 1555). Tazón, without giving any reason, states that Stukeley's first wife was not Anne Curtis, but 'a woman from Devon whose name is unknown' (p. 40).

15 *APC* 5: 259 (2 Apr. 1556).

16 *SP Dom. Mary*, v. 13 (27 Aug. 1558); see also *APC* 6: 340 (1 June 1558).

17 *SP For.* (25 Nov. 1559).

18 George North, *The Description of Swedland, Gotland, and Finland, the auncient estate of theyr Kynges . . . collected and gathered out of sundry laten aucthors, but chieflye out of Sebastian Mounster*, London, 1561, sig A3r–v.

19 *CSP For.* (1563), p. 268 (3 Apr.). Five years later, when Stukeley was in Ireland, Sir Hugh wrote a similar letter to Lord Burghley, *SP Dom. Eliz.* v. 46 (19 June 1568).

20 Camden, Bk 1, pp. 61–2.

21 Henry Machyn, *The Diary of H. Machyn, Citizen and Merchant Taylor of London, from A.D. 1550 to A.D. 1563*, ed. J. G. Nichols, London, 1848, pp. 275, 277.
22 Machyn, p. 309.
23 *CSP Spn.* (1558–67), pp. 322–3 (1 May 1563).
24 Robert Seall, *A Comendation of the adventerus viage of the wurthy Captain. M. Thomas Stutely Esquyer and others, towards the land called Terra Florida*, London, 1563.
25 *CSP Spn.* (1558–67), p. 323 (1 May 1563).
26 *CSP Spn.* (1558–67), pp. 334–5 (19 June 1563).
27 *CSP Spn.* (1558–67), p. 343 (15 July 1563).
28 Samuel Haynes, ed., *A collection of state papers relating to affairs in the reigns of King Henry VIII, King Edward VI, Queen Mary, and Queen Elizabeth from the year 1542 to 1570*, v. 1, London, 1740, p. 401.
29 *CSP For.* (1563), p. 619 (22 Jan.); *CSP Spn.* (1558–67), pp. 359–60 (22 Jan. 1564), 397 (4 Dec. 1564).
30 *CSP For.* (1564–65), p. 272 (24 Dec. 1564).
31 *CSP Ire.* (1509–73), p. 263 (18 June 1565).
32 M. V. Ronan, *The Reformation in Ireland under Elizabeth 1558–1580*, London, 1930, p. 155.
33 *CSP Ire.* (1509–73), p. 278 (4 Nov. 1565).
34 *CSP Spn.* (1558–67), p. 488 (8 Oct. 1565).
35 Cardinal Michael Bonelli's report of his conversations with Stukeley in Spain (see pp. 7–8), dated 5 February 1571, included the information that 'nearly nine years ago a son named William' was born (*CSP Rom.* (1558–71), p. 79).
36 *CSP Ire*, p. 277 (27 Oct. 1565).
37 *CSP Ire.* (1509–73), p. 49 (12 Aug. 1539).
38 Raimond de Fourquevaux, *Dépêches de M. de Fourquevaux, Ambassadeur du Roi Charles IX en Espagne, 1565–1572*, 3 v., Paris, 1896–1904, 2: 268; *CSP For.* (1572–74), p. 451 (30 Dec. 1573); James Morrin, ed., *Calendar of the Patent and Close Rolls of Chancery in Ireland, from th 18th to the 45th of Queen Elizabeth*, v. 2, Dublin, 1862, p. 47. That Tazón should fail to mention Elizabeth is odd, since he quotes Fourquevaux's letter in another context (p. 119).
39 *CSP Spn.* (1558–67), p. 555 (1 June 1566).
40 Thomas Wright, *Queen Elizabeth and Her Times: A Series of Original Letters*, 2 v., London, 1838, 1: 246.
41 Daniel A. Binchy, 'An Irish Ambassador at the Spanish Court, 1569–74', *Studies: An Irish Quarterly Review* 11 (1922): 209. Lord Burghley wrote to Sidney, expressing the hope that White's qualifications in civil law would make up for his lack of military knowledge, *CSP Ire.* (1509–73), p. 397 (15 Dec. 1568).
42 *SP Ire.* v. 28 (10 June 1569).
43 *SP Dom. Eliz.* v. 80 (29 Aug. 1571).
44 *CSP Rom.* (1558–71), pp. 353–4 (24 Sept. 1570).
45 *CSP Rom.* (1558–71), p. 385 (5 Feb. 1571).
46 *CSP Rom.* (1558–71), p. 376 (5 Feb. 1571).
47 *CSP Rom.* (1558–71), p. 379 (5 Feb. 1571).
48 *CSP Rom.* (1558–71), p. 385 (8 Feb. 1571).
49 *CSP Spn.* (1568–79), p. 305 (23 Apr. 1571).
50 *CSP Rom.* (1558–71), p. 474 (6 Dec. 1571).
51 *CSP Ire.* (1509–73), p. 469 (30 Mar. 1572), 472 (29 May 1572); how or why Stukeley joined up with Don John, and his service at Lepanto, are not well documented.

52 *CSP Rom.* (1572–78), pp. 2–3 (11 Jan. 1572); Norfolk was executed six months later, on 5 June 1572.
53 *CSP For.* (1575–77), p. 71 (13 June 1575).
54 *CSP For.* (1575–77), p. 523 (19 Feb. 1577).
55 Wright, 2: 250.
56 *CSP Rom.* (1572–78), p. 367 (14 Jan. 1578); other letters give the number of Italian troops as 900 and 2000.
57 *CSP Rom.* (1572–78), pp. 380–1 (14 Feb. 1578).
58 H. de Castries, ed., *Les Sources Inédites de L'Histoire du Maroc: Archives et Bibliothèques d'Angleterre*, 2 v., Paris, 1918–25, 1: 297–8.
59 Castries, 1: 298–9.
60 Wright, 2: 85–6.
61 Westcote, p. 272.
62 Moroccan names and places are given a variety of spellings in modern texts. I have relied mostly on E. W. Bovill's *The Battle of Alcazar*, London, 1952, and Stephan and Nandy Ronart's *Concise Encyclopaedia of Arabic Civilization: The Arab West*, Amsterdam, 1966. Unless otherwise indicated, original spelling is retained in quotations.
63 Robert Brown, ed., *The History and Description of Africa: and of the notable things therein contained. Written by al-Hassan ibn Mohammed al-Wezaz, al-Fasi, a Moor, baptized as Giovanni Leone, but better known as Leo Africanus; done into English in the year 1600 by John Pory*, London, 1896, pp. 496, 498.
64 Richard Johnson, 'The life and death of the famous Thomas Stukely: an English gallant in time of Queen Elizabeth, who ended his dayes in a battaile of Kings in Barbarie', in *A Crowne-Garland of Golden Roses: Gathered Out of England's Royall Garden*, London, 1612.
65 John Polemon, *The Second part of the booke of Battailes fought in our age: taken out of the best authors and writers in sundrie languages, published for the profit of those that practise armes and for the pleasure of such as love to be harmlesse hearers of bloudie broiles*, London, 1587, sig. R3r. This book was Peele's principal source, as discussed pp. 26–7.
66 Ronart, *West*, pp. 335–8.
67 Ronart, *West*, p. 336.
68 *A Dolorous Discourse of a most terrible and bloudy Battel, fought in Barbarie, the fowrth day of August, last past, 1578*, London, 1579, sig A55.
69 *Dolorous Discourse*, sig. A5r.
70 See pp. 23–4.
71 Bovill, p. 21.
72 Dahiru Yahya, *Morocco in the Sixteenth Century: Problems and Patterns in African Foreign Policy*, Harlow, Essex, 1981, pp. 48–9.
73 *Dolorous Discourse*, sig. A5v.
74 Weston F. Cook Jr, *The Hundred Years War for Morocco: Gunpowder and the Military Revolution in the Early Modern Muslim World*, Boulder, 1994, p. 242.
75 Yahya, pp. 51–2.
76 Yahya, p. 66.
77 *A True Historicall discourse of Muley Hamets rising to the three Kingdomes of Moruecos, Fes, and Sus by Cottington, R.*, London, 1609, sig. A4r (Cottington may be a pseudonym).
78 Polemon, sig. T3r.
79 Cook, p. 247.
80 Cook, p. 247.

81 Cook, p. 247.
82 'The Ambassage of M. Edmund Hogan, one of the sworne Esquires of her Majesties person, from her Highnesse to Mully Abdelmelech . . . in the yeere 1577', in Richard Hakluyt, *The Principal Navigations, Voyages, Traffiques, and Discoveries of the English Nation*, 12 v., Glasgow, 1903, 6: 285–92.
83 Bovill, p. 97; Cook, p. 248.
84 Bovill, pp. 105–7.
85 Polemon, sig. X2v.
86 Bovill and Cook provide excellent accounts.
87 Cook, p. 252.
88 *Explanation*, p. 4; for details of this work see n. 144, below.
89 *CSP Rom.* (1572–78), p. 510 (29 Sept. 1578).
90 *CSP Rom.* (1572–78), pp. 509–10 (29 Sept. 1578).
91 *The Uniting*, p. 55. For details of this work see n. 149 below.
92 Victor von Klarwill, ed., *The Fugger News-Letters*, 2 v., London, 1924, 1: 27.
93 See *Stukeley*, n. 19 OSD.
94 Sebastian was the son of Philip's younger sister, Juana.
95 R. B. Wernham, *Before the Armada: The Growth of English Foreign Policy 1485–1588*, London, 1966, p. 381.
96 *Englands Parnassus: or The choysest Flowers of our Moderne Poets*, London, 1600, sig. D3r.
97 The fleet sailed for Plymouth on 16 March, but did not leave for Spain until 17 April (John Sugden, *Sir Francis Drake*, New York, 1990, pp. 268, 270).
98 At the time, a title often given to naval commanders (see Edelman, *Shakespeare's Military Language: A Dictionary*, London, 2002, p. 147).
99 All quotations from Peele's other works are from C. T. Prouty, gen. ed., *The Life and Works of George Peele*, 3 v., New Haven, 1952–70.
100 John Yoklavich, introd., *The Battle of Alcazar*, in *The Life and Works of George Peele*, v. 2, New Haven, 1961, pp. 223–4.
101 See p. 26.
102 Yoklavich, p. 225.
103 Edelman, *Military*, pp. 17–18.
104 W. W. Greg, *Two Elizabethan Stage Abridgements: The Battle of Alcazar & Orlando Furioso*, London, 1922.
105 See Appendix II.
106 See Andrew Gurr, ed., *King Henry V*, Cambridge, 1992, pp. 56–63.
107 See below, pp. 20–1.
108 Greg, pp. 15–16.
109 Greg, p. 16.
110 David Bradley, *From Text to Performance in the Elizabethan Theatre: Preparing the Play for the Stage*, Cambridge, 1992, p. 58.
111 Andrew Gurr, *The Shakespearian Playing Companies*, Oxford, 1996, pp. 41–3.
112 Bradley, pp. 73–4.
113 Greg, p. 121.
114 Greg, p. 118; R. A. Foakes, ed., *Henslowe's Diary*, Cambridge, 2002, p. 318.
115 Greg, p. 96. Greg also discusses the matter of some of Q's stage directions being in roman, not italic type. Dover Wilson suggested to him that 'the [original] transcriber followed the habitual practice of writing the stage directions in an Italian script (hence the italic type), while the reviser, who was not a regular scribe, when he had to restore or insert directions himself, did so in the English hand he used for the text . . . the roman directions are consistent with the revised text, the italic often are not' (Greg, pp. 99, 100). How Greg, who had seen many a

dramatic manuscript, could say that the printer's convention of italic directions came from the *scribe* having used two different hands, one for dialogue and one for directions, is a mystery. He goes on to comment that although Wilson's theory is 'probably correct it is hardly sufficiently certain to form a satisfactory basis for any further conjecture' (p. 100), but then proceeds to adopt the theory without reservation in his analysis of the quarto and Plot.

116 Bradley, p. 167.

117 See *Alcazar*, n. 4.2.29, 4.2.37.

118 Alfred Hart, *Stolne and Surreptitious Copies: A Comparative Study of Shakespeare's Bad Quartos*, Melbourne, 1942, p. 122.

119 Bradley, p. 129.

120 Greg, pp. 2, 22.

121 Greg, p. 21.

122 Bradley, p. 84.

123 Bradley, p. 89.

124 Bradley, p. 171.

125 Foakes, pp. 16–19.

126 They are, in alphabetical order: mulamulluco, mule muloco, mulemuloco, mulimu-lucko, mullo mulluco, mullomuloco, mulo mullocco, mulo mulluco, mulo muloc, mulo mulocko, mulo muloco, mulomulluco, mulomurco.

127 Yoklavich, pp. 221–2; citing Greg, pp. 10–12.

128 Yoklavich, pp. 222, 223.

129 Gurr, p. 259.

130 For a fuller discussion of this point see Edelman, '*The Battle of Alcazar*, *Muly Molocco*, and Shakespeare's 2 and 3 *Henry VI*', *N&Q* 49 (2002): 215–18.

131 1613 is the probable date of *Henry VIII*, when carrying out the direction *Drum and trumpet. Chambers discharged* (1.4.50SD) resulted in the Globe being burnt to the ground.

132 Michael Hattaway, ed., 2 *Henry VI*, Cambridge, 1991, pp. 64–7, 216–17.

133 The old categories of 'authorial' and 'playhouse' directions, written in by the book-keeper, have rightfully been discarded as overly simplistic.

134 Foakes, pp. 329–30.

135 My thanks to Robert Smallwood for bringing this point to my attention.

136 S. P. Ceresano, 'Edward Alleyn's "Retirement"', *Medieval and Renaissance Drama in England* 10 (1998): 98–112; Foakes, pp. 329–30.

137 Martin Wiggins, 'A Choice of Impossible Things: Dating the Revival of *The Battle of Alcazar*', in *Shakespeare & ses contemporains: Actes de colloque 2002 de la Société Française Shakespeare*, ed. Patricia Dorval, Montpellier, 2002, pp. 189–90.

138 The other unassigned part in the Plot is Calipolis.

139 Foakes, pp. 329–30; Wiggins, 'Choice', p. 198.

140 W. G. Rice, 'A Principal Source of *The Battle of Alcazar*', *Modern Language Notes* 58 (1943): 428–31.

141 Polemon, sig. R3r.

142 These details are from Yoklavich, p. 230.

143 The sources for particular passages in both plays are discussed in the textual notes.

144 *The Explanation of the true and lawful right and tytle of the Most Excellent Prince Anthonie the First of that Name, King of Portugall, concerning his warres, again-ste Phillip King of Castile, and against his subjectes and adherentes, for the recov-erie of his kingdome*, London, 1585, cited as *Explanation* hereafter.

145 This theme is more prominent in *Stukeley*; see pp. 43–4.

146 George Whetstone, *The English Myrror. A regard wherein al estates may behold the conquests of envy: containing ruine of common weales, murther of princes, cause of heresies, and in all ages, spoile of devine and humane blessings, unto which is adjoyned, envy conquered by vertues*, London, 1586.

147 Yoklavich, p. 371.

148 Bovill, pp. 125, 142, 165.

149 Gerolamo Franchi di Conestaggio [attrib.], *The Historie of the Uniting of the Kingdom of Portugall to the Crowne of Castill: containing the last warres of the Portugals against the Moores of Africke, the end of the house of Portugall, and change of that government*, London, 1600.

150 See *Alcazar*, n. 2.3.94.

151 G. K. Hunter, *English Drama 1586–1642: The Age of Shakespeare*, Oxford, 1997, p. 49.

152 Alvin B. Kernan, 'The Plays and the Playwrights', in *The Revels History of Drama in English*, v. 3, London, 1975, pp. 255–6.

153 Kernan, p. 256.

154 G. K. Hunter, *Lyly and Peele*, Harlow, 1968, pp. 40–1.

155 A. C. Swinburne, *Contemporaries of Shakespeare*, ed. E. Gosse and T. J. Wise, London, 1919, p. 8; D. H. Horne, in *Life and Works of George Peele*, v. 1, New Haven, 1952, p. 78.

156 G. K. Hunter likens the Hollywood epics of DeMille and D. W. Griffith to plays such as *Tamburlaine*, *Alphonsus King of Aragon*, *The Battle of Alcazar* and *Captain Thomas Stukeley* ('The Making of a Popular Repertory: Hollywood and the Elizabethans', in *Shakespearean Continuities: Essays in Honour of E. A. J. Honigmann*, ed. John Batchelor, Tom Cain and Claire Lamont, Basingstoke, 1997, p. 252).

157 A. R. Braunmuller, *George Peele*, Boston, 1983, p. 73.

158 Braunmuller, p. 73; Thelma N. Greenfield, *The Induction in Elizabethan Drama*, Eugene, 1969, p. 31.

159 Dieter Mehl, *The Elizabethan Dumb Show*, London, 1965, pp. 177–8.

160 Jonathan Bate, 'Othello and the Other–Turning Turk: the Subtleties of Shakespeare's Treatment of Islam', *TLS*, 19 October 2001; see also Michael Neill, ' "Mulattos", "Blacks", and "Indian Moors": *Othello* and the Early Modern Constructions of Human Difference', *SQ* 49 (1998): 364.

161 Polemon, sig. R3r–v.

162 Dympna Callaghan, ' "Othello was a White Man": Properties of Race on Shakespeare's Stage', in *Alternative Shakespeares*, v. 2, ed., Terence Hawkes, London, 1996, p. 195.

163 See Richard Levin, 'The Longleat Manuscript and *Titus Andronicus*', *SQ* 53 (2002): 323–40.

164 Eldred Jones, *Othello's Countrymen: The African in English Renaissance Drama*, London, 1965, p. 64.

165 Jones, p. 66.

166 *The Essays of Montaigne: John Florio's Translation*, ed. J. I. M. Stewart, New York, 1933, pp. 612–13. Book II of Montaigne's *Essais* was published in 1580; his work was widely known in England well before Florio's translation of 1603.

167 The view that Peele and Shakespeare collaborated in writing *Titus Andronicus* has gained increased acceptance; see Brian Vickers, *Shakespeare, Co-Author: A Historical Study of Five Collaborative Plays*, Oxford, 2002, and Jonathan Bate's review, *TLS*, 18 April 2003.

168 Polemon, sig. Y2r.

169 Castries, 1: 513.

170 Castries, 1: 513–14.

171 Castries, 1: 514.

172 Castries, 1: 520–1.

173 Castries, 1: 517.

174 As referred to by John Chamberlain, *Letters Written by John Chamberlain During the Reign of Queen Elizabeth*, ed. Sarah Williams, London, 1861, p. 91.

175 Bate, 'Othello and the Other'.

176 Lord Mayor Nicholas Mosley to Sir Robert Cecil, cited by Bernard Harris, 'A Portrait of a Moor', *Shakespeare Survey 11*, Cambridge, 1958, p. 94.

177 Edmund Howes, *The Annales, or Generall Chronicle of England, begun first by maister John Stow, and after him continued and augmented with matters forreyne, and domestique, auncient and moderne, unto the ende of this present yeere 1614*, London, 1615, p. 790.

178 Bradley, p. 152.

179 Foakes, p. 50.

180 Foakes, pp. 55–9.

181 Levinson, p. v.

182 On the numbering of scenes see pp. 45–8.

183 See n. 3.

184 Simpson, p. 140.

185 The 'missing' sequences may not have actually been written; see pp. 44–5.

186 Simpson, p. 141, italics in original.

187 Simpson, p. 141.

188 E. H. C. Oliphant, 'Capt. Thomas Stukeley', *N&Q* 10th ser., 3 (1905): 301–2, 342–3, 382–5.

189 Joseph Quincy Adams, 'Captaine Thomas Stukeley', *Journal of English and Germanic Philology* 15 (1916): 107.

190 See *Stukeley*, n. 3 OSD, 3. 27 SD.

191 Adams, pp. 108, 110.

192 Adams, p. 109.

193 Levinson, p. vi.

194 Wiggins, 'Things that Go Bump in the Text: *Captain Thomas Stukely*', *Publications of the Bibliographical Society of America* 98 (2004): 9

195 Adams, p. 108.

196 Adams, p. 109.

197 Adams, p. 111.

198 See *Stukeley*, n. 26.6.

199 Simpson, p. 142.

200 Wiggins, 'Things', p. 10.

201 Wiggins, 'Things', p. 11. He notes that Levinson's hypothesis (p. vii) that the revision was the work of the printer is even less likely: no printer would turn two marketable plays into one.

202 Carol Chillington Rutter, *Documents of the Rose Playhouse*, 2nd edn, Manchester, 1999, pp. 26–7.

203 Gurr, p. 102.

204 Rutter, p. 28.

205 Neil Carson, *A Companion to Henslowe's Diary*, Cambridge, 1988, p. 57.

206 Adams, p. 116.

207 Adams, p. 120.

208 *Literature Online: English Drama (1280–1915)*, www.chadwyck.com.

209 *Q* reads 'evety'.
210 British Library, MS Egerton 1994.
211 E. A. J. Honigmann, *The Stability of Shakespeare's Text*, London, 1965, p. 201.
212 Paul Werstine argues convincingly that the old categories of 'foul papers', 'fair copy' etc. are inadequate; plays found their way into print through a much wider variety of means ('Narratives About Printed Shakespeare Texts: "Foul Papers" and "Bad" Quartos', *SQ* 41 (1990): 65–87).
213 Stephen Orgel, *The Authentic Shakespeare and Other Problems of the Early Modern Stage*, New York, 2002, p. 36.
214 Martin Gilbert, *The Churchill War Papers*, v. 2, London, 1994, pp. 83–90.
215 Paul Merchant, ed., *Three Marriage Plays*, Manchester, 1996, p. 30.
216 Heywood, *The English Traveller*, London, 1633, sig. A3r.
217 Rutter. p. 106.
218 Vittorio Gabrieli and Giorgio Melchiori, ed., *Sir Thomas More*, Manchester, 1990, p. 22.
219 E. K. Chambers, *The Elizabethan Stage*, 4 v., Oxford, 1923, 4: 246.
220 Mary Ann Weber Gasior, ed., *Thomas Heywood's The Four Prentices of London: A Critical Old Spelling Edition*, New York, 1980, p. xiv.
221 Gabrieli and Melchiori, p. 27.
222 The words 'Hawodes bocke' do not make Heywood the sole author, since collaboration could take many different forms, but someone must have been responsible for assigning and collecting the contributions, organising further revisions before and/or after the Master of the Revels had read the play, etc.; see Gurr, p. 102, Carson pp. 57–60, Gabrieli and Melchiori, pp. 20–6.
223 Oliphant, p. 301.
224 Irving Ribner, *The English History Play in the Age of Shakespeare*, Princeton, 1957, p. 194.
225 Wiggins, 'Things', p. 12.
226 *The Famous History of Stout Stukley: or, His Valiant Life and Death*, London, 1650, sig. A7r.
227 See Yoklavich, '*Captain Thomas Stukeley*', *N&Q* 10 (1963): 96–8; Levinson, 'The Sources of *Captain Thomas Stukeley*', *English Language Notes* 9 (1971): 85–90.
228 Simpson, p. 139.
229 E.g. *Stukeley*, 14.16, where Abdelmelec and Muly Mahamet are brothers, not uncle and nephew.
230 See *Alcazar*, 1.2 OSD; Levinson, 'Sources', p. 90.
231 Adams, p. 111.
232 Wiggins, 'Things', pp. 18–19.
233 We must be careful here. It might have been a single direction split at the last minute to fill in extra space, but the page shows evidence of compression elsewhere.
234 Levinson, p. vii.
235 Wiggins, accepting that *Q*'s 'After antonio's going out / Enter Muly hamet with victorie' is one direction, proposes that Stukeley's death was meant to be *two* scenes earlier, before the capture of Don Antonio ('Things', pp. 19–20). I differ on this point, because I do not think the Chorus would fail to say anything about Stukeley if his death was shown beforehand.

The Battle of Alcazar by George Peele

EDITIONS AND TEXTUAL CONVENTIONS

This edition relies on W. W. Greg's Malone Society reprint of the 1594 quarto. Greg notes only a few (and insignificant) variations in the printing of the four extant original copies, and Yoklavich observes that Greg's facsimile is 'scrupulously accurate'.[1]

Four modern editions are cited in the textual collation. Alexander Dyce's *Works of George Peele* [Dyce[1]] was published in 1828. This edition had several reprints, but without significant change to the text; in 1861, Dyce completely re-edited the play for his one-volume collection, *The Dramatic and Poetical Works of Robert Greene and George Peele* [Dyce[2]]. In the collation, when only Dyce[1] is cited, it may be assumed that this reading was reproduced in Dyce[2]; emendations appearing for the first time in Dyce[2] are so indicated. A. H. Bullen's text, in *The Works of George Peele*, v. 1, appeared in 1888. Bullen almost always accepts Dyce's readings, so he is seldom cited, except for those few instances where he disagrees with Dyce, or offers a new emendation. John Yoklavich's edition for Yale University Press, 1961, is in old spelling, and bears little textual apparatus. Other than regularising speech headings and stage directions, including the insertion of some directions from the Plot, he substantially reproduces Greg's edition of *Q*; hence Yoklavich, like Bullen, is rarely cited.

This edition follows Yoklavich in inserting material from the Plot; unless otherwise indicated, my authority is David Bradley's reconstruction.[2]

NOTES

1 Yoklavich, p. 286.
2 Bradley, pp. 172–3.

LIST OF CHARACTERS

The PRESENTER.

Moroccans

ABDELMELEC, *also known as Muly Molocco, rightful King of Morocco.*
ABDIL RAYES, *his Queen.*
CALSEPIUS BASHAW, *general of the Turkish troops supporting Abdelmelec.*
ZAREO, *a Moor of Argier, follower of Abdelmelec.*
CELYBIN, *a captain in Abdelmelec's army.*
MULY MAHAMET SETH, *brother to Abdelmelec.*
RUBIN ARCHIS, *widow of Abdelmelec's brother, Abdelmunen.*
Rubin's Young Son.*
MULY MAHAMET, *the Moor, nephew to Abdelmelec.*
CALIPOLIS, *Muly Mahamet's wife.*
MULY MAHAMET'S SON.
PISANO, *Muly Mahamet's Captain.*
MESSENGER.
A BOY serving Muly Mahamet.
ATTENDANT.
AMBASSADORS *from Muly Mahamet to the King of Portugal.*

Portuguese and Spaniards

SEBASTIAN, *King of Portugal.*
DIEGO LOPES, *Governor of Lisbon.*
DUKE OF AVERO.
DON DE MENESES, *Governor of Tangier.*
Duke of Barceles.*
Lewes de Silva.*
CHRISTOPHERO DE TAVORA.
Lord Lodovico Caesar.*
County Vimioso.*
AMBASSADORS *from King Philip of Spain to the King of Portugal.*
PORTUGUESE SOLDIER.
TWO CAPTAINS.
SOLDIERS.

English and Irish

Captain Thomas STUKELEY.
JONAS and HERCULES, *two English captains serving Stukeley.*
An Irish BISHOP.

Others

TWO ITALIAN SOLDIERS.
　Pages, janissaries, ladies.

Characters in the Dumb Shows

Two Young Princes, *brothers to Muly Mahamet.*
Abdelmunen, *brother of Abdelmelec, murdered by his nephew Muly Mahamet.*
Two Murderers.
Ghosts, Nemesis, Furies, Death, Fame.

* mute character.

ACT I

[1.Prol.]

[*Sound sennet.*] *Enter the* PRESENTER [, *a Portugal*].

Presenter. Honour, the spur that pricks the princely mind
    To follow rule and climb the stately chair,
    With great desire inflames the Portugal,
    An honourable and courageous king,
    To undertake a dangerous dreadful war   5
    And aid with Christian arms the barbarous Moor,
    The negro Muly Hamet that withholds
    The kingdom from his uncle Abdelmelec
    (Whom proud Abdallas wronged),
    And in his throne installs his cruel son   10
    That now usurps upon this prince,
    This brave Barbarian lord Muly Molocco.
    The passage to the crown by murder made,
    Abdallas dies, and deigns this tyrant king

Act 1] *This ed.*; Actus I *Dyce¹*; Act I *Dyce²*; *not in* Q. 1.Prol.] *This ed.*; *not in* Q.
OSD. *This ed.*; Enter the Presenter Q; Sound sennet, Enter a Portingall *Plot.* 1 SH.]
This ed.; *not in* Q. 3. Portugal] *This ed.*; Portingall Q; Portingal *Dyce¹*. 14. deigns]
This ed.; deisnes Q; leaves *Dyce²*; desines *Yoklavich*.

---

3. *the Portugal*] Sebastian, the King of Portugal. Q has 'Portingall' here, but 'Portugall' or 'Portugal(s)' elsewhere. Both forms are common in early modern texts.

7. *negro Muly Hamet*] Muly Mahamet, the Moor.

9. *Abdallas*] Muly Abdallas, father of Muly Mahamet the Moor, and elder brother
of Abdelmelec (see fig. 1).

12. *Muly Molocco*] One of only two times Abdelmelec is referred to as Muly
Molocco; the other is at 2.1.53 (see also pp. 23–4).

13. *passage to the crown*] The remainder of the Presenter's speech makes Muly
Mahamet directly responsible for the murders described. In Polemon (sig. S2r), 'Muley
Abdallas . . . privelie compassed the murther of his brothers, that hee might safelie leave
the kingdome to his sonnes', but Peele follows the *Uniting* (p. 14), where Abdallas
'although he were cruel, yet did he refraine from muthering his three brethren'. Muly
Mahamet 'practised against his uncles, sending a Moore to Tremisenne to kill the eldest,
who was detained by the Turkes, the which he did effect'; see also pp. 12–13.

14. *deigns this tyrant king*] Dyce, observing that 'something seems to be wanting
here', substitutes 'leaves' for 'deigns' (*Dyce²*). Bradley (p. 141) argues for 'desines' i.e.
'designs' in its original sense of 'nominates' or 'appoints' (*OED v* 1), but I have found
no examples in Elizabethan verse of 'design' with emphasis on the first syllable, as

Of whom we treat, sprung from the Arabian Moor,   15
Black in his look and bloody in his deeds,
And in his shirt, stained with a cloud of gore,
Presents himself with naked sword in hand,
Accompanied, as now you may behold,
With devils coated in the shapes of men.   20

The first dumb show.

[*Sound sennet. Enter* MULY MAHAMET *the Moor, his son, three*
Moors *attendant and two* Pages *to attend the Moor. To them the*
Moor's two young Brethren.] *The Moor showeth them the bed, and*
then takes his leave of them, and they betake them to their rest. And
then the PRESENTER *speaketh:*

Like those that were by kind of murder mummed,
Sit down and see what heinous stratagems
These damnèd wits contrive. And lo, alas,
How like poor lambs prepared for sacrifice
This traitor king hales to their longest home,   25
These tender lords his younger brethren both.

---

20 SD.] *This ed.;* Enter Muly Mahamet and his sonne, and his two young brethren,
the Moore sheweth them the bed, and then takes his leave of them, and they betake
them to their rest. And then the presenter speaketh *Q;* Sennet. Enter Muly Mahamett
mr Ed. Allen, his sonne Antho. Jeffes, moores attendant. mr Sam, mr Hunt & w.
Cartwright, ii Pages to attend the moore, mr Allens boy, mr Townes boy. To them 2
young bretheren, Dab & Harry. To them Abdelmenen w. Kendall *Plot.*   21. mummed]
This ed.; mumd *Q;* mumm'd *Dyce¹.*   26 SD.] *subst. Q.*

---

would be required for this line. Since 'deigns' can be taken to mean 'grants' (*OED v* 2),
and is metrically apt, this seems the better choice: the passage might be understood as
'deigns this tyrant [to be] king'. Further confusion arises in that Abdallas first 'installs'
his son as successor (1.Prol.10) and then 'deigns' the same thing four lines later.

   20. *devils . . . men*] these must be the 'Moors attendant' given an entrance in the
Plot, there to assist in the murders.

   20. SD.] The first part of this direction is from the Plot. The dumb show would have
been elaborate, as the Plotter provides Muly Mahamet with three attendants and two
pages. 'To them' indicates that the entrance of the 'two young brethren' is slightly
delayed, and Yoklavich places it after l. 26, but since the Presenter would be speaking
while the pantomime was going on, any placement of his lines in relationship to the
dumb show would be arbitrary, so the *Q* direction remains intact in this edition.

   21. *kind of murder mummed*] The sense seems to be 'like those mummed, i.e.
silenced [*OED v* 1], by murder done by their kind (kin), sit down . . .'; cf. Yoklavich,
p. 349.

   22. *Sit down and see*] The Presenter addresses the seated patrons, ignoring those in
the yard, as does the Chorus in *Henry V*, 'Yet sit and see / Minding true things by what
their mock'ries be' (4.Cho.52–3).

   26. SD.] So labelled in *Q*; the Plotter numbers the dumb show preceding Act 2 '2
domb show', and accordingly for subsequent acts.

The second dumb show.

Enter [MULY MAHAMET] *the Moor and two* Murderers *bringing
in his uncle* Abdelmunen, *then they draw the curtains and smother
the young* Princes *in the bed. Which done in sight of the uncle,
they strangle him in his chair, and then go forth, and then the*
PRESENTER *saith:*

His brethren thus in fatal bed behearsed,
His father's brother of too light belief,
This negro puts to death by proud command.
Say not these things are feigned, for true they are,   30
And understand how eager to enjoy
His father's crown this unbelieving Moor,
Murdering his uncle and his brethren,
Triumphs in his ambitious tyranny
Till Nemesis, high mistress of revenge,   35
That with her scourge keeps all the world in awe,
With thundering drums awakes the god of war
And calls the furies from Avernus' crags,
To range and rage and vengeance to inflict
Vengeance on this accursèd Moor for sin.   40
And now behold how Abdelmelec comes,
Uncle to this unhappy traitor king,
Armed with great aid that Amurath had sent,
Great Amurath, Emperor of the East,
For service done to Sultan Solimon,   45

Abdelmunen] Abd al-Mumin, Abd al-Malek's brother, appointed governor of
Tlemcen (in what is now northern Algeria) and later assassinated (Yahya, pp. 31, 93;
see fig. 1).

35–6. *Nemesis . . . scourge*] Nemesis, the goddess of revenge, is given a scourge in
Marston's *Antonio's Revenge*, 'There is a thing call'd scourging Nemesis' (4.1.248).

38. *Avernus*] from the Greek for 'birdless'. In Virgil, Aeneas enters the underworld
through a cave near Cumae in Italy: 'And there th'unnavigable lake extends, / O'er
whose unhappy waters, void of light, / No bird presumes to steer his airy flight; / Such
deadly stenches from the depths arise, / And steaming sulphur, that infects the skies. /
From hence the Grecian bards their legends make, / And give the name Avernus to the
lake' (6.341–7). As a lake does not have 'crags', Peele appears to use Avernus as a
general term for the underworld.

44. *Amurath*] Murad III, who became Sultan upon the death of his father Selim II
(known to historians as 'Selim the Sot') in 1574. He promptly murdered all his
brothers, hence the newly crowned Henry V reassures his brothers in *2 Henry IV*,
'This is the English not the Turkish court / Not Amurath an Amurath succeeds / But
Harry, Harry' (5.2.47–9).

45. *Sultan Solimon*] Amurath was grandson to Suleiman the Great (reigned
1520–66), not son; Abdelmelec's service was done for Selim. The error is in Polemon
(sig. S3r); see Yoklavich, p. 350.

Under whose colours he had served in field,
Flying the fury of this negro's father,
That wronged his brethren to install his son.
Sit you and see this true and tragic war,
A modern matter full of blood and ruth,   50
Where three bold kings confounded in their height
Fell to the earth contending for a crown,
And call this war *The Battle of Alcazar*.   *Exit.*

[1.1]

Sound drums and trumpets, and enter ABDELMELEC *with*
CALSEPIUS BASHAW *and his guard, and* ZAREO, *a Moor,*
with soldiers.

Abdelmelec. All hail, Argier! Zareo and ye Moors,
Salute the frontiers of your native home.
Cease, rattling drums, and Abdelmelec here
Throw up thy trembling hands to heaven's throne,
Pay to thy god due thanks and thanks to him   5

1.1] *This ed.;* Scene I *Dyce²; not in* Q.   OSD.] *subst.* Q, *Bullen;* Enter Abdelmelec mr
Doughton, Calcepius bassa mr Jubie, Zareo mr Charles, attendate with the Bassa
w. Kendall, Ro. Tailor & George *Plot.*   Bashaw] *This ed.;* Bassa Q.   and Zareo] *Q,*
Bullen; and Argerd Zareo *Dyce².*   1 SH.] *This ed.;* Abdel., Abdelm., Abdilm., Abdil.
Q; Abdilm *Dyce¹;* Abdelm. *Dyce²;* Abdel. *Yoklavich.*   Argier! Zareo] *This ed.;* Argerd
Zareo *Q, Dyce¹.*   5. god] *This ed.;* God Q.

1.1.] The action of this scene takes place near Argier (Algiers).
   OSD. BASHAW] a Turkish general or governor. One of the two modern forms of
Q's 'Bassa', the other being 'Pasha'; 'Bashaw' was more common in military use.
   ZAREO] For Dyce's naming the character 'Argerd Zareo' see following note. The
Plot entry direction is substantially the same as in Q, but there is no mention of Zareo
being 'a Moor'. Bradley argues that the Plotter saw him as a white character, which led
to difficulties in the doubling of roles later; Zareo's 'native home' is 'Argier' (ll. 1–2),
but there is no explicit reference to his race in the dialogue; see n. 2.3.47.SH and pp.
29–30.
   1. All hail, Argier] Abdelmelec's greeting in Q, 'Alhaile Argerd Zareo and yee
Moores', has troubled commentators, who assume that he is addressing his lieutenant,
'Argerd Zareo'. But he is clearly saluting the city of Argier, upon returning after a long
absence. In *Eastward Ho*, Slitgut arrives at Cuckold's Haven and proclaims 'All haile,
faire haven of married men onely' (sig. E3v), while in *The Fair Maid of Bristow*, King
Richard arrives at Bristol with 'All haile thou blessed bosome of my peace / Richard
findes instance of his home returne' (sig. D3v); see Edelman, 'The Battle of Alcazar',
Explicator 61 (2003): 196–7.
   5. thy god] All previous editions read 'God', but Peele seems to follow the popular
conception of the time that Moslems were pagans, as implied by the 'thy', and many
subsequent appeals to 'the gods'. On three occasions, however, a Moroccan character
invokes 'God' (see n. 4.1.69).

That strengthens thee with mighty gracious arms
Against the proud usurper of thy right,
The royal seat and crown of Barbary.
Great Amurath, great Emperor of the world,
The world bear witness how I do adore   10
The sacred name of Amurath the Great.
Calsepius Bashaw, Bashaw Calsepius,
To thee and to thy trusty band of men
That carefully attend us in our camp,
Picked soldiers comparable to the guard   15
Of Myrmidons that kept Achilles' tent,
Such thanks we give to thee and to them all,
As may concern a poor distressèd king
In honour and in princely courtesy.
Calsepius Bashaw. Courteous and honourable Abdelmelec,   20
We are not come at Amurath's command
As mercenary men to serve for pay,
But as sure friends by our great master sent
To gratify and to remunerate
Thy love, thy loyalty and forwardness,   25
Thy service in his father's dangerous war,
And to perform in view of all the world
The true office of right and royalty,
To see thee in thy kingly chair enthroned,

12ff. Bashaw] *This ed.*; Bassa *Q.*   20 SH.] *This ed.*; Bassa, Bas. *Q*; Bas. *Dyce¹*; Cal.
Bas. *Dyce²*; Bassa *Yoklavich.*

9. *world*] Dyce suggests 'East', the 'transcriber's or compositor's eye having caught
["world"] in the next line' (*Dyce²*).

12. *Calsepius Bashaw*] The general of the Turkish troops was actually a Venetian
renegade called Ramdan (Bovill, p. 22). In Polemon, Abdelmelec 'determined to rest a
little while in the Citie of Fes, and there dismissed the Turkish forces which came with
him under the leading of Rabadan Bassa' (sig. S4v). The name Calsepius is probably
Peele's invention (Bradley, p. 142).

16. *Myrmidons*] 'According to the *Iliad*, Achilles led a band of warlike Myrmidons
from Thessaly at Troy; Zeus had created them out of ants, or *murmekes*' (David
Bevington, ed., *Troilus and Cressida*, London, 1998, p. 180).

20–33.] This fourteen-line speech, all one sentence with the repetition of opening
words, is but one of many in which Peele imitates Marlowe's rhetorical devices (see pp.
27–9).

26. *service . . . war*] Polemon (sig. S2v) records, 'to avoide the furie of [his] brother
. . . Muley Abdelmelec went to Constantinople, where he did serve so well both by sea
and land . . . and through his valiant acts and victories gotten of his enimies, he wan
the fame of a great name, not onely among the people, but also with the Prince of the
Turkes himselfe'. In the *Uniting* (p. 14), Abdelmelec gave 'an honorable testemonie of
himself in the last sea fight at Navarin, betwixt the armies of the league and the Turke,
and at the taking of Golette [La Goulette]'.

> To settle and to seat thee in the same,   30
> To make thee Emperor of this Barbary,
> Are come the viceroys and sturdy janissaries
> Of Amurath, son to Sultan Solimon.

> [*Sound sennet.*] *Enter* MULY MAHAMET [SETH],
>   RUBIN ARCHIS, ABDIL RAYES, *with others.*

Abdil Rayes. Long live my lord, the sovereign of my heart,
   Lord Abdelmelec, whom the god of kings,   35
   The mighty Amurath, hath happy made,
   And long live Amurath for this good deed.
Muly Mahamet Seth. Our Moors have seen the silver moons to wave
   In banners bravely spreading o'er the plain,
   And in these semicircles have descried,   40
   All in a golden field, a star to rise,
   A glorious comet that begins to blaze,
   Promising happy sorting to us all.

---

33 SD.] *This ed.;* Enter Muly Mahamet Xeque, Rubin Arches, Abdil Rayes, with others *Q;* Sound. To them Muly mahamet Xeque, Abdula Rais, & Ruben H Jeffes, dick Jubie & Jeames *Plot;* Enter Muly Mahamet Seth, Rubin Archis, Abdel Rayes, with others *Dyce¹.* 34 SH.] *Q exc.* Abd. Ra. *l. 30;* Abd. Rayes *Dyce¹;* Abd. Ra. *Yoklavich.* 38 SH.] *This ed.;* Muly Mah., Muly Xe., Muly *Q;* Muly Mah. Seth *Dyce¹;* Muly Mah. S. *Yoklavich.* wave] *Dyce²;* wane *Q.* 40. these] *Dyce¹;* this *Q.*

---

32. *janissaries*] *yeni tscheri* or 'new troops', taken from their parents as infants and moulded into the renowned and feared Turkish infantry. According to Giovanni Botero (*The Travellers Breviat*, London, 1601, pp. 44–5), the Turks recruited Christian boys from Europe, 'for they alwaies accounted the Asians effeminate and cowardly, alwaies more readie to flie then willing to fight; but the Europians, hardy, couragious and good men of warre'; see Edelman, *Military*, pp. 369–71.

33. SD. MULY MAHAMET SETH] Abd al-Malek's younger brother and eventual successor, Muly Ahmed al-Monsour, is known simply as 'Muly Hamet' in Polemon and *Stukeley.* Q has 'Muly Mahamet Xeque' in this direction, but 'Muly Mahamet Seth' in all subsequent scenes; see pp. 31–3 and fig. 1; for 'Xeque' see n. 1.1.70.

with others] As Bradley notes, the 'others' of the Q direction would have to be the 'dames of Fez', addressed by Abdelmelec at l. 49. Although the Plotter does not include them, 'there can be no question that [they] are an original part of the play, and provide with spectacular visual effect the impression given in the sources of the inhabitants of Morocco greeting Abdelmelec with rich presents' (Bradley, p. 180).

38. *silver moons*] the Ottoman symbol of the crescent (Yoklavich, p. 351).

42. *comet*] This comet, also mentioned in the Act 5 dumb show (5.Prol.14 SD) and in *Stukeley* (20.21 SD), inspired the Portuguese as well as the Moroccans. Botulphe Holder, an English merchant who provided Burghley with intelligence, wrote to him on 9 December 1577: 'Saturday at nyght, rose owt of [the WSW] from thys place a greate blasyng star [its beams] towarde the east, inclynyng somethyng towarde the south . . . suche sorte as the lyke has fewe tymes byn seene as they say, & styll contynuse to the wonder of manye' (*SP Dom. Eliz. Addenda* 1566–79, v. 27).

43. *sorting*] divine ordaining of events (*OED v¹* 1b); cf. *Richard III*, 'All may be well, but if God sort it so' (2.3.36).

Rubin Archis. Brave man at arms whom Amurath hath sent
    To sow the lawful true succeeding seed   45
    In Barbary, that bows and groans withal
    Under a proud usurping tyrant's mace,
    Right thou the wrongs this rightful king hath borne.
Abdelmelec. Distressèd ladies and ye dames of Fez,
    Sprung from the true Arabian Muly Sharif,   50
    The lodestar and the honour of our line,
    Now clear your watery eyes, wipe tears away
    And cheerfully give welcome to these arms.
    Amurath hath sent scourges by his men
    To whip that tyrant traitor king from hence,   55
    That hath usurped from us and maimed you all.
    Soldiers, since rightful quarrels [. . .] aid
    Successful are, and men that manage them
    Fight not in fear as traitors and their feres,
    That you may understand what arms we bear,   60
    What lawful arms against our brother's son,
    In sight of heaven, even of mine honour's worth,
    Truly I will deliver and discourse
    The sum of all. Descended from the line
    Of Mahomet, our grandsire Muly Sharif   65
    With store of gold and treasure leaves Arabia
    And strongly plants himself in Barbary.
    And of the Moors that now with us do wend
    Our grandsire Muly Sharif was the first,

44 SH.] *This ed.*; Rubyn, Rub. Ar., Rub. *Q*; Rub. *Dyce¹*; Rub. Ar. *Dyce²*, *Yoklavich.*
man at arms] *Q*; man-at-arms *Dyce²*.   49ff. Fez] *This ed.*; Fesse *Q*, *Dyce¹*; Fess *Dyce²*.
50. Sharif] *This ed.*; Xarif *Q (& l. 69).*   65. Muly Sharif] *This ed.*; Muli zaref *Q*;
Muly Xarif *Dyce¹*.

---

49. *Fez*] Both the powerful kingdom in northern Africa and its capital, to Leo
Africanus the 'principall citie of all Barbarie . . . a world it is to see, how large, how
populous, how well-fortified and walled this citie is' (Leo Africanus, ed. Brown, pp.
416, 419). The spellings 'Fez', 'Fes,' 'Fesse' and 'Fess' are all found in early modern
texts: *Q* of *Alcazar* consistently uses 'Fesse', while *Stukeley* has the first three spellings;
in any event the difference in pronunciation would have been slight.
    50. *Muly Sharif*] Peele drew the genealogy in this speech from Polemon (sig. R3r–v),
and follows Polemon's 'Xarif' for 'Sharif', meaning 'noble, or sublime', a title given to
descendants of Mohammed's second grandson al-Hasan. I have followed Ronart's
spelling (Ronart, *West*, p. 483); cf. *OED*'s 'shereef'; see also p. 12.
    57.] This short line appears to have a word or words missing between 'quarrels' and
'aid'. Bullen suggests 'quarrels [by heaven's] aid'.
    59. *feres*] companions (*OED* sb¹ 1); cf. *Solyman and Perseda*, 'When didst thou,
with thy sampler in the Sunne / Sit sowing with thy feres, but I was by' (sig. A2v); see
n. 3.3.40.
    64–5.] See n. l. 50.

From him well wot ye Muly Mahamet Sheikh,   70
Who in his lifetime made a perfect law,
Confirmed with general voice of all his peers,
That in his kingdom should successively
His sons succeed. Abdallas was the first,
Eldest of four, Abdelmunen the second   75
And we the rest, my brother and myself.
Abdallas reigned his time, but see the change:
He labours to invest his son in all,
To disannul the law our father made
And disinherit us his brethren,   80
And in his lifetime wrongfully proclaims
His son for king that now contends with us.
Therefore I crave to reobtain my right,
That Muly Mahamet the traitor holds,
Traitor and bloody tyrant both at once,   85
That murderèd his younger brethren both,
But on this damnèd wretch, this traitor king,
The gods shall pour down showers of sharp revenge.
And thus a matter not to you unknown
I have delivered; yet for no distrust   90
Of loyalty, my well belovèd friends,
But that the occasions fresh in memory
Of these encumbers so may move your minds
As for the lawful true succeeding prince,
Ye neither think your lives nor honours dear   95
Spent in a quarrel just and honourable.
Calsepius Bashaw. Such and no other we repute the cause
That forwardly for thee we undertake,
Thrice puissant and renownèd Abdelmelec,
And for thine honour, safety and crown,   100
Our lives and honours frankly to expose
To all the dangers that our war attends,

---

70. Sheikh] *This ed.;* Xeque *Q.*   74. Abdallas] *Dyce¹;* Abdullas *Q (& l. 77).*   75. four, Abdelmunen] *Dyce¹;* faire Abdelmenen *Q.*   91. friends] *Dyce²;* friend *Q.*   102. our war attends] *subst. Q;* on war attend *Dyce².*

---

70. *Muly Mahamet Sheikh*] Q follows Polemon's spelling, 'Xeque' for 'Sheikh' or 'Shaykh', lit. 'old man', the title given to the patriarchal chief of a tribe or clan (Ronart, *East,* pp. 484–5; see fig. 1).

79. *disannul*] make null and void (*OED v* 1), cf. *Comedy of Errors,* 'our laws / Which princes, would they, may not disannul' (1.1.142–3).

93. *encumbers*] encumbrances, annoyances (*OED sb*); cf. Dekker's *If It Be Not Good, the Devil Is in It,* 'Raves he for bonds and incombers' (5.4.259).

102. *attends*] awaits, expects (*OED v* 13); Dyce suggests 'on war attend', but Q's line makes sense with OED's alternative, albeit less common, definition.

As freely and as resolutely all
As any Moor whom thou commandest most.
Muly Mahamet Seth. And why is Abdelmelec then so slow   105
    To chastise him with fury of the sword,
    Whose pride doth swell to sway beyond his reach?
    Follow this pride, then, with fury of revenge.
Rubin Archis. Of death, of blood, of wreak and deep revenge
    Shall Rubin Archis frame her tragic songs;   110
    In blood, in death, in murder and misdeed,
    This heaven's malice did begin and end.
                      [RUBIN ARCHIS *sings.*]
Abdelmelec. Rubin, these rites to Abdelmunen's ghost
    Have pierced by this to Pluto's grave below;
    The bells of Pluto ring revenge amain,   115
    The furies and the fiends conspire with thee,
    War bids me draw my weapons for revenge
    Of my deep wrongs, and my dear brother's death.
Muly Mahamet Seth. Sheathe not your swords, you soldiers of
    Amurath,
    Sheathe not your swords, you Moors of Barbary   120
    That fight in right of your anointed king,
    But follow to the gates of death and hell,
    Pale death and hell to entertain his soul.
    Follow, I say, to burning Phlegethon
    This traitor tyrant and his companies.   125
Calsepius Bashaw. Heave up your swords against these stony holds,
    Wherein these barbarous rebels are inclosed;
    Called for is Abdelmelec by the gods
    To sit upon the throne of Barbary.
Abdil Rayes. Bashaw, great thanks, the honour of the Turks.   130
    Forward, brave lords, unto this rightful war.

---

107. reach?] *Dyce¹;* reach, Q.   112 SD.] *This ed.; not in* Q.   130 the honour] Q,
Bullen; thou honour *Dyce².*

---

109. *wreak*] 'Pain or punishment inflicted in return for an injury, wrong, offence,
etc.' (*OED sb* 1); cf. Chapman's *Revenge of Bussy D'Ambois*, 'can you but appease
your great-spleen'd sister / For our delay'd wreak of your brother's slaughter'
(2.1.51–2).
    112. SD.] Bradley's surmise (p. 142) that Rubin may sing a lament here is supported
by 'these rites', l. 113.
    114. *Pluto's grave*] the underworld, cf. Wilson, *The Three Ladies of London*, 'We
search not Plutos pensive pit, nor taste of Limbo lake' (sig. A2r).
    115. *amain*] with full force (*OED adv* 1).
    124. *Phlegethon*] See n. 5.1.108.
    130. *the honour*] i.e. 'thou who art the honour' (Bullen).

How can this battle but successful be
Where courage meeteth with a rightful cause?
Rubin Archis. Go in good time, my best belovèd lord,
Successful in thy work thou undertakes.   135

[*Exeunt.*]

[1.2]

> *Sound sennet. Enter* [MULY MAHAMET] *the Moor in his chariot,*
> *attended with his* SON, [*his wife* CALIPOLIS, *and*] PISANO *his*
> *captain, with his guard and treasure.*

Muly Mahamet. Pisano, take a cornet of our horse,
As many argolets and armèd pikes,

135 SD.] *Plot, Dyce'*; Exit Q.

1.2] *This ed.*; Scene II *Dyce²; not in* Q. OSD.] *This ed.*; Enter the Moore in his
Chariot, attended with his sonne. Pisano his captaine with his gard and treasure *Q*;
Enter in a charriott Muly Mahamett & Calipolis, on each side a page, moores atten-
dant Pisano mr Hunt & w. Cartwright and young Mahamet Anthony Jeffes *Plot*; ...
with his guard and treasure and his Queen *Dyce¹*; Enter, in his chariot, the Moor.
Calipolis, and their Son, Pisano with the Moor's Guard and treasure *Dyce²*. 1 SH.]
This ed.; Moore., More, Mu. Mah., Muly Mah., Muly Ma. *Q*; Moor *Dyce¹*; The Moor
Dyce²; Moore *Yoklavich.*

135. *undertakes*] a common form of the second person singular (Abbott, p. 242).

1.2.] The action occurs in northern Fez, 'in a certain valley three leagues from the
river of Sala towardes the west, along the sea coast, in a place called Motha Arraca-
hana [ar-Rukn] ... where the 29. of June at three of the clocke, in the after noone, a
cruell and bloudie battaile was fought' (Polemon, sig. T1r); see also *Stukeley* n. 25.15.
OSD.] The chariot entrance is an example of the spectacular staging Rose audiences
seemed to savour; cf. 2 *Tamburlaine* (5.1.62SD) and p. 28.
CALIPOLIS] Muly Mahamet's queen is not in the *Q* direction, nor does she speak,
but she is named in the Plot and is the only candidate for 'Madam' at l. 8. How Peele
thought of the name has been the cause of some speculation: Rice (p. 430) suggests he
read of galleys from the Turkish town of Callipolis (now Gallipoli) in Polemon's account
of the battle of Lepanto, but the scholarly Peele must have been familiar with the 'beautiful city' of Plato's *Republic*; cf. Jonson's masque *Love's Triumph Through Callipolis*:
'Euphemus, sent downe from Heaven to Callipolis, which is understood the Citty of
Beauty or Goodnes' (ll. 17–18).
1. SH.] *Q* uses 'Muly Mahamet' or 'The Moor' in various abbreviated forms; in the
Plot he is always 'Muly Mahamet'.
Pisano] see Appendix I.
cornet] a company of cavalry, so called from its horn (*cornum*)-shaped standard; cf.
1 *Henry VI*, 'O God, that Somerset, who in proud heart / Doth stop my cornets, were
in Talbot's place' (4.3.24–5).
2. *argolets*] light-armed horse-soldiers, originally mounted bowmen.

And with our carriage march away before
By Scyras, and those plots of ground
That to Morocco leads the lower way.   5
Our enemies keep upon the mountain tops,
And have encamped themselves not far from Fez.
Madam,
Gold is the glue, sinews and strength of war,
And we must see our treasure may go safe.   10
Away!
                                                    [*Exit* PISANO.]
Now, boy, what's the news?
Muly Mahamet's Son. The news, my lord, is war, war and revenge;
And if I shall declare the circumstance,
'Tis thus: 15
Rubin, our uncle's wife, that wrings her hands
For Abdelmunen's death, accompanied
With many dames of Fez in mourning weeds,
Near to Argier encountered Abdelmelec,
That bends his force, puffed up with Amurath's aid,   20
Against your holds and castles of defence.
The younger brother, Muly Mahamet Seth,

---

5. Morocco] *This ed.;* Moroccus *Q.* 8. Madam, / Gold] *Dyce²;* Madame, gold *Q,*
Bullen. 11 SD.] *subst.* Plot, *Yoklavich;* Exit Pisano & c. *Dyce¹;* Exit Pisano with the
treasure and some of the Guard *Dyce²; not in Q.* 13 SH.] *This ed.;* Muly Mah., Mah.,
The Moores sonne *Q;* The Moor's Son *Dyce¹;* The Moores sonne *Yoklavich.*

3. *carriage*] baggage train (*OED sb* 19); cf. Hooker's *History of Ireland*, 'The carriage was dragging after the armie, and slenderlie manned' (Holinshed, 6: 279).
4. *Scyras*] Possibly the plain of Azgar, lying on the west coast of Morocco (Sugden),
but more probably the place is Peele's invention, perhaps inspired by Scyros, the island
where Thetis hid her son Achilles after learning that he was fated to die at Troy.
5. *Morocco*] Written as Moroccus, Maroccus, Marocco or Morocco in *Q*. The
inconsistency follows no pattern, e.g. of Europeans pronouncing the word one way and
Africans another; I have regularised all to 'Morocco'.
8–9.] 'Madam' is part of the next line in *Q* – the compositor did not always
separate extra-metrical vocatives or exclamations as he does at l. 15.
9.] Yoklavich (p. 352) notes that this aphorism appears in Cicero's *Philippics*, '*nervos
belli, pecuniam infinitam*' (5.2.5); cf. Massinger's *Believe As You List*, 'the saphir, rubie,
iacinth, amber, currall / . . . they are indeede the nurses / and sinnewes of your war'
(1.2.84–7).
11. *Away*] this order evidently to Pisano, who exits alone; the Plot shows '*exit m*ʳ
Sam [actor Sam Rowley] *manet the rest*'.
12. *boy*] According to the *Uniting* (p. 30), 'Mulei Cheque son to the Cheriffe [was]
of the age of twelve yeeres'.
13–26.] Muly Mahamet's Son is already on stage; for him to possess the information he then gives is not credible (Bradley, p. 147). Probably, part or all of the speech
originally belonged to a messenger, who entered at this point.

Greets the great Bashaw, that the King of Turks
Sends to invade your right and royal realm
And basely beg revenge, arch-rebels all,   25
To be inflict upon our progeny.
Muly Mahamet. Why, boy, is Amurath's Bashaw such a bug
That he is marked to do this doughty deed?
Then, Bashaw, lock the winds in wards of brass,
Thunder from heaven, damn wretched men to death,   30
Bear all the offices of Saturn's sons,
Be Pluto then in hell and bar the fiends,
Take Neptune's force to thee and calm the seas,
And execute Jove's justice on the world,
Convey Tamburlaine into our Afric here,   35
To chastise and to menace lawful kings.
Tamburlaine, triumph not, for thou must die.
As Philip did, Caesar, and Caesar's peers.
Muly Mahamet's Son. The Bashaw grossly flattered to his face
And Amurath's praise advanced above the sound   40
Upon the plains, the soldiers being spread,
And that brave guard of sturdy janissaries
That Amurath to Abdelmelec gave,
And bade him boldly be to them as safe
As if he slept within a wallèd town [. . .]   45
Who take them to their weapons threatening revenge,
Bloody revenge, bloody revengeful war.
Muly Mahamet. Away, and let me hear no more of this.
Why, boy,
Are we successors to the great Abdallas   50

---

31. Bear] *Dyce²*; Barre Q.   35. Tamburlaine] *Dyce¹*; Tamberlaine *Q (& l. 37)*.   49.
boy, / Are] *Dyce²*; boy, are *Q*.   50 Abdallas] *Bullen*; Abdilmelec *Q*; Abdelmunen
Dyce².

---

27. *bug*] bugbear, an imaginary object of terror (*OED sb¹* 1a).

28. *doughty*] valiant, brave (*OED a* 1b).

31. *Saturn's sons*] Pluto, Neptune and Jove (i.e. Hades, Poseidon and Zeus) were
sons of the Titan Cronus, whom the Romans associated with their god Saturn.

37. cf. the hero's dying words in 2 *Tamburlaine*, 'Tamburlaine, the scourge of God,
must die' (5.3.248).

38. *Philip*] Philip of Macedon.

39–47.] Greg (p. 106) observes, 'these lines, a mere jumble of participial and relative clauses, are clearly impossible as they stand'; there could well be lines missing after
l. 45 (Bradley, p. 147).

45.] Some lines must have dropped out of the text here, a common occurrence. Most
of these omissions are noted by Bradley (p. 167), who credits them to 'a careless compositor'; see also pp. 19–21.

50. *Abdallas*] Bullen's emendation for *Q*'s 'Abdilmelec' must be correct, since
Abdallas was Muly Mahamet's father, and is metrical.

Descended from the Arabian Muly Sharif,
And shall we be afraid of Bashaws and of bugs,
Raw head and bloody bone?
Boy, seest here this scimitar by my side?
Sith they begin to bathe in blood,   55
Blood be the theme whereon our time shall tread.
Such slaughter with my weapon shall I make
As through the stream and bloody channels deep,
Our Moors shall sail in ships and pinnaces
From Tangier shore unto the gates of Fez.   60
Muly Mahamet's Son. And of those slaughtered bodies shall thy son
A hugy tower erect like Nimrod's frame,
To threaten those unjust and partial gods
That to Abdallas' lawful seed deny
A long, a happy and triumphant reign.   65

Sound an alarum within, and enter a MESSENGER.

Messenger. Fly, King of Fez, King of Morocco, fly,
Fly with thy friends, Emperor of Barbary,
O fly the sword and fury of the foe
That rageth as the ramping lioness
In rescue of her younglings from the bear.   70
Thy towns and holds by numbers basely yield,
Thy land to Abdelmelec's rule resigns,
Thy carriage and thy treasure taken is
By Amurath's soldiers, that have sworn thy death.
Fly Amurath's power, and Abdelmelec's threats,   75
Or thou and thine look here to breathe your last.
Muly Mahamet. Villain, what dreadful sound of death and flight
Is this, wherewith thou dost afflict our ears?
But if there be no safety to abide
The favour, fortune and success of war,   80
Away in haste, roll on my chariot wheels,
Restless till I be safely set in shade

---

51. Sharif] *This ed.*; *Zarif* Q; *Xarif* Dyce[1], Yoklavich.   62. hugy] Dyce[2]; huge Q;
hugie Yoklavich.   66 SH.] *This ed.*; Mes. Q; Mess. Dyce[1].   Morocco] *This ed.*;
Moroccus Q.   77. flight] Dyce[1]; fight Q.

62. *hugy*] a common form of 'huge'; cf. *1 Tamburlaine*, 'Your threefold army and
my hugy host / Shall swallow up these base-born Persians' (3.3.94–5).
Nimrod's frame] the Tower of Babel (Genesis, chs 10–11).
65. SD.] It is not unusual, in Elizabethan plays, for an entire battle and its aftermath to take place off-stage within a few moments.
66–76.] This messenger speech may have been taken by the returning Pisano
(Bradley, p. 182).

Of some unhaunted place, some blasted grove
Of deadly yew or dismal cypress tree,
Far from the light or comfort of the sun,   85
There to curse heaven, and he that heaves me hence,
To sick as Envy at Cecropia's gate
And pine the thought and terror of mishaps.
Away!

                                             [*Exeunt.*]

---

83. unhaunted] *Dyce¹;* unhanted *Q.*   84. yew] *Dyce²;* hue *Q.*   87. sick] *Dyce²;*
seeke *Q.*   Cecropia's] *Dyce¹;* Cecropes *Q.*   89 SD.] *Plot;* Exit *Q.*

---

83. *unhaunted*] not frequented, lonely, solitary (*OED ppl* 2); cf. *The Maid's Meta-
morphosis,* 'But pray ye maide, it will be very good / To take the shade, in this
unhaunted wood' (sig. D3r).

84. *deadly yew*] Q reads 'hue', but in Elizabethan handwriting an 'h' goes below
the line, and is easily mistaken for a 'y'. The yew tree was 'deadly' in two senses, being
both poisonous and the wood from which the English longbow was fashioned; cf.
Richard II, 'The very beadsmen learn to bend their bows / Of double-fatal yew'
(3.2.112–13).

87. *sick . . . gate*] Q reads 'seeke', but 'sick', in the sense of 'sicken', was not unusual
in Peele's time; Bullen supports Dyce's emendation by citing 2 *Henry IV,* 'Say it did so
a little time before / That our great grandsire Edward sicked and died' (4.3.127–8).
Muly Mahamet alludes to the story of Aglauros, the daughter of Cecrops, King of
Athens, in Ovid's *Metamorphoses* (2.711–835). She was envious of her sister Herse,
loved by the god Mercury, and, when she barred the door of Herse's house, Mercury
turned her to stone.

ACT 2

Alarum. [Enter the PRESENTER,] *and then the* PRESENTER *speaketh.*

Presenter. Now war begins his rage and ruthless reign
And Nemesis with bloody whip in hand
Thunders for vengeance on this negro Moor.

                      [Enter above Nemesis.]

Nor may the silence of the speechless night,
Divine architect of murders and misdeeds,   5
Of tragedies and tragic tyrannies,
Hide or contain this barbarous cruelty
Of this usurper to his progeny.

          [Enter] three Ghosts *crying 'vindicta'.*

Hark, lords, as in a hollow place afar,
The dreadful shrieks and clamours that resound   10
And sound revenge upon this traitor's soul,
Traitor to kin and kind, to gods and men.
Now Nemesis upon her doubling drum,
Moved with this ghastly moan, this sad complaint,

Act 2] *This ed.;* Actus Secunda. Scæna prima *Q;* Actus Secundi. Scena prima *Dyce¹;*
Act II *Dyce².* 2. Prol.] *This ed.; not in Q.* OSD.] *This ed.;* Alarum. And then the
presenter speaketh *Q;* Enter the Presenter *Plot.* 1 SH.] *This ed.; not in Q.* 3 SD.]
Plot; not in Q. 5. Divine architect] *Dyce¹;* Divine Architects *Q;* Dire architect *Dyce².*
8 SD.] *subst. Q.* 10. shrieks] *Dyce¹;* shrikes *Q.*

---

2. *Nemesis with bloody whip*] cf. the 'third addition' to the *Spanish Tragedy* (Q
1602), 'And there is Nemesis and Furies / And things called whippes / And they sometimes doe meete with murderers' (sig. G4r).
3 SD.] Q has no dumb show, but the Plot has directions for one that is consistent
with the Presenter's speech. I follow Yoklavich in inserting a direction here, and others
at ll. 25 and 31.
5. *Divine architect*] Q has 'architects', but the singular makes sense, as the Presenter
must be referring to 'speechless night'; the unmetrical 'divine' is probably a compositor's
error, but there is no clear candidate for substitution. Greg (p. 107) and Dyce propose
that the architect be 'dire'; M. K. Nellis offers 'dumme', as it relates nicely to 'speechless
night' ('Peele's Night: Dumb or Divine Architect', *N&Q* 30 (1983): 132–3), but Bradley
(p. 149), for precisely the same reason, considers 'dimme architect' to be 'obvious'.
8 SD.] 'It was the stage-practice of ghosts to cry "Vindicta"' (Bullen, p. 241).

'Larums aloud into Alecto's ears,   15
And with her thundering wakes whereas they lie,
In cave as dark as hell and beds of steel,
The furies, just imps of dire revenge.
'Revenge', cries Abdelmunen's grievèd ghost,
And rouseth with the terror of this noise   20
These nymphs of Erebus. 'Wreak and revenge',
Ring out the souls of his unhappy brethren,
And now start up these torments of the world,
Waked with the thunder of Rhamnusia's drum,
And fearful echoes of these grievèd ghosts,   25

[*To them lying behind the curtains three* Furies, *one with
a whip, another with a bloody torch, and the third with
a chopping knife.*]

Alecto with her brand and bloody torch,
Megaera with her whip and snaky hair,
Tisiphone with her fatal murdering iron,
These three conspire, these three complain and moan.
Thus, Muly Mahamet, is a council held   30

---

19. Abdelmunen's] *Dyce²*, *Yoklavich;* Abdilmelecs *Q*; Abdilmunen's *Dyce¹*.
24. Rhamnusia's] *Dyce¹;* Ramusians *Q*; Ramnusias *Yoklavich*. 25 SD.] *This ed.;* To
them lying behind the Curtaines 3 furies: Parsons, George & Ro. Tailor, one with a
whipp, another with a blody torch, and the 3ᵈ with a Chopping knife *Plot; not in Q*.

---

15. *Alecto*] see n. ll. 26–9.
16. *whereas*] where (*OED rel. adv.* 1).
17–18.] The furies, or erinyes, were the mythological tormenters of criminals, especially when the offence was against blood kin; 'imp', in this context, is a child of the
devil or hell (*OED sb* 4). The 'beds of steel', also found at 4.2.70, are probably drawn
from the *Aeneid*, 'The Furies' iron beds; and Strife, that shakes / Her hissing tresses
and unfolds her snakes' (6.392–3).
21. *nymphs of Erebus*] an oxymoron. Nymphs, the female divinities who resided
in natural phenomena such as trees, mountains and lakes, can hardly be equated
with furies roused from Erebus, i.e. the 'primeval darkness' (Harvey, p. 168); cf.
Shakespeare's frequent use of 'nymph' in *The Tempest*; see also n. 4.2.73.
24. *Rhamnusia*] another name for Nemesis, whose 'chief cult center' was the town
of Rhamnus on the north-eastern coast of Attica (Edward Tripp, *The Meridian Hand-
book of Classical Mythology*, New York, 1970, p. 512).
26–9.] The appearance in Peele's dumb show of the 'three sisters born of Night', as
Ovid calls them in the *Metamorphoses* (4.452), is similar to that described over twenty
years earlier in *Gorboduc*: 'First the Musick of Howeboies began to plaie, duringe
whiche there came forth from under the Stage, as thoughe out of Hell three Furies.
Alecto, Megera & Ctisiphone clad in blacke garments sprinkled with bloud & flames,
their bodies girt with snakes, their heds spread with Serpents in steade of heare, the
one bearinge in her hande a Snake, the other a whip, & the thirde a burning Firebrande'
(sig. C5r). Peele, unlike Norton and Sackville, gives only one fury (Alecto) snaky hair,

To wreak the wrongs and murders thou hast done.
[*Exeunt show.*]
By this imagine was this barbarous Moor
Chased from his dignity and his diadem
And lives forlorn among the mountain shrubs,
And makes his food the flesh of savage beasts.   35
Amurath's soldiers have by this installed
Good Abdelmelec in his royal seat,
The dames of Fez and ladies of the land
In honour of the son of Solimon,
Erect a statue made of beaten gold   40
And sing to Amurath songs of lasting praise.
Muly Mahamet's fury overruled,
His cruelty controlled and pride rebuked,
Now at last, when sober thoughts renewed
Care of his kingdom and desirèd crown,   45
The aid, that once was offered and refused,
By messengers he furiously implores
Sebastian's aid. Brave King of Portugal!
He, forward in all arms and chivalry,
Hearkens to his ambassadors, and grants   50
What they in letters and by words entreat.
Now listen, lordings, now begins the game,
Sebastian's tragedy in this tragic war.
[*Exit.*]

31 SD.] *Yoklavich;* exeunt *Plot; not in Q.*   39. Solimon] *Dyce¹, Yoklavich;* Soliman
Q.   47. implores] *Dyce¹, Yoklavich;* imployes *Q.*   48. aid. Brave] *This ed.;* aide
brave *Q;* aid, brave *Dyce¹.*   53 SD.] *Yoklavich;* exeunt *Plot; not in Q.*

and specifies the properties to be held by each, adding visual colour to the scene – the
Plot calls for 'whip, bloody torch, and chopping knife'. Ancient Pistol undoubtedly has
this speech in mind when he states, 'Rouse up Revenge from ebon den with fell Alecto's
snake / For Doll is in' (2H4, 5.5.37–8).
    31 SD.] Yoklavich's placement of 'exeunt show' here is reasonable, although any
choice must be considered somewhat arbitrary.
    32. *By this imagine was*] OED gives this passage as its only example of 'imagine'
as a noun, meaning 'device, contrivance'. A more likely reading, although 'was' is syn-
tactically odd, would be 'imagine' as an imperative – the Presenter is telling spectators
what to picture in their minds.
    40. *statue . . . gold*] The events described in this speech are in Polemon, except for
the golden statue. Although neither the stage directions nor the Plot mentions it, Bradley
(p. 149) argues for a statue to be placed or revealed on stage, the scene including 'a
strange attempt at an oriental ceremony'.
    47. *implores*] As 'furiously' does not fit well with Q's 'imployes', Dyce's substitu-
tion of 'implores' seems sensible.

[2.1]

> *Alarum within, and then enter* ABDELMELEC, MULY MAHAMET
> SETH, [ZAREO,] CALSEPIUS BASHAW, *with Moors and*
> *janissaries, and the Ladies* [*and* Rubin's young son].

Abdelmelec. Now hath the sun displayed his golden beams
    And dusky clouds dispersed, the welkin clears
    Wherein the twenty-coloured rainbow shows.
    After this fight happy and fortunate,
    Wherein our Moors have won the day,   5
    And victory, adorned with fortune's plumes,
    Alights on Abdelmelec's glorious crest.
    Here find we time to breathe; and now begin
    To pay thy due and duties thou dost owe
    To heaven and earth, to gods and Amurath.   10

                                Sound Trumpets.

    And now draw near and heaven and earth give ear,
    Give ear and record, heaven and earth with me.
    Ye lords of Barbary, hearken and attend,
    Hark to the words I speak and vow I make
    To plant the true succession of the crown: 15
    Lo, lords, in our seat royal to succeed
    Our only brother here we do install,
    And by the name of Muly Mahamet Seth
    Entitle him true heir unto the crown.
    Ye gods of heaven gratulate this deed,   20
    That men on earth may therewith stand content.

2.1] *This ed.;* Scene I *Dyce²; not in* Q. OSD.] *subst.* Yoklavich*;* Alarum within, and
then enter Abdilmelec, Muly Mahamet Seth, Calsepius Bassa, with Moores and
Janizaries, and the Ladies *Q;* Sound. Enter Abdelmelec, mahamet Xeque, Zareo,
Calcepius Bassa, Abdula Rais, & Ruben. Attendants. mr Hunt & George & young
sonne Dab *Plot.* 5. Moors have won] *This ed.;* Moors have lost *Q, Bullen;* trait'rous
Moors have lost *Dyce².*

    2.1.] The action of the scene is not localised, but may be imagined to be taking place
in Fez.
    OSD.] Rubin's son is a mute part, but, as the Plot and ll. 32–47 require, he must be
present (see Bradley, p. 184).
    3. *twenty-coloured*] perhaps a misreading of 'thousand coloured'. 'Twentie' and
'thousande' or 'thowsande' are fairly similar in Elizabethan handwriting, and Virgil's
description of Iris (goddess of the rainbow) descending to visit the dying Dido (see n.
5.Prol.9) reads 'Downward the various goddess took her flight / And drew a thousand
colors from the light' (*Aeneid*, 4.1005–6).
    5. *our . . . day*] Q's 'lost the day' makes no sense. Dyce inserts 'traitorous', adding
needed syllables, but then Abdelmelec would not say 'our traitorous Moors'.
    8. *and now begin*] Here Abdelmelec begins speaking to himself.

Lo, thus my due and duties do I pay
To heaven and earth, to gods and Amurath.
                                 Sound trumpets.
Muly Mahamet Seth. Renownèd Bashaw, to remunerate
  Thy worthiness and magnanimity,   25
  Behold the noblest ladies of the land
  Bring present tokens of their gratitude.
Rubin Archis. Rubin, that breathes but for revenge,
  Bashaw, by this commends herself to thee [. . .]
  Resigns the token of her thankfulness.   30
  To Amurath, the god of earthly kings,
  Doth Rubin give and sacrifice her son,
  Not with sweet smoke of fire or sweet perfume,
  But with his father's sword his mother's thanks
  Doth Rubin give her son to Amurath.   35
Abdil Rayes. As Rubin gives her son, so we ourselves
  To Amurath give, and fall before his face.
  Bashaw, wear thou the gold of Barbary,
  And glister like the palace of the sun,
  In honour of the deed that thou hast done.   40
Calsepius Bashaw. Well worthy of the aid of Amurath
  Is Abdelmelec and these noble dames.
  Rubin, thy son I shall ere long bestow
  Where thou dost him bequeath in honour's fee
  On Amurath, mighty Emperor of the East,   45
  That shall receive the imp of royal race
  With cheerful looks and gleams of princely grace.
  This chosen guard of Amurath's janissaries
  I leave to honour and attend on thee.
  King of Morocco, conqueror of thy foes,   50
  True King of Fez, Emperor of Barbary,
  Muly Molocco, live and keep thy seat

---

22. my due and duties do I pay] *Dyce²*; due and duetie is done, I paie *Q*.   30. Resigns]
Bullen; Resigne *Q*; Receive *Dyce²*; Resignes *Yoklavich*.   36 SH.] *This ed.*; Queene *Q*;
Queen *Dyce¹*; Abd. Ra. *Yoklavich*.

29.] Part of Rubin's speech after 'thee' appears to be missing.

36. SH. *Abdil Rayes*] Yoklavich correctly identifies *Q*'s 'Queen' as Abdil Rayes;
Dyce assumes she is a separate character, 'a petty princess'; see also p. 25.

39. *palace of the sun*] Possibly a reference to Phaethon's journey through Ethiopia
and India in search of his father Apollo in *Metamorphoses*, 'The Palace of the Sun rose
high aloft / On soaring columns, bright with flashing gold' (2.1–2); cf. *Stukeley*,
n. 21.27–8.

46. *imp*] here, the scion of a noble house (*OED sb* 3); Pistol's greeting the newly
crowned Henry V as 'most royal imp of fame' (5.5.42) is probably one of the several
parodies of Peele in *2 Henry IV* (see n. 2.3.94; also p. 27).

In spite of fortune's spite or enemies' threats.
Ride, Bashaw, now, bold Bashaw homeward ride
As glorious as great Pompey in his pride.   55

                                                    [*Exeunt.*]

[2.2]

Enter DIEGO LOPES *the Governor of Lisbon, the Irish* BISHOP,
          STUKELEY, JONAS *and* HERCULES.

Diego Lopes. Welcome to Lisbon, valiant Catholics,
    Welcome brave Englishmen to Portugal.
    Most reverent primate of the Irish church
    And noble Stukeley, famous by thy name,
    Welcome, thrice welcome to Sebastian's town,   5
    And welcome, English captains, to you all.
    It joyeth us to see his Holiness' fleet,
    Cast anchor happily upon our coast.
Bishop. These welcomes, worthy governor of Lisbon,
    Argue an honorable mind in thee,   10
    But treat of our misfortune therewithal.
    To Ireland by Pope Gregory's command,
    Were we all bound, and therefore thus embarked
    To land our forces there at unawares,
    Conquering the land for his Holiness,   15
    And so restore it to the Roman faith.
    This was the cause of our expedition,

55 SD.] *Plot, Dyce²*; Exit omnes *Q.*

2.2] *This ed.*; Scene II *Dyce²*; *not in Q.* OSD.] *subst. Q*; Enter Diego Lopis, Governor of Lisborne mr Rich. Allen, Stukeley, Jonas, Hercules, & an Irish Bishopp mr Towne, Ro. Tailor, w Kendall & mr Shaa *Plot.* STUKELEY] Stukeley, Stukley *Q*; Stukeley *Dyce¹*; Stukley *Yoklavich.* 1 SH.] *This ed.*; Die. *Q.* Lisbon] *Dyce¹*; Lisborne *Q (exc.* Lishborne *5.1.164).* 9 SH.] *This ed.*; Bishop, Bish. *Q*; Bish. *Dyce¹*, *Yoklavich.*

————————————————————————————————

55. *great Pompey*] i.e. Pompey the Great (106–48 BC), defeated by Julius Caesar at the battle of Pharsalia.

2.2.] Our story now goes to Lisbon.

OSD. JONAS *and* HERCULES] Peele's making Stukeley's captains, Jonas and Hercules, English causes no end of confusion later; see Appendix I.

1. *Lisbon*] *Q* is consistent with 'Lisborne', but 'Lisbon' is far more common in plays of the period. Since the actors' pronunciation would probably not have changed from play to play, the modern spelling is employed here.

14. *unawares*] without intimation or warning (*OED adv* 4); cf. *3 Henry VI*, 'Either betrayed by falsehood of his guard / Or by his foe surprised at unawares' (4.5.8–9).

And Ireland long ere this had been subdued
Had not foul weather brought us to this bay.
Diego Lopes. Under correction, are ye not all Englishmen,   20
And 'longs not Ireland to that kingdom, lords?
Then may I speak my conscience in the cause,
Sans scandal to the Holy See of Rome:
Unhonourable is this expedition,
And misbeseeming you to meddle in.   25
Stukeley. Lord Governor of Lisbon, understand
As we are Englishmen, so are we men,
And I am Stukeley so resolved in all
To follow rule, honour and empery,
Not to be bent so strictly to the place   30
Wherein at first I blew the fire of life,
But that I may at liberty make choice
Of all the continents that bounds the world.
For why, I make it not so great desert
To be begot or born in any place,   35
Sith that's a thing of pleasure and of ease,
That might have been performed elsewhere as well.
Diego Lopes. Follow what your good pleasure will,
Good Captain Stukeley, be it far from me
To take exceptions beyond my privilege.   40
Bishop. Yet, captain, give me leave to speak:
We must affect our country as our parents,
And if at any time we alienate
Our love or industry from doing it honour,
It must respect effects and touch the soul [. . .]   45
Matter of conscience and religion,
And not desire of rule or benefit.

26 SH.] *This ed.;* Stuk. Q *(exc.* Stukley 4.2.68), *Dyce¹;* Stuke *Dyce²;* Stuk. *Yoklavich.*

29. *follow . . . empery*] Stukeley uses 'follow' in the sense of 'strive after' (*OED v* 6), 'empery' being 'the status, dignity, or dominion of an emperor' (*OED sb* 1); see n. 2.4.44.
33. *bounds*] The singular verb following a plural subject is common in early modern usage (Abbott, pp. 235–7).
42. *affect*] love, have affection for (*OED v¹* 2a).
45.] Some text may be missing after this line, as Hercules' rejoinder (ll. 50–5) seems out of proportion to whatever point the Bishop may be making.
45. *effects*] affects, i.e. motives or intentions, contrary to *OED*'s misleading definition. The dictionary gives no alternative spelling for 'affect' (*OED sb* 1), while citing an 1850 edition of Tyndale's *Supper of the Lord*, 'God is searcher of heart and reins, thoughts and affects'. The 1553 octavo of this work, however, reads 'thoughts and *effectis*' (sig. D8r).

Stukeley. Well said, Bishop, spoken like yourself,
   The reverent lordly Bishop of Saint Asses.
Hercules. The Bishop talks according to his coat,   50
   And takes not measure of it by his mind.
   You see he hath it made thus large and wide
   Because he may convert it as he list,
   To any form may fit the fashion best.
Bishop. Captain, you do me wrong to descant thus   55
   Upon my coat or double conscience,
   And cannot answer it in another place.
Diego Lopes. 'Tis but in jest, Lord Bishop, put it up,
   And all as friends deign to be entertained
   As my ability here can make provision.   60
   Shortly shall I conduct you to the King,
   Whose welcomes evermore to strangers are
   Princely and honourable as his state becomes.
Stukeley. Thanks, worthy Governor. Come, Bishop, come,
   Will you show fruits of quarrel and of wrath?   65
   Come, let's in with my lord of Lisbon here,
   And put all conscience into one carouse,
   Letting it out again, as we may live. [. . .]
                    [*Exeunt, manet* STUKELEY.]
   There shall no action pass my hand or sword
   That cannot make a step to gain a crown,   70
   No word shall pass the office of my tongue
   That sounds not of affection to a crown,
   No thought have being in my lordly breast
   That works not every way to win a crown.
   Deeds, words and thoughts shall all be as a king's,   75
   My chiefest company shall be with kings,
   And my deserts shall counterpoise a king's.
   Why should not I then look to be a king?
   I am the Marquess now of Ireland made
   And will be shortly King of Ireland.   80
   King of a mole-hill had I rather be

---

66. let's] *Dyce²;* let us *Q.*   68 SD.] *subst. Dyce²; not in Q.*   79. Marquess] *This ed.;*
marques *Q;* Marquis *Dyce¹.*

49. *Bishop of Saint Asses*] Obviously a pun on 'Asaph', but our Bishop is Irish, not
Welsh; see Appendix II.
   68.] Some lines must be missing after 'live'. Q has no 'exeunt' here, but the rest of
Stukeley's speech reads like a soliloquy.
   79. *Marquess*] William Pillen, an English merchant, witnessed Stukeley's arrival in
Lisbon, and noted 'the same Stukley there was called by noe other name than Marques'
(Castries, 1: 52); see pp. 9–10.
   81. *King of a mole-hill*] a statement widely associated with Stukeley. In *Pierce's
Supererogation*, published a year before the quarto of *Alcazar*, Gabriel Harvey objects

Than the richest subject of a monarchy.
Huff it, brave mind, and never cease t'aspire,
Before thou reign sole king of thy desire.

                                                              [*Exit.*]

[2.3]

    Enter [MULY MAHAMET] *the Moor with* CALIPOLIS *his wife,*
        his SON *and two others.*

Muly Mahamet. Where art thou boy? Where is Calipolis?
O deadly wound that passeth by mine eye,
The fatal prison of my swelling heart!
O fortune constant in unconstancy!
Fight earthquakes in the entrails of the earth   5
And eastern whirlwinds in the hellish shades,
Some foul contagion of the infected heaven,
Blast all the trees, and in their cursèd tops
The dismal night raven and tragic owl
Breed, and become foretellers of my fall,   10
The fatal ruin of my name and me.
Adders and serpents hiss at my disgrace,
And wound the earth with anguish of their stings.
Now, Abdelmelec, now triumph in Fez,
Fortune hath made thee King of Barbary.   15

84 SD.] *This ed.;* Exeunt *Q.*
2.3] *This ed.;* Scene III *Dyce²; not in Q.* OSD.] *subst. Q;* Enter Mully Mahamet,
Calipolis, young mahamet & 2 moores w Cartwright and mr Hunt *Plot.* 3. prison]
Q; poison *Dyce².*

---

to the Puritans' denial of church hierarchy, and ironically suggests that every parish
minister be made equal to a Pope: 'onely let the sayd Pontife beware, he prove not a
great Pope in a little Roome; or discover the humour of aspiring Stukely, that would
rather be king of a moulhill, then the second in Ireland, or England' (*Pierce's
Supererogation*, London, 1593, p. 85).
    83. *Huff*] to puff or swell with pride or arrogance (*OED v* 4). When Sir Jerome
Horsey tried to deliver an edict from Queen Elizabeth to the Hanse towns forbidding
them to trade with Spain, the Burgermeister of Lübeck 'hufft therat, saienge they would
pass with their shippinge in spight of the Quen of Englands power' (*Travels of Sir
Jerome Horsey* (1591), in *Russia at the Close of the Sixteenth Century*, ed. Edward A.
Bond, London, 1856, p. 238).
    2.3.] The action takes place somewhere in the Atlas Mountains.
    1.] This line is quoted by Jonson in *The Poetaster* (3.4.346–52), while two theatre
boys, one perched on the other's shoulders, strut the stage in imitation of Edward Alleyn
(Bradley, p. 153).
    2–3.] 'There is no sense to be got out of these lines' (Greg, p. 110).

Calipolis. Alas, my lord, what boots these huge exclaims
    To advantage us in this distressed estate?
    O pity our perplexed estate, my lord,
    And turn all curses to submiss complaints,
    And those complaints to actions of relief.   20
    I faint, my lord, and naught may cursing plaints
    Refresh the fading substance of my life.
Muly Mahamet. Faint all the world, consume and be accursed,
    Since my state faints and is accursed.
Calipolis. Yet patience, lord, to conquer sorrows so.   25
Muly Mahamet. What patience is for him that lacks his crown?
    There is no patience where the loss is such,
    The shame of my disgrace hath put on wings
    And swiftly flies about this earthly ball.
    Car'st thou to live then, fond Calipolis,   30
    When he that should give essence to thy soul,
    He on whose glory all thy joy should stay,
    Is soulless, gloryless, and desperate,
    Crying for battle, famine, sword and fire,
    Rather then calling for relief or life.   35
    But be content, thy hunger shall have end,
    Famine shall pine to death and thou shalt live.
    I will go hunt these cursèd solitaries,
    And make the sword and target here my hound,
    To pull down lions and untamèd beasts.   40
                                          Exit.
Muly Mahamet's Son. Tush, mother, cherish your unhearty soul
    And feed with hope of happiness and ease,
    For if by valour or by policy
    My kingly father can be fortunate,
    We shall be Jove's commanders once again,   45
    And flourish in a threefold happiness.

---

16 SH.] *This ed.*; Caly., Calyp. *Q*; Calip. *Dyce¹*; Calyp. *Yoklavich.*   41 SD.] *Q*; Exit
Muly Mahamet, manet the rest *Plot.*

---

   19. *submiss*] common form of 'submissive' (*OED a* 1).

   25. *to conquer sorrows so*] the 'so' at the end of the line is odd, and implies
that this line was part of a longer speech than is retained in *Q* (see Yoklavich,
p. 357).

   34. *famine, sword and fire*] the traditional instruments of war; cf. *Henry V*,
'Leashed in like hounds, should famine, sword, and fire / Crouch for employment'
(1.Prol.7–8).

   38. *solitaries*] deserts; cf. Dekker, *Satiro-mastix*, 'I meane I will go solus, or in solitaries alone' (4.2.161–2).

Attendant. His majesty hath sent Sebastian,
The good and harmless King of Portugal,
A promise to resign the royalty
And kingdom of Morocco to his hands.   50
But when this haughty offer takes effect
And works affiance in Sebastian,
My gracious lord, warned wisely to advise,
I doubt not but will watch occasion
And take her foretop by the slenderest hair,   55
To rid us of this miserable life.
Muly Mahamet's Son. Good madam, cheer yourself, my father's wife,
He can submit himself and live below,
Make show of friendship, promise, vow and swear,
Till by the virtue of his fair pretence,   60
Sebastian trusting his integrity,
He makes himself possessor of such fruits
As grow upon such great advantages.
Calipolis. But more dishonour hangs on such misdeeds
Than all the profit their return can bear.   65
Such secret judgements hath the heavens imposed
Upon the drooping state of Barbary,
As public merits in such lewd attempts
Hath drawn with violence upon our heads.

Enter MULY MAHAMET *with [raw] flesh upon his sword.*

Muly Mahamet. Hold thee, Calipolis, feed and faint no more.   70
This flesh I forcèd from a lioness,

---

47 SH.] *Yoklavich;* Zareo *Q.* 69 SD.] *This ed.;* Enter Muly Mahamet with lyons flesh upon his sworde *Q;* to them muly mahamet a gains wth raw flesh *Plot.*

---

47 SH.] *Q* gives this speech to Zareo, although he obviously cannot be present. Greg (pp. 110–11) surmises that Peele intended that the actor playing Zareo would double as the attendant. Bradley agrees, noting that a 'blacked-up' actor would be needed, but argues that the Plotter saw Zareo as white-skinned, and, since black make-up could not be removed and re-applied quickly, this caused casting problems elsewhere in the Plotter's production. See Bradley (pp. 37–8, 127, 142, 161–2, 178, 183–4, 197) for an intriguing discussion of this matter, which cannot be given in detail here.

48. *harmless*] innocent (*OED a* 3).

52. *works affiance*] creates faith, trust (*OED sb* 1).

53. *advise*] consider, think over (*OED v* 3); cf. n. 2.4.130.

54–5.] That 'occasion' or 'opportunity' had a foretop (a lock of hair from the forepart of the head) to be seized was a common expression; cf. Marston, *Antonio's Revenge,* 'Opportunity shakes us his foretop' (5.1.81–2).

69 SD.] Muly Mahamet's speech indicates that he carries 'lion's flesh' (*Q* stage direction) in that a lioness previously owned it, i.e. he has stolen some of her dinner.

Meat of a princess, for a princess meet.
Learn by her noble stomach to esteem
Penury plenty, in extremest dearth,
Who when she saw her foragement bereft,   75
Pined not in melancholy or childish fear,
But as brave minds are strongest in extremes,
So she redoubling her former force
Ranged thorough the woods, and rent the breeding vaults
Of proudest savages to save herself.   80
Feed then and faint not fair Calipolis,
For rather than fierce famine shall prevail
To gnaw thy entrails with her thorny teeth,
The conquering lioness shall attend on thee
And lay huge heaps of slaughtered carcasses   85
As bulwarks in her way to keep her back.
I will provide thee of a princely osprey,
That as she flieth over fish in pools,
The fish shall turn their glistering bellies up
And thou shalt take thy liberal choice of all.   90
Jove's stately bird with wide commanding wings
Shall hover still about thy princely head
And beat down fowl by shoals into thy lap.
Feed then and faint not, fair Calipolis.
Calipolis. Thanks, good my lord, and though my stomach be   95
Too queasy to digest such bloody meat,
Yet strength I it with virtue of my mind;
I doubt no whit but I shall live, my lord.
Muly Mahamet. Into the shades then, fair Calipolis,
And make thy son and negroes here good cheer.   100
Feed and be fat that we may meet the foe
With strength and terror to revenge our wrong.

                                        [*Exeunt.*]

---

72. meet] *Dyce¹*; meate *Q*.   96. digest] *Dyce¹*; disgest *Q, Bullen*.   102 SD.] *Dyce¹*, *Yoklavich*; exeunt manet muly *Plot; not in Q*.

87–9.] The osprey's supposed power to make any fish instantly surrender to be eaten is metaphorically ascribed to Coriolanus: 'I think he'll be to Rome / As is the osprey to the fish, who takes it / By sovereignty of nature' (4.7.33–5).

94. *feed then and faint not*] famously parodied by Shakespeare in 2 *Henry IV*, 'Then feed and be fat, my fair Calipolis / Come, give's some sack' (2.4.176–7), as well as in Dekker's *Satiro-mastix*, 'Feede and be fat my faire Calipolis, stir not my beauteous wriggle-tailes' (4.1.150–1), and Marston's *What You Will*, 'Feed and be fat my fair Calipolis' (5.1.1). See p. 27.

97. *strength*] obsolete form of 'strengthen' (*OED*).

102 SD.] The Plot shows '*exeunt manet muly*'. As Muly Mahamet's speech does not end in a couplet, he may have remained on stage to deliver a soliloquy which has been omitted from *Q* (Greg, p. 110).

[2.4]

> [*Sound sennet.*] *Enter* SEBASTIAN *King of Portugal, the*
> DUKE OF AVERO, *the* Duke of Barceles, Lewes de Silva,
> CHRISTOPHERO DE TAVORA [*and the* County Vimioso].

Sebastian. Call forth those Moors, those men of Barbary,
That came with letters from the King of Fez.
                  Exit one [*who brings in the* AMBASSADORS].
Ye warlike lords and men of chivalry,
Honourable ambassadors of this high regent,
Hark to Sebastian, King of Portugal.   5
These letters sent from your distressèd lord,
Torn from his throne by Abdelmelec's hand,
Strengthened and raised by furious Amurath,
Imports a kingly favour at our hands
For aid to reobtain his royal seat,   10
And place his fortunes in their former height.
For quittal of which honourable arms,
By these his letters he doth firmly vow
Wholly to yield and to surrender up
The kingdom of Morocco to our hands,   15

2.4] *This ed.*; Scene IV *Dyce²; not in Q.* OSD. County Vimioso] *This ed.*; County
Vinioso *Plot; not in Q.* 1 SH.] *This ed.*; Sebast., Seb. *Q*; K. Seb. *Dyce¹*; Sebast.
Yoklavich. 2 SD.] *This ed.*; Exit one *Q*: To them 2 moores embassadors mr Sam mr
Hunt & 2 pages *Plot*; Exit one and brings in the Embass. *Dyce¹*; The Moorish Ambas-
sadors are brought in by an Attendant *Dyce²*; The Moorish Ambassadors are brought
in *Bullen.* 9. Imports] *Q*; Import *Dyce¹.* 12. quittal] *This ed.*; quitall *Q*; 'quital
Dyce¹. 15. Morocco] *This ed.*; Maroccus *Q.*

2.4.] The setting is Lisbon, the royal palace.
   OSD.] The Plot direction includes the wrongly spelled 'County Vinioso', who
neither speaks nor is spoken of in *Q*. The powerful Don Alfonso of Portugal (1519–79),
Count of Vimioso, is portrayed in the *Uniting* as something of a 'yes-man': with
Sebastian determined to go to Africa, 'one of the chiefe that did most applaud his
humour was Alphonso of Portugall, Earle [*sic*] of Vimioso, who had beene (in the
Kings former voyage into Affricke) Chamberlaine, and had charge of the victuals;
wherein he behaved himselfe so sparingly, as if they had continued any longer in
Affricke, or else at sea, they had beene starved' (p. 35). He is listed amongst 'the named
of the chiefe slaine in the battle' (p. 52), although in fact he was captured, dying of his
wounds soon after. His son Don Francisco, who succeeded him, was also captured, and
later released through the intercession of Philip II (Castries, 1: 388); the *Dolorous
Discourse*, probably confusing him with his father, mistakenly lists Francisco among
the dead (sig. B3v). Various theories, based on likely doubling patterns, have been
offered for this textual oddity (see Greg, pp. 110–11; Yoklavich, p. 358; Bradley,
pp. 189–90).
   9. Imports] see n. 2.2.33.
   12. quittal] abbreviated form of 'requital'; cf. *Rape of Lucrece*, 'As in revenge or
quittal of such strife' (l. 236).

And to become to us contributary,
And to content himself with the realm of Fez.
These lines, my lords, writ in extremity,
Contain therefore but during fortune's day,
How shall Sebastian then believe the same?   20
Moorish Ambassador. Viceroys, and most Christian King of Portugal,
To satisfy thy doubtful mind herein,
Command forthwith a blazing brand of fire
Be brought in presence of thy majesty,
Then shalt thou see by our religious vows   25
And ceremonies most inviolate
How firm our sovereign's protestations are.
                   [*A brand is brought in by an attendant.*]
Behold, my lord, this binds our faith to thee:
In token that great Muly Mahamet's hand
Hath writ no more than his stout heart allows,   30
And will perform to thee and to thine heirs,
We offer here our hands into this flame
And as this flame doth fasten on this flesh,
So from our souls we wish it may consume
The heart of our great lord and sovereign,   35
Muly Mahamet, King of Barbary,
If his intent agree not with his words.
Sebastian. These ceremonies and protestations
Sufficeth us, ye lords of Barbary.
Therefore return this answer to your king: 40
Assure him by the honour of my crown
And by Sebastian's true unfeignèd faith,
He shall have aid and succour to recover,
And seat him in his former empery.

---

19. day] *This ed.;* date *Q.*   21 SH.] *This ed.;* Embas., Emb. *Q;* Emb. *Dyce¹;* First
Amb. *Dyce²;* Embas. *Yoklavich.*   27 SD.] *Dyce²; not in Q.*

---

16. *contributary*] one who pays tribute (*OED sb*).

19. *fortune's day*] *Q* shows 'fortunes date', but 'daie' makes slightly more sense, cf.
Middleton's *Phoenix,* ''Twas first my birthday, now my fortune's day' (5.1.6). *OED*
notes that 'contain' could be used reflexively, so the meaning might be that Muly
Mahamet's 'lines', written under duress, are valid only as long as his luck remains bad.

21. *Viceroys*] 'corruption again, seemingly' (Bullen). Perhaps the ambassador is
using 'viceroys', a more exotic term than 'my lords', as an honorific for Sebastian's
courtiers, but it would be discourteous so to address them before the King.

27 SD. A brand is brought in] the Plot does not mention the brand, but 'we offer
here our hands . . .' demands its presence. Yoklavich (p. 359) notes, 'some "Turkish"
and frightful stage business must be imagined'.

44. *empery*] 'absolute dominion' (*OED sb* 1b); as in *Henry V,* the king promising
to rule France 'in large and ample empery' (1.2.226); cf. 2.2.29.

Let him rely upon our princely word;   45
Tell him by August we will come to him
With such a power of brave impatient minds,
As Abdelmelec and great Amurath
Shall tremble at the strength of Portugal.
Moorish Ambassador. Thanks to the renowned King of Portugal   50
On whose stout promises our state depends.
Sebastian. Barbarians, go glad your distressed king,
And say Sebastian lives to right his wrong.
                                        [Exeunt AMBASSADORS.]
Duke of Avero, call in those Englishmen,
Don Stukeley and those captains of the fleet   55
That lately landed in our bay of Lisbon.
Now breathe, Sebastian, and in breathing blow
Some gentle gale of thy new formèd joys.
Duke of Avero, it shall be your charge,
To take the muster of the Portugals   60
And bravest bloods of all our country.
Lewes de Silva, you shall be dispatched
With letters unto Philip King of Spain.
Tell him we crave his aid in this behalf;
I know our brother Philip nill deny   65
His furtherance in this holy Christian war.
Duke of Barceles, as thy ancestors
Have always loyal been to Portugal,
So now in honour of thy toward youth

---

51. depends] *Dyce¹*; depend *Q*. 53 SD.] *Dyce²*; Exit *Q*; Exeunt *Dyce¹*. 62. de
Silva] *Dyce¹*; de Sylva *Q*.

54. *Duke of Avero*] Jorge de Lencastre, the second Duke of Aveiro, named in the
Uniting as 'George d'Alencastro, Duke of Avero ... slaine with a shot' at Alcazar (pp.
42, 49). Bradley (p. 189) notes a 'textual peculiarity' in that Avero is instructed to 'call
in' the Englishmen, but is present to receive another order five lines later. *Q* has no
direction for Avero's exit or re-entry with Stukeley, however the 'calling in' could easily
be done with a signal towards the door. In *Henry V*, the King says 'Call in the messengers sent from the Dauphin' (1.2.221), but *F* has no exit direction for anyone in
response, and the Ambassadors, like the Englishmen in this scene, enter unattended.
60. *Portugals*] Peele always uses this term for 'Portuguese'; cf. *Stukeley*, where we
find both 'Portingalls' and 'Portuguese'.
62. *Lewes de Silva*] a mute character in the *Q* text. According to the *Uniting* (p.
35), he was 'one of the kings chiefe favorites', who tried to dissuade Sebastian from
marching overland to Larissa 'saying there was no reason for an armie to march by
land, that went to a towne adjoyning upon the sea' (see n. 4.2.42).
65. *nill*] will not (*OED v* 1), as in the phrase 'will-he nill-he'.
69. *in ... youth*] 'toward youth' is something of an understatement, since 'yoong
Theodore, Duke of Barcellos, for so they call the eldest sonne of the Dukes of
Bragançe' (*Uniting*, p. 42), was all of ten years old. He nevertheless travelled to Africa,

Thy charge shall be to Antwerp speedily,   70
To hire us mercenary men at arms.
Promise them princely pay, and be thou sure
Thy word is ours: Sebastian speaks the word.
Christophero de Tavora. I beseech your majesty employ me in this war.
Sebastian. Christophero de Tavora, next unto my self,   75
My good Hephaestion and my bedfellow,
Thy cares and mine shall be alike in this,
And thou and I will live and die together.

> [*Sound sennet.*] *Enter* STUKELEY
> [, JONAS, HERCULES, *and the Irish* BISHOP].

And now, brave Englishmen, to you
Whom angry storms have put into our bay,   80
Hold not your fortune e'er the worse in this:
We hold our strangers' honours in our hand,
And for distressèd frank and free relief.
Tell me then, Stukeley, for that's thy name I trow,
Wilt thou, in honour of thy country's fame,   85
Hazard thy person in this brave exploit
And follow us to fruitful Barbary,
With these six thousand soldiers thou hast brought
And choicely picked through wanton Italy?

---

74 SH.] *This ed.;* Chri. *Q;* Christo. *Dyce¹.* 75. Christophero de Tavora] *This ed.;* Christopher de Tavera *Q.* 76. Hephaestion] *Dyce¹;* Efestian *Q.* 78 SD.] *This ed.;* Enter Stukley and the rest *Q (after l. 77);* to them Stukeley, Jonas, Hercules & Irish Bishopp *Plot;* Re-enter the Duke of Avero, with the Irish Bishop, Stukeley, Jonas, Hercules, and others *Dyce².*

---

representing his father who was too ill to go, taking with him twenty-two pavilions for his personal use (Bovill, p. 102). He was taken prisoner at Alcazar, and according to the *Dolorous Discourse,* 'there is offered for the raunsome of the Duke of Bargansa his sonne 10000 duccats: but it is refused' (sig. B4v). A mute character in *Q.*

75. *Christophero de Tavora*] Sebastian's 'chamberlaine, and master of his horse (whom he loved entirely) was made commander of all the nobilitie that should go into Affricke' (*Uniting,* p. 25). Both parts of his name have been emended: *Q* has 'Christophero' in the entry direction (see n. 2.4.OSD) and 'Christopher' here, but the Plot has 'Christoporo'. As vocative lines are commonly extra-metrical but not unmetrical, it is hard to believe that Peele would have discarded the four-syllable 'Christophero'. The family name, from the city and river in Portugal, is Tavora, as is found in the Plot and all chronicle sources; *Q* has 'Tavera' in the stage direction and here, and 'Alvaro Peres de Tavero' (this character's brother) at 4.1.30.

76. *Hephaestion*] the companion of Alexander the Great, a standard trope for 'royal friend'; cf. *A Knack to Know a Knave,* 'Dunston will say as once Hefestion did / When Alexander wan rich Macedone' (sig. A3v).

88. *six thousand soldiers*] Both chronicle sources and diplomatic papers of the time vary widely in giving the number of Stukeley's troops (see pp. 8–9).

Thou art a man of gallant personage,   90
Proud in thy looks, and famous every way;
Frankly tell me, wilt thou go with me?
Stukeley. Courageous King, the wonder of my thoughts [. . .]
And yet my lord, with pardon understand,
Myself and these, whom weather hath enforced   95
To lie at road upon thy gracious coast,
Did bend our course and made amain for Ireland.
Sebastian. For Ireland, Stukeley? Thou mistak'st wondrous much,
With seven ships, two pinnaces, and six thousand men?
I tell thee, Stukeley, they are far too weak   100
To violate the Queen of Ireland's right,
For Ireland's queen commandeth England's force.
Were every ship ten thousand on the seas,
Manned with the strength of all the eastern kings,
Conveying all the monarchs of the world   105
To invade the island where her highness reigns,
'Twere all in vain, for heavens and destinies
Attend and wait upon her majesty.
Sacred, imperial and holy is her seat,
Shining with wisdom, love and mightiness.   110
Nature that every thing imperfect made,
Fortune that never yet was constant found,
Time that defaceth every golden show,
Dare not decay, remove, or be impure;
Both nature, time and fortune, all agree   115
To bless and serve her royal majesty.
The wallowing ocean hems her round about,
Whose raging floods do swallow up her foes,
And on the rocks their ships in pieces split.
And even in Spain, where all the traitors dance,   120
And play themselves upon a sunny day [. . .]
Securely guard the west part of her isle,
The south the narrow Britain sea begirts,
Where Neptune sits in triumph, to direct

---

98. Thou mistak'st wondrous much] *Bullen*; thou mistakst me wonderous much *Q*;
thou mak'st me wonder much *Dyce²*.

93.] Some text following this line must be missing (Dyce²).
98. *Thou . . . much*] Bullen's emendation seems correct. Q's 'mistakst me' is nonsensical, since Stukeley has not misunderstood anything King Sebastian has said, but
appears to have 'mistaken' in the general sense of 'erred' (mistake *OED v* 6a). The
speech, as Yoklavich (p. 359) observes, 'is probably the most corrupt in the play, [and]
it is impossible to know just where there have been imperfect revisions and deletions'.
120.] This and the following lines are, as Bullen notes, 'hideously corrupt'; lines are
probably missing after l. 121.

Their course to hell that aim at her disgrace,   125
The German seas alongst the east do run,
Where Venus banquets all her water nymphs
That with her beauty glancing on the waves,
Distains the cheek of fair Proserpina.
Advise thee then, proud Stukeley, ere thou pass   130
To wrong the wonder of the highest God,
Sith danger, death and hell doth follow thee,
Thee and them all that seek to danger her.
If honour be the mark whereat thou aim'st,
Then follow me in holy Christian wars,   135
And leave to seek thy country's overthrow.
Stukeley. Rather, my lord, let me admire these words,
Than answer to your firm objections.
His holiness Pope Gregory the Seventh
Hath made us four the leaders of the rest: 140
Amongst the rest, my lord, I am but one;
If they agree, Stukeley will be the first
To die with honour for Sebastian.
Sebastian. Tell me, Lord Bishop, captains, tell me all,
Are you content to leave this enterprise   145
Against your country and your countrymen,
To aid Mahamet, King of Barbary?
Bishop. To aid Mahamet, King of Barbary,
'Tis 'gainst our vows, great King of Portugal.
Sebastian. Then, captains, what say you?   150
Jonas. I say, my lord, as the Bishop said,
We may not turn from conquering Ireland.
Hercules. Our country and our countrymen will condemn
Us worthy of death, if we neglect our vows.

---

129. Distains the cheek] *Dyce²; disdaines the checke* Q.   151 SH.] Q; Jon. *Dyce¹*.
153 SH.] *This ed.;* Herc. Q.

---

126. *German seas*] a common name for what is now called the North Sea; cf. Peter Heylyn, *Microcosmus: or a Little Description of the Great World* (Oxford, 1621, p. 241), 'England is bounded on the East with the German, on the West with the Irish, on the South with the British Ocean'.
129. *Distains the cheek*] Dyce's plausible emendation of Q's 'disdaines the checke', taking 'distain' as 'to deprive of colour' (*OED v* 3). Venus quarrelled with Proserpina over Adonis, and the image may refer, in a missing line, to Proserpina shedding tears; cf. Zenocrate in *1 Tamburlaine*, 'Thence rise the tears that so distain my cheeks' (3.2.64).
130. *Advise thee*] consider, reflect (*OED v* 5); cf. *Twelfth Night*, 'Advise you what you say, the minister is here' (4.2.96); See n. 2.3.53.
132. *danger, death and hell doth*] See n. 2.2.33.
139. *Gregory the Seventh*] Peele is six Gregorys astray; Gregory XIII was Pope at the time; cf. n. 5.1.156.

Sebastian. Consider, lords, you are now in Portugal,   155
And I may now dispose of you and yours.
Hath not the wind and weather given you up,
And made you captives to our royal will?
Jonas. It hath, my lord, and willingly we yield
To be commanded by your majesty;   160
But if you make us voluntary men
Our course is then direct for Ireland.
Sebastian. That course will we direct for Barbary.
Follow me, lords, Sebastian leads the way
To plant the Christian faith in Africa.   165
Stukeley. Saint George for England, and Ireland now adieu,
For here Tom Stukeley shapes his course anew.

                                                          [*Exeunt.*]

---

167 SD.] *Plot, Dyce²;* Exit Q.

161. *voluntary*] volunteer, rather than conscripted soldiers; cf. Thersites in *Troilus and Cressida*, 'I serve here voluntary' (2.1.96). Greg (p. 111) rightly notes that the suddenness of Jonas's conversion implies that this scene has been pruned.

ACT 3

[3.Prol.]

          [*Sound sennet.*] *Enter the* PRESENTER *and speaks.*

Presenter. Lo, thus into a lake of blood and gore
    The brave courageous King of Portugal
    Hath drenched himself, and now prepares amain
    With sails and oars to cross the swelling seas
    With men and ships, courage and cannon shot,   5
    To plant this cursèd Moor in fatal hour,
    And in this Catholic case the King of Spain
    Is called upon by sweet Sebastian,
    Who surfeiting in prime time of his youth
    Upon ambitious poison, dies thereon.   10

    [*Enter* Nemesis *above. To her three* Furies *bringing in the scales.*
    To them enter three Devils. *Then enter to them three* Ghosts.
    The Furies *first fetch in* SEBASTIAN *and carry him out again, which*
    done they fetch in STUKELEY *and carry him out, then bring in the*
    Moor *and carry him out. Exeunt.*]

Act 3] *This ed.*; Actus III *Dyce¹*; Act III *Dyce²*; *not in Q.* 3. Prol.] *This ed.*; *not in*
Q. OSD.] *This ed.*; Sound, Enter the Presenter *Plot*; Enter the presenter and speakes
Q. 1 SH.] *This ed.*; *not in Q.* 7. case] *Q*; cause *Dyce²*. 10. ambitious] *Q*; ambition's *Bullen.* SD.] *subst. Yoklavich*; Enter Nemesis above Tho. Drum. To her 3 Furies
bringing in the scales: Georg Somersett Tom Parsons and Robin Tailor. To them 3
divells: mr Sam, H. Jeffes & Antho. Jeffes. To them 3 ghosts: w. Kendall, Dab & Harry.
The Furies First Fech in Sebastian & carrie him out again, then which done they Fech
in Stukeley & Carrie him out, then bring in the Moore & Carrie him out. Exeunt. *Plot*;
not in Q.

---

   7. *this Catholic case*] Dyce's 'cause' seems apt in this context, but since 'case' is
repeated at 3.3.44 with the same sense, it was probably intended.
   9. *surfeiting*] feeding to excess or satiety (surfeit *OED v* 1); cf. *2 Henry IV*, 'I have
long dreamt of such a kind of man / So surfeit-swelled, so old, and so profane'
(5.5.49–50).
   10 SD.] Although there is no direction in *Q*, the Plot provides for a dumb show.
Along with scales to be carried by the Furies, the Plotter calls for '3 violls of blood &
a sheeps gather' (heart, lungs and liver), presumably for removal of the guts of Sebastian, Stukeley and Muly Mahamet after the Furies have weighed their fates. This Presenter speech, unlike the others, does not allude to the actions described in the Plot;
Greg's conjecture that the original speech was pruned, the missing portion being
between ll. 10 and 11, is probably correct (see Yoklavich, pp. 359–60).

By this time is the Moor to Tangier come,
A city 'longing to the Portugal;
And now doth Spain promise with holy face,
As favouring the honour of the cause,
His aid of arms, and levies men apace.   15
But nothing less than King Sebastian's good
He means, yet at Guadalupea
He met, some say, in person with the Portugal
And treateth of a marriage with the King.
But 'ware ambitious wiles and poisoned eyes: 20
There was nor aid of arms nor marriage,
For on his way without those Spaniards King Sebastian went.
                                                          [*Exit.*]

[3.1]

        [*Sound sennet. Enter two, bringing in a chair of state.*]
        Enter [*at one door* SEBASTIAN] *the King of Portugal,*
        the DUKE OF AVERO, [STUKELEY. *To them at another door*]
        Lewes de Silva *and the* AMBASSADORS *of Spain.*

11. Tangier] *Dyce²*; Tangar *Q*.   17. Guadalupea] *This ed.*; Sucor de Tupea *Q*.
22. Spaniards King] *Q*; Spaniards / King *Dyce¹*.   SD.] *Dyce¹*; *not in Q*.
3.1] *This ed.*; Scene I *Dyce²*; *not in Q*.   OSD.] *This ed.*; Enter the king of Portugall
and his Lordes, Lewes de Sylva, and the Embassadors of Spaine *Q*; Sound. Enter 2

---

11. *Tangier*] the principal seaport of Morocco, 'built by the Romanes upon the
Ocean sea shore' (Leo Africanus, ed. Brown, p. 507).
    12. *'longing to the Portugal*] The Portuguese became masters of Tangier in 1471; in
1662 they ceded it to the English as part of the dowry of Catherine of Braganza, Queen
of Charles II (Brown, p. 627).
    13. *with holy face*] Peele is emphasising the treachery of the Spanish, who have no
intention of keeping their promise of aid to Sebastian (Bradley, pp. 158–9).
    17. *Guadalupea*] *Q*'s 'Sucor de Tupea' must be a compositor's not very good guess
for 'Guadalupea [Guadalupe], a citie of Castilia' (Polemon, sig. T3v). London received
intelligence from Spain that Sebastian's counsellors proposed the meeting in the hope
that Philip II would prevent his nephew from invading Africa: 'they thought they could
not use a better meane then to procure the meeting of the unkle and nephew, that the
Kinge of Spayne by his autoritie and experience might diswade him from that so charge-
able and daungerous an enterprise' (Castries, 1: 190–1).
    19. *marriage with the King*] Negotiations for Sebastian to marry one of the Spanish
infantas are not in Polemon, an indication that Peele saw the *Uniting* in the original
Italian (see p. 27). The English translation (1600) relates that Philip gave Sebastian 'the
promise of marriage with one of his daughters, when she should come to yeeres, for as
yet they were too yoong' (p. 16).
    22. Dyce proposes a new line at 'King Sebastian', but the Presenter's fourth-act
speech also ends with a heptameter (4.Prol.13).
    3.1.] The action continues in Lisbon's royal palace.
    OSD.] The *Q* direction is badly deficient in not naming Stukeley, but enough remains
of the damaged Plot to give an idea of how the entrance was staged. Stukeley is included,

Sebastian. Honourable lords, Ambassadors of Spain,
     The many favours by our meetings done
     From our belovèd and renownèd brother,
     Philip the Catholic King of Spain,
     Say, therefore, good my lord Ambassador,   5
     Say how your mighty master minded is
     To propagate the fame of Portugal.
First Ambassador. To propagate the fame of Portugal
     And plant religious truth in Africa,
     Philip, the great and puissant King of Spain,   10
     For love and honour of Sebastian's name,
     Promiseth aide of arms and swears by us
     To do your majesty all the good he can
     With men, munition, and supply of war,
     Of Spaniards proud in King Sebastian's aid,   15
     To spend their bloods in honour of their Christ.
Second Ambassador. And farther to manifest unto your majesty
     How much the Catholic king of Spain affects
     This war with Moors and men of little faith,
     The honour of your everlasting praise,   20
     Behold, to honour and enlarge thy name,
     He maketh offer of his daughter Isabel
     To link in marriage with the brave Sebastian;
     And to enrich Sebastian's noble wife,

---

bringing in a chair of state mr Hunt, w. Kendall Dab & Harry. Enter at one dore Sebastian, Duke of Avero, Stukeley, 1 Page Jeames, Jonas & Hercules. To them at another dore Embassadors of Spaine mr Jones mr Charles, attendants George & w. Cartwright *Plot;* Enter Sebastian the king of Portugal and his lords, Lewes de Silva and the Embassadors of Spain *Dyce¹;* Enter King Sebastian, Lords, Lewes de Silva, and the Ambassadors and Legate of Spain *Dyce²;* Enter the King of Portugal and his Lords, Lewes de Silva, and the Ambassadors and Legate of Spain *Bullen.*   8 SH.] *This ed.;* Embas. *Q;* Emb. *Dyce¹;* First Amb. *Dyce².*   17 SH.] *This ed.;* Legate *Q.*

---

as is De Silva, who does not speak in the scene, but, since he was dispatched with a message to Philip II in 2.4, it makes sense for him to return with the Spanish ambassadors. The Plot also has Jonas and Hercules present, but it is unclear if the original production would have allowed for them; Bradley ascribes such discrepancies between the Q and Plot stage directions to the Plotter's production having a different doubling pattern (Bradley, pp. 160, 195–6).
     3. *brother*] meant metaphorically here.
     4. *Catholic King of Spain*] some of Sebastian's speech might be missing after this line, although the passage can be made to make some sense by cutting l. 2.
     17 SH.] Q's speech heading of 'Legate' is justifiable: although the term usually refers to a Papal envoy, it can indicate 'ambassador' in a general sense (*OED sb¹*). But since he represents the King of Spain, and the word 'legate' is not spoken, to the audience he would simply be the Second Ambassador.
     23.] See n. 3.Prol.19.

His majesty doth promise to resign   25
The titles of the Islands of Moloccus,
That by his royalty in India he commands.
These favours with unfeignèd love and zeal,
Voweth King Philip to King Sebastian.
Sebastian. And God so deal with King Sebastian's soul   30
As justly he intends to fight for Christ.
Nobles of Spain, since our renownèd brother,
Philip, the king of honour and of zeal,
By you the chosen orators of Spain [...]
The offer of the holds he makes   35
Are not so precious in our account
As is the peerless dame whom we adore:
His daughter, in whose loyalty consists
The life and honour of Sebastian.
As for the aid of arms he promiseth,   40
We will expect and thankfully receive
At Cadiz, as we sail alongst the coast.
Sebastian, clap thy hands for joy,
Honoured by this meeting and this match.
Go, lords, and follow to the famous war   45
Your king, and be his fortune such in all
As he intends to manage arms in right.
     Exeunt. Manent STUKELEY *and* [*the* DUKE OF AVERO].

25. doth] *Dyce¹;* with   Q.   27. India] *Dyce²;* Iudah   Q.   commands.] *Dyce²,*
Yoklavich; commands; *Dyce¹;* commands Q.   42. Cadiz] *Dyce¹;* Cardis Q.   47 SD.]
Plot; Exeunt. Manet Stukley and another Q; Exeunt King and Train. Manet Stukeley
and another *Dyce¹;* Exeunt all except Stukeley and Another *Dyce²; Exeunt.* Manent
Stukeley and another *Bullen.*

26. *Islands of Moloccus*] the Moluccas, or 'Spice Islands' of the East Indies, between
Celebes and New Guinea (Sugden).

27. *India*] the Indies. Yoklavich (p. 361) suggests that Q's 'Iudah', i.e. Judah, might
be correct, since 'Jerusalem was sometimes considered to be part of the "Indies"', but
Philip II would not 'command' the Moluccas from there; see E. A. J. Honigmann's commentary on the 'Indian/Judean' crux in Othello's final speech, *The Arden Shakespeare:
Othello*, London, 1996, pp. 342–3.

34.] The syntax of the speech begins to disappear here; as Greg notes (p. 96), some
lines must be missing.

35. *holds*] fortresses (*OED sb¹* 10). There has been no mention of Philip offering
Sebastian any such 'holds', although we learn of such an offer from Abdelmelec to
Philip at 3.2.18. 'It is impossible to suggest any tolerable emendation; for a line or more
seems to have been dropped' (Bullen).

42. *Cadiz*] Q's 'Cardis' has been modernised; stress was on the first syllable. Cf.
Stukeley, where 'Cales' (the more common form at the time) is maintained for metrical purposes.

Stukeley. Sit fast, Sebastian, and in this work
　　God and good men labour for Portugal.
　　For Spain, disguising with a double face,   50
　　Flatters thy youth and forwardness, good King.
　　Philip, whom some call the Catholic king,
　　I fear me much thy faith will not be firm,
　　But disagree with thy profession.
Avero. What then shall of these men of war become,   55
　　Those numbers that do multiply in Spain?
Stukeley. Spain hath a vent for them and their supplies.
　　The Spaniard ready to embark himself
　　Here gathers to a head, but all too sure
　　Flanders, I fear, shall feel the force of Spain.   60
　　Let Portugal fare as he may or can,
　　Spain means to spend no powder on the Moors.
Avero. If kings do dally so with holy oaths,
　　The heavens will right the wrongs that they sustain.
　　Philip, if these forgeries be in thee,   65
　　Assure thee, King, 'twill light on thee at last,
　　And when proud Spain hopes soundly to prevail,
　　The time may come that thou and thine shall fail.   [*Exeunt.*]

[3.2]

　　　　Enter ABDELMELEC, MULY MAHAMET SETH, ZAREO *and*
　　　　　　　　　　　　their train.

Abdelmelec. The Portugal, led with deceiving hope,
　　Hath raised his power and received our foe
　　With honourable welcomes and regard,
　　And left his country bounds, and hither bends
　　In hope to help Mahamet to a crown   5
　　And chase us hence, and plant this negro Moor
　　That clads himself in coat of hammered steel
　　To heave us from the honour we possess.
　　But for I have myself a soldier been,
　　I have in pity to the Portugal   10
　　Sent secret messengers to counsel him.
　　As for the aid of Spain whereof they hoped,
　　We have dispatched our letters to their prince
　　To crave that in a quarrel so unjust,

55 SH.] *This ed.;* The other *Q (and at l. 63).*   68 SD.] *Plot, Dyce¹;* Exit *Q.*

3.2] *This ed.;* Scene II *Dyce²; not in Q.*

67–8.] Possibly a post-Armada sentiment, but see p. 18.

3.2.] The action is set in Fez. This scene was not played in the Plotter's production
(see Bradley, p. 161).

He that entitled is the Catholic king   15
Would not assist a careless Christian prince.
And as by letters we are let to know,
Our offer of the seven holds we made
He thankfully receives, with all conditions,
Differing in mind as far from all his words   20
And promises to King Sebastian
As we would wish, or you my lords desire.
Zareo. What resteth then but Abdelmelec may
Beat back this proud invading Portugal,
And chastise this ambitious negro Moor   25
With thousand deaths for thousand damnèd deeds?
Abdelmelec. Forward, Zareo and ye manly Moors!
Sebastian, see in time unto thy self,
If thou and thine misled do thrive amiss,
Guiltless is Abdelmelec of thy blood.   *Exeunt.*   30

[3.3]

    Enter DON DE MENESES, *Governor of Tangier, with his company,*
        speaking to the CAPTAIN[S].

Don de Meneses. Captains,
    We have receivèd letters from the King,

20. mind as far] *Dyce²;* mind far *Q.*

3.3] *This ed.;* Scene III *Dyce²; not in Q.*   OSD.] *subst. Q;* Enter Governor of Tanger
& Captains mr Shaa, H Jeffes *Plot;* Enter Don de Menysis, with Captains and others
Dyce².   1 SH.] *This ed.;* Gover., Govern. *Q;* Gov. *Dyce¹;* De Men. *Dyce².* Gover.
Yoklavich.   Captains, / We] *Dyce¹;* Captaine, we *Q;* Captains, we *Bullen.*

18. *seven holds*] There is no direct reference to an offer of seven fortresses in the
chronicle sources. According to the *Uniting* (p. 20), 'in the meane time Mulei Moluck
[Muly Molocco] hearing of these preparatives, fearing the Catholique king should joyne
with the Portugals, sent wisely unto him to will him to advise what part of his territories he pleased to have, the which he would give to be his friend and confederate'.
In general, Abdelmelec's many overtures to Philip II were no secret: from the moment
he regained Fez in 1576, Abdelmelec actively sought a mutual security treaty with Spain,
as both countries feared Ottoman domination of the region. He emphasised his pro-
western sentiments at every opportunity, and Philip, on his part, was anxious to procure
Moroccan saltpetre (see pp. 12–14). Spain's failure to provide more than token support
to Sebastian points to the success of Moroccan diplomacy (see Yahya, pp. 66–80).
    3.3.] The action takes place in Tangier.
    OSD. DON DE MENESES] Don Duarte de Meneses, Governor of Tangier and 'great
maister of the campe', named in the *Dolorous Discourse* amongst those 'as were taken,
and arc knowen to remaine alive in Barbary' (sig. B4r).
    1. *Captains*] The Plotter calls for only one captain; Bradley (p. 199) credits this to
his doubling pattern. This edition follows Dyce in giving the vocative a separate line
(see n. 1.2.8–9).

That with such signs and arguments of love
We entertain the King of Barbary,
That marcheth toward Tangier with his men,   5
The poor remainders of those that fled from Fez,
When Abdelmelec got the glorious day
And stalled himself in his imperial throne.
First Captain. Lord Governor, we are in readiness
To welcome and receive this hapless king,   10
Chased from his land by angry Amurath.
And if the right rest in this lusty Moor,
Bearing a princely heart unvanquishable,
A noble resolution then it is
In brave Sebastian our Christian king   15
To aid this Moor with his victorious arms,
Thereby to propagate religious truth
And plant his springing praise in Africa.
Second Captain. But when arrives this brave Sebastian
To knit his forces with this manly Moor,   20
That both in one, and one in both may join
In this attempt of noble consequence?
Our men of Tangier long to see their king,
Whose princely face, that like the summer's sun,
Glads all these hither parts of Barbary.   25
Don de Meneses. Captains, he cometh hitherward amain,
Top and top gallant, all in brave array.
The six-and-twentieth day of June he left

---

6. remainders] *Q;* remains *conj. Dyce².*   9 SH.] *This ed.;* Cap. *Q;* First Cap. *Dyce²;*
Capt. *Yoklavich.*   19 SH.] *This ed.;* Ano. Capt. *Q;* Sec. Cap. *Dyce².*   28–31.] 4 *ll.*
Dyce¹; 3 ll. Q.   28. six-and-twentieth] *Bullen;* 26 *Q;* twenty-sixth *Dyce¹.*

6. *remainders*] Dyce suggests 'remains', but Peele's verse is sufficiently variable to
allow 'remainders'.

8. *stalled*] a common form of 'installed' or 'placed'; cf. *Richard III,* 'I see thee now
/ Decked in thy rights, as thou art stalled in mine' (1.3.203).

27. *top and top gallant*] short for 'topsail and topgallant sail', hence 'with all sail
set, in full array or career' ('top' *OED sb¹* 9c).

28–31.] These four lines are printed as three in Q, but 'read "six-and-twentieth" [for
Q's '26.'] and make four lines of the passage' (Greg, p. 115).

28. *six-and-twentieth day of June*] This detail comes from Polemon (sig. T4v): 'King
Sebastian (having nominated before seaven of the chiefe of the Realme governours of

The Bay of Lisbon, and with all his fleet
At Cadiz happily he arrived in Spain   30
The eighth of July, tarrying for the aid
That Philip King of Spain, had promisèd;
And fifteen days he there remained aboard
Expecting when this Spanish force would come,
Nor stepped ashore as he were going still.   35
But Spain that meant and minded nothing less
Pretends a sudden fear and care, to keep
His own from Amurath's fierce invasion,
And to excuse his promise to our king;
For which he storms as great Achilles erst   40
Lying for want of wind in Aulis gulf,
And hoisteth up his sails and anchors weighs
And hitherward he comes, and looks to meet
This manly Moor, whose case he undertakes.
Therefore go we to welcome and receive   45
With cannon shot and shouts of young and old,
This fleet of Portugals and troop of Moors.
                                                  [*Exeunt.*]

---

30. Cadiz] *Dyce¹*; Cardis Q.   31. eighth] *Dyce¹*; eight Q.   41. Aulis] *Dyce¹*; Aldest
Q.   42. hoisteth] *This ed.*; hoiseth Q.   45. receive] *Dyce¹*; rescue Q; reserve
Yoklavich.   47 SD.] *Plot, Dyce¹*; Exit Q.

the kingdome) because the Cardinall his unkle had refused the government, for that he
could not intreate the king to relinquish the voiage, launched out of the haven, and
hoised up sailes the 26. of June, with ten or twelve galleons, in whom were embarked
the whole nobilitie of his kingdome'.
    39.] As noted by Yoklavich (pp. 276–7), Philip II's excuse comes from the *Expla-nation* (p. 3): 'The King of Castile graunting this petition, promised to ayde him, with
fiftye gallyes well appointed and furnished, and foure thousand armed souldiours. King
Sebastian trusting thereunto, with all care and dilligence prepared his armye . . . But the
King of Castile, under pretence that the greate Turke, prepared an armye for that yeare,
not onelye denyed to performe his promise, but also (that is farre worse) caused a
proclamation to bee made and published thorowoute all Spayne, subject to his juris-diction, whereby all his subjectes were commaunded uppon great pennalties that none
of them should accompanye Kinge Sebastian in that voyage'.
    40–1.] The Greek fleet was unable to sail from Aulis until Agamemnon appeased the
anger of Artemis by sacrificing his daughter, Iphigeneia. Achilles' 'storming' is obscure:
in Euripides' *Iphigeneia at Aulis*, as Iphigeneia's betrothed he strongly opposes the sac-rifice, although in the end he does nothing to stop it. Peele may be alluding to his first
dramatic effort, a translation of one of Euripides' *Iphigeneia* plays, written while he
was a student at Oxford (see Horne, pp. 42–6).

[3.4]

The trumpets sound, the chambers are discharged. Then enter
[at one door the Portugal army with drum and colours:
SEBASTIAN, CHRISTOPHERO DE TAVORA, *the* DUKE OF AVERO,
STUKELEY, JONAS, HERCULES, Lodovico Caesar. *At another door*
*[*DON DE MENESES*] the Governor of Tangier, and two* CAPTAINS.
From behind the curtains to them MULY MAHAMET *and*
CALIPOLIS *in their chariot with Moors, one on each side,*
attending young MAHAMET].

Sebastian. Muly Mahamet, King of Barbary,
    Well met and welcome to our town of Tangier
    After this sudden shock and hapless war.
    Welcome, brave Queen of Moors, repose thee here,
    Thou and thy noble son, and soldiers all,   5
    Repose you here in King Sebastian's town.
    Thus far in honour of thy name and aid,
    Lord Mahamet, we have adventurèd
    To win for thee a kingdom, for ourselves
    Fame, and performance of those promises   10
    That in thy faith and royalty thou hast
    Sworn to Sebastian King of Portugal.
    And thrive it so with thee as thou dost mean,
    And mean thou so as thou dost wish to thrive;
    And if our Christ, for whom in chief we fight   15
    Hereby to enlarge the bounds of Christendom,
    Favour this war, and as I do not doubt,
    Send victory to light upon my crest,
    Brave Moor, I will advance thy kingly son

3.4] *This ed.;* Scene IV *Dyce²; not in* Q. OSD.] *subst.* Yoklavich; The Trumpets
sound, the chambers are dischargde. Then enter the king of Portugall and the Moore,
with all theyr traine Q, *subst. Dyce¹, Bullen;* Enter at one dore the Portingall army with
drom & Cullors, Sebastian, Christoporo Duke of Avero, Stukeley, Jonas & Hercules,
Lodovico Caesar mr Jones. Att another dore Governor of Tanger mr Shaa & 2 Captains H Jeffes & mr Sam. From behind the curtains to them muly mahamet & Calipolis in their chariott with moores, one on each side & attending young mahamet, & w.
Cartwright & George *Plot;* Trumpets sound and chambers are discharged within. Then
enter King Sebastian, the Duke of Avero, Lord Lodowick, Stukeley, &c.; the Moor,
Calipolis, their Son, &c. *Dyce².*

3.4.] The setting is Tangier: 'the King with his five galleis and fower galleons (leaving
the rest of the ships) went to Tanger, where he made a short abode' (*Uniting*, p. 30).
    OSD.] The latter part of the entry direction is based on Greg's reconstruction of the
damaged Plot; Bradley investigates the matter independently and finds himself in agree-
ment (Greg, pp. 35–6; Bradley, pp. 172–3, 200–3).
    chambers are discharged] See p. 24.

And with a diadem of pearl and gold   20
Adorn thy temples and enrich thy head.
Muly Mahamet. O brave Sebastian, noble Portugal,
Renowned and honoured, ever mayst thou be
Triumpher over those that menace thee.
The hellish prince, grim Pluto, with his mace   25
Ding down my soul to hell, and with this soul
This son of mine, the honour of my house,
But I perform religiously to thee
That I have holily erst underta'en.
And that thy lords and captains may perceive   30
My mind in this single and pure to be,
As pure as is the water of the brook,
My dearest son to thee I do engage.
Receive him, lord, in hostage of my vow [. . .]
For even my mind presageth to myself   35
That in some slavish sort I shall behold
Him dragged along this running river shore,
A spectacle to daunt the pride of those
That climb aloft by force, and not by right.
Muly Mahamet's Son. Nor can it otherwise befall the man   40
That keeps his seat and sceptre all in fear,
That wears his crown in eye of all the world
Reputed theft and not inheritance.
What title then hath Abdelmelec here,
To bar our father or his progeny?   45
Right royal prince, hereof you make no doubt [. . .]
Agreeing with your wholesome Christian laws:
Help then, courageous lord, with hand and sword
To clear his way, whose lets are lawless men,
And for this deed ye all shall be renowned,   50
Renowned and chronicled in books of fame,

---

26. *Ding*] beat (OED *v* 1).

28. *But*] unless

34. *in hostage*] The sense of 'hostage' as a person taken captive and threatened with harm unless demands are met was not in early modern usage. Polemon (sig. U1v) relates that Muly Mahamet 'promised also to give the King of Portugall two or three havens in Barbarie, with their territories adjoyning, for suretie thereof hee gave his sonne in hostage'.

35. As Greg notes (p. 115), there must be lines missing before this one, as the 'him' to be 'dragged along this running river' (l. 37) is Abdelmelec, not Muly Mahamet's son.

presageth] augurs, predicts; cf. *Edward III*, 'a Country swaine / Whose habit rude, and manners blunt and playne / Presageth nought' (sig. B4v).

46.] This speech, like the previous one, seems to have lines omitted.

49. *lets*] hindrances (OED *sb¹*).

In books of fame and characters of brass,
Of brass, nay beaten gold. Fight then for fame,
And find the Arabian Muly Hamet here,
Adventurous, bold, and full of rich reward.   55
Stukeley. Brave boy, how plain this princely mind in thee
Argues the height and honour of thy birth,
And well have I observed thy forwardness,
Which being tendered by your majesty,
No doubt the quarrel opened by the mouth   60
Of this young prince unpartially to us
May animate and hearten all the host
To fight against the devil for Lord Mahamet.
Sebastian. True, Stukeley, and so freshly to my mind,
Hath this young prince reduced his father's wrong,   65
That in good time I hope this honour's fire,
Kindled already with regard of right,
Bursts into open flames and calls for wars,
Wars, wars to plant the true succeeding prince.
Lord Mahamet, I take thy noble son,   70
A pledge of honour and shall use him so.
Lord Lodovic, and my good lord of Avero,
See this young prince conveyed safe to Mazagan,
And there accompanied as him fitteth best,
And to this war prepare ye more and less,   75
This rightful war, that Christians' God will bless.

Exeunt.

72. Lodovic] *This ed.;* Lodowicke *Q;* Lodowick *Dyce¹.*   73. Mazagan] *This ed.;*
Messegon *Q.*

56–63.] a very different Stukeley from the one who delivers a similar speech in
Captain Thomas Stukeley (21.52–8).

72. *Lodovic*] Like Lewes de Silva (see n. 2.4.62), Lodovico Caesar (the 'o' dropped
here for metrical reasons) is named in stage directions and dialogue, but remains mute
in the Q text. In describing the Portuguese formations at Alcazar, Polemon has, 'The
fourth battaile were Portugals, under the conduct of a certaine noble man of that nation,
whose name was Ludovicke Caesar' (sig. X2r).

73. *Mazagan*] a town built by the Portuguese in 1506; Muly Mahamet commanded
the Moorish army that failed to take it in 1562 (Brown, p. 379; Bovill, p. 22).

ACT 4

[4.Prol.]

[*Enter the* PRESENTER.]

Presenter.   Now hardened is this hapless heathen prince
And strengthened by the arms of Portugal,
This Moor, this murderer of his progeny,
And war and weapons now, and blood and death
Wait on the counsels of this cursèd king: 5
And to a bloody banquet he invites
The brave Sebastian and his noble peers.

> [*Enter a banquet brought in by two Moors. Enter to the bloody
> banquet* SEBASTIAN, MULY MAHAMET, *the* DUKE OF AVERO, *and*
> STUKELEY. *To them enter* Death *and three* Furies, *one with blood, one
> with dead men's heads in dishes, another with dead men's bones.*]

In fatal hour arrived this peerless prince
To lose his life, his life and many lives
Of lusty men, courageous Portugals,   10
Drawn by ambitious golden looks.

Act 4] *This ed.*; Actus 4 *Q*; Actus IV *Dyce¹*; Act IV *Dyce².*   4. Prol.] *This ed.; not in*
Q.   OSD.] *Plot, Dyce²*; The Presenter speaketh *Q.*   1 SH.] *This ed.; not in Q.*   6.
banquet] *Dyce¹*; banket *Q, Bullen.*   7 SD.] *subst.* *Yoklavich*; Enter to the bloudie
banket *Q*; Enter a banquett brought in by mr Hunt and w. Cartwright. To the banquet
enter Sebastian, Muly mahamet, Duke of Avero & Stukeley. To them Death & 3 Furies
mr Sam, Ro. Tailor, George & Parsons, one wᵗʰ blood to dyppe lights, one with dead
mens heads in dishes, and another with dead men's bones *Plot.*   9. lose] *Dyce¹*; loose
Q.   11. ambitious] *Q*; ambition's *Bullen.*

OSD.] Bradley (p. 163) notes that the *Q* direction, where the Presenter simply
'speaketh' without a preceding entry direction, might indicate that he, a 'Portingall',
was intended to double as Don de Meneses and could have remained on stage.
   6. *banquet*] pronounced as in the *Q* spelling, 'banket'.
   7. SD.] The section of the Plot containing this dumb show survives nearly intact. I
follow Yoklavich in inserting the Plotter's direction at this point.
   11. *drawn by ambitious*] Dyce suggests 'drawn hither by', Bullen 'drawn by proud',
to repair the metre, but as 'drawn by' ('drawen by' in *Q*) could be effectively spoken
as a spondee, the line is reasonably good as it stands.

Let fame of him no wrongful censure sound,
Honour was object of his thoughts, ambition was his ground.

[*Exeunt.*]

[4.1]

[*Enter with drum and colours* ABDELMELEC, MULY MAHAMET SETH,
CELYBIN, ZAREO *and attendants.*]

Abdelmelec. Now tell me, Celybin, what doth the enemy?
Celybin. The enemy, dread lord, hath left the town
Of Arzil, with a thousand soldiers armed,
To guard his fleet of thirteen hundred sail,
And mustering of his men before the walls,   5
He found he had two thousand armèd horse
And fourteen thousand men that serve on foot,
Three thousand pioneers, and a thousand coachmen,
Besides a number almost numberless
Of drudges, negroes, slaves and muleteers,   10

13 SD.] *Plot; Exit Q.*

4.1] *This ed.;* Scene I *Dyce²; not in Q.* OSD.] *Plot;* Enter Abdelmelec and his
traine *Q, subst. Bullen;* Enter Abdelmelec, Argerd Zareo, and others *Dyce²;* Enter
Abdelmelec and his traine [with Celybin and Zareo] *Yoklavich.* 1. doth] *Dyce¹;* doeth
Q. 2 SH.] *Q (later Cely.);* Cel. *Dyce¹;* Cely. *Yoklavich.* 3. Arzil] *Dyce¹;* Areil *Q.*

13. SD.] 'Exeunt', rather than Q's 'exit', as the dumb show and the Presenter would
presumably depart at about the same time.

4.1.] The action is set near Alcazar.

OSD.] Bradley agrees with Greg's reconstruction, from a fragment, of the Plot's 4.1
entry direction. When the damaged right-hand column of the Plot was first pasted
together, this fragment was incorrectly placed (see Greg, pp. 37–8; Bradley, pp. 172–3,
204–5).

1. *Celybin*] Rice (p. 430) suggests that, like Calipolis (see n. 1.2 OSD), this name
derives from Polemon's account of the battle of Lepanto, where Celybin is the surname of several Turkish captains; another possible inspiration is 'Celebinus', one of
Tamburlaine's sons. Peele may have invented a name because Abdelmelec's master of
the horse was a Cordovan renegade named 'Solimano' in *Dell'unione* (sig. E2r), and
he would not have wanted to use the great Sultan's name again (see 1.Prol.45).

3. *Arzil*] Leo Africanus writes, 'The great citie of Arzilla called by the Africans
Azella, was built by the Romans upon the Ocean sea shore, about seventie miles from
the streits of Gibraltar, and an hundred and fortie miles from Fez' (Brown, p. 504).
Polemon notes that 'the king himselfe marched by land thitherwards [to Larissa], going
out of Arzil the 29. of June' (sig. U3v).

8. *pioneers*] foot-soldiers of low rank, often assigned to dig trenches or mines; see
Edelman, *Military*, pp. 255–7.

Horse-boys, laundresses and courtesans
And fifteen hundred waggons full of stuff
For noble men brought up in delicate.
Abdelmelec. Alas, good King, thy foresight hath been small
To come with women into Barbary,   15
With laundresses, with baggage, and with trash,
Numbers unfit to multiply thy host.
Celybin. Their payment in the camp is passing slow,
And victuals scarce, that many faint and die.
Abdelmelec. But whither marcheth he in all this haste?   20
Celybin. Some thinks he marcheth hitherward
And means to take this city of Alcazar.
Abdelmelec. Unto Alcazar, O unconstant chance!
Celybin. The brave and valiant King of Portugal
Quarters his power in four battalions –   25
Afront the which, to welcome us withal
Are six and thirty roaring pieces placed –
The first, consisting of light armèd horse,
And of the garrisons from Tangier brought,
Is led by Alvaro Peres de Tavora.   30

---

11. laundresses] *Dyce¹;* landresses *Q.*   courtesans] *This ed.;* curtizans *Q;* courtezans
Dyce¹.   16. laundresses] *Dyce¹;* landresse *Q.*   21. some thinks he] *Q;* some think he
Dyce¹; some think, my lord, he *Bullen.*   30. Tavora] *This ed.;* Tavero *Q.*

---

11. *laundresses and courtesans*] Polemon has Sebastian's army including 'almost an
infinite number of drudges, slaves, negroes, mulletters, horse boies, landresses, and
those sweete wenches that the Frenchmen doe merrilie call the daughters of delight'
(sig. U2v). Yoklavich's comment (p. 365), that 'by "landresses" we are probably to
understand "prostitutes"' is hard to accept: Clayton's *Approved Order of Martial Discipline* (London, 1591, p. 34) states that only 'victualers or laundresses, which shall be
licensed by the Marshalls byll' shall follow the camp; see also Edelman, *Military,* p. 95.
    12–13.] 'He had also sixe and thirtie field pieces and 1500 waggons full of mattes,
vessell, and household stuffe onelie for noble men' (Polemon, sig. U2v). In using the
words 'in delicate', Peele seems to emphasise Portuguese effeminacy; cf. Peele's *Edward
I,* where Queen Elinor is 'brought up in nicenesse and in delicacie' (l. 2342).
    21. *Some thinks*] As this is a short line, there may be corruption here, but the seem-
ingly ungrammatical 'some thinks' is probably intended; cf. *Edward I,* 'Some thinkes
he praies Lluellen were in heaven' (l. 801), and Rowley, *When You See Me, You Know
Me,* 'some thinkes he's a shepheard' (sig. D2r).
    25. *his . . . battalions*] Peele is relying on Polemon, who writes that Sebastian
'divided his whole armie into 4. battailes' (sig. X2r); the *Uniting* (p. 41) reports that
'the front, was in a manner divided into three'.
    26. *Afront*] in front of (*OED prep*).
    28. *The first*] not the first of the 'roaring pieces' (cannon) but the battalions of l. 25.
    30. *Alvaro Peres de Tavora*] Christophero's brother, 'Alvaro Pirez, brother and lieu-
tenant to Christopher of Tavora' (*Uniting,* p. 41); see n. 2.4.75.

The left or middle battle of Italians
And German horsemen Stukeley doth command,
A warlike Englishman sent by the Pope
That vainly calls himself Marquess of Ireland.
Alonso Aguilar conducts the third: 35
That wing of German soldiers most consists.
The fourth legion is none but Portugals,
Of whom Lodovico Caesar hath the chiefest charge.
Besides there stand six thousand horse
Bravely attirèd, pressed where need requires.   40
Thus have I told your royal majesty
How he is placed to brave his fight.
Abdelmelec. But where's our nephew Muly Mahamet?
Celybin. He marcheth in the middle, guarded about
With full five hundred harquebus on foot,   45
And twice three thousand needless armèd pikes.
Zareo. Great sovereign, vouchsafe to hear me speak,
And let Zareo's counsel now prevail:
Whilst time doth serve and that these Christians dare
Approach the field with warlike ensigns spread,   50
Let us in haste with all our forces meet
And hem them in, that not a man escape.

---

34. Marquess] *This ed.;* Marques *Q;* Marquis *Dyce¹.*   35. Aguilar] *This ed.;* Aquilaz
Q.   38. Lodovico] *This ed.;* Lodevico *Q.*   42. brave his fight] *Q;* brave us in the
fight *Dyce².*   45. harquebus] *This ed.;* hargubuze *Q;* harquebuze *Dyce¹.*

---

32. *German horsemen*] Polemon (sig. T4r) has the German mercenaries as infantry,
not horse: 'they were also fresh water souldiour [*sic*], and unskilfull of martiall matters'.
    35. *Alonso Aguilar*] Philip II sent a small Castilian regiment, 'the Captaine whereof
was Alonzo Aquilar' (Polemon, sig. X2r); *Dell'unione* has 'Alfonso di Aguilar' (sig.
D8r), the *Uniting* 'Alphonso d'Aguilar' (p. 41).
    38–42. Peele has done well so far, but lists of troop numbers and commanders are
hard to keep metrical; cf. 2.4.99.
    42. *brave his fight*] Dyce's 'brave us in the fight' gives the line two needed syllables,
but the original may have been intended: 'to brave' can be taken as 'to array or deck
out'; cf. *Richard III*, 'He [the sun] should have braved the east an hour ago' (5.6.9). A
'fight' can be an army in formation for battle, as in Drayton's *Second Part, or a Con-
tinuance of Poly-Olbion* (London, 1622, 'XXII Song', p. 32), 'The King into three fights
his forces doth divide'.
    45. *harquebus*] A common type of firearm in the sixteenth century, eventually
replaced by the musket.
    46.] In describing the army that Sebastian brought to Africa, Polemon notes 'eight
thousand that bare long pikes, then the which kinde of souldiours there is none of lesse
use and service, and more unfit for wars in Barbarie'. When placed in its final formation, Muly Mahamet's battle had 'five hundreth harguebuziers and five hundreth
speares' (sig. U3r).

So will they be advised another time
How they do touch the shore of Barbary.
Abdelmelec.   Zareo, hear our resolution,   55
And thus our forces we will first dispose:
Hamet, my brother, with a thousand shot
On horseback, and choice harquebusiers all,
Having ten thousand horse with spear and shield,
Shall make the right wing of the battle up;   60
Zareo, you shall have in charge the left,
Two thousand argolets and ten thousand horse.
The main battle of harquebus on foot,
And twenty thousand horsemen in their troops.
Myself environed with my trusty guard   65
Of janissaries, fortunate in war [. . .]
And toward Arzil will we take our way.
If then our enemy will balk our force,
In God's name let him, it will be his best.
But if he level at Alcazar walls,   70
Then beat him back with bullets as thick as hail,
And make him know and rue his oversight
That rashly seeks the ruin of this land.   *Exeunt.*

---

58. harquebusiers] *This ed.*; harguebuziers *Q*; harquebuziers *Dyce¹*.   59. ten
thousand horse with] *Yoklavich*; ten thousand with *Q*; ten thousand foot with *conj.*
Dyce².   63. harquebus] *This ed.*; hargubuze *Q*; harquebuze *Dyce¹*.   69. God's]
Dyce¹; Gods *Q*.

59. *ten thousand horse*] the word 'horse', not in *Q*, was obviously intended, as the
line paraphrases Polemon, 'he had also ten thousand horsemen with speare and sheelde'
(Yoklavich, p. 365).
   66.] Greg notes (p. 116), 'something is clearly wanting after this, since the sense is:
"The maine battell . . . My selfe [will lead]"'. Polemon reads (sig. X2r), 'The third battaile, which was the maine battaile, wherein king Abdelmelec stoode, was defenced with
harquebuziers on foote. Then dyd the king followe, environed with his garde of two
hundreth souldiours, that had forsworne the faith, who were all weaponed with hal-
berdes'; for 'janissaries' see n. 1.1.32.
   68. *will balk our force*] A seemingly corrupt passage is made clear by understanding 'balk', in this context, as 'to pass by,' or 'shun' (*OED v¹* 2). Peele would have
read in Polemon how Abdelmelec was trying to avoid a fight: 'But when Abdelmelec
knew by espies almost everie houre what was done in the campe of the Christians, and
how weake the Portugall forces were, and how coldly all things were ordered, and
therefore did see that the wretched king being in the prime of his yeares, was neere to
death and destruction: he wrought by all meanes he could, that he should not be forced
to fight a battaile, because he was not otherwise verie ill affected towards Christians'
(sig. U3r).
   69. *In God's name*] *Q* has 'Gods', which may be a misreading. Except for this line,
5.1.205 and 5.1.215, Moroccans generally refer to 'the gods' or 'Jove'. One possible
emendation is 'i' the gods' name'; see also n. 1.1.5.

[4.2]

[*Enter by torchlight to council* SEBASTIAN, *the* DUKE OF AVERO,
STUKELEY, JONAS, *with attendants and soldiers, a guard.*]

Sebastian. Why tell me lords, why left ye Portugal
And crossed the seas with us to Barbary?
Was it to see the country and no more,
Or else to fly before ye were assailed?
I am ashamed to think that such as you,   5
Whose deeds have been renownèd heretofore,
Should slack in such an act of consequence.
We come to fight, and fighting vow to die,
Or else to win the thing for which we came.
Because Abdelmelec, as pitying us,   10
Sends messages to counsel quietness,
You stand amazed and think it sound advice,
As if our enemy would wish us any good.
No, let him know we scorn his courtesy,
And will resist his forces whatsoe'er.   15
Cast fear aside, myself will lead the way,
And make a passage with my conquering sword
Knee-deep in blood of these accursèd Moors,

4.2] *This ed.;* Scene II *Dyce²; not in* Q.   OSD.] *Plot;* Enter Sebastian king of Portugall, the Duke of Avero, Stukley, and others *Q;* Enter King Sebastian, the Duke of Avero,
Stukeley, Hercules, and others *Dyce².*   4. fly] *Dyce¹;* slay *Q.*

4.2.] The action is at the Portuguese camp, near Alcazar, on the eve of the battle.
Peele conflates what are three Portuguese councils in Polemon: the first was 'when the
King of Portugall was come the Saturdaie morning [2 August] to the river of Larissa
[i.e. Lixus, see n. 4.2.42], & was encamped neere to the place where he thought ther
might be a foord found to pass over his ordenance, & was minded to go to Larissa'.
He broke camp on Sunday morning, and 'when he had found a foord' to cross over
the river, he stopped and commanded his men 'to make it readie against the next daie'.
That night, Sunday 3 August, 'the King of Portugall sawe that his enimies were retired
into their camp, he also did the like, and lodged in the verie same place from whence
he came. He assembling his counsaile the chiefe men of the armie that night, determined the next daie, being mundaie, to offer the enimie battaile' (sig. U3v–U4r, X1r).
    OSD.] As the Plotter calls for torches, we should imagine this scene as taking place
on Sunday, the night before the battle. The 'guard' probably refers to the soldiers, not
a separate office.
    4. fly] Q has 'slay'. The initial 'f' and 's' were very similar in Elizabethan hand-
writing, and the compositor probably misread 'fly' or 'flie'.
    11. *messages to counsel quietness*] Polemon (sig. U3r) mentions Abdelmelec's urging
Sebastian to abandon the fight: 'he laboured privilie and secretly by certaine men
and they mostly merchants, to certifie the King of Portugall of the guiles and deceits
of Mahamet, that had brought him into these daungers, and to present ruine and
jeoperdie of life'.

And they that love my honour follow me.
Were you as resolute as is your king,   20
Alcazar walls should fall before your face
And all the force of this Barbarian lord
Should be confounded, were it ten times more.

Avero. So well become these words a kingly mouth,
That are of force to make a coward fight,   25
But when advice and prudent foresight
Is joinèd with such magnanimity,
Trophies of victory and kingly spoils
Adorn his crown, his kingdom and his fame [. . .]

[*Enter* CHRISTOPHERO DE TAVORA, DON DE MENESES
and HERCULES.]

Hercules. We have descried upon the mountain tops   30
A hugy company of invading Moors,
And they, my lord, as thick as winter's hail
Will fall upon our heads at unawares.
Best then betimes t'avoid this gloomy storm,
It is in vain to strive with such a stream.   35

Enter MULY MAHAMET.

Muly Mahamet. Behold thrice noble lord, uncalled I come
To counsel where necessity commands,

---

28. Trophies] *Dyce¹*; Troupes *Q*; Trophes *Yoklavich*.   29 SD.] *Subst. Yoklavich;* To
them Christoporo Dick Jubie, the Governor of Tanger & W. Kendall *Plot; not in Q.*
31. hugy] *Dyce¹*; hugie *Q.*

---

28. *Trophies*] *Q*'s 'Troupes' is obviously meant to be 'Trophes', sometimes pronounced with two syllables; cf. *The Tragedie of Caesar and Pompey*, 'Grac'd with eter-
nall trophes of renowne' (sig. H1v); Heywood, *2 Fair Maid of the West*, 'We reckon
as a trophe of your loves' (sig. I2v); see 5.1.197.
29.] Some of Avero's speech must be missing, as he does not say what 'prudent foresight' demands. It is likely that a sizeable portion of the original text was omitted here;
what remains implies that Peele intended to follow Polemon and have Sebastian agree
to march to Larissa, as the Portuguese commanders unanimously advise: 'his Counsaile
laboured to their uttermost, to disuade the king from joyning in battaile, but rather
advised him to march to Larissa, and they wrought so much by blaming and urging
him, that the king at length yeelded to go to Larissa' (sig. U3r–v). Muly Mahamet's
appeal for an immediate attack and Sebastian's reversal would provide for some exciting drama.
29. SD.] I follow Yoklavich in inserting the entry direction, based on the Plot, here.
33. *at unawares*] See n. 2.2.14.
36–60.] In Polemon, Abdelmelec was willing to let Sebastian march to the sea, 'for
he would have suffered his enimie to have taken Larissa, thinking that the Portugall
being contented with the taking of it, would from thence returne home'. This is exactly

And honour of undoubted victory
Makes me exclaim upon this dastard flight.
Why, King Sebastian, wilt thou now forslow   40
And let so great a glory slip thy hands?
Say you do march unto Larissa now,
The forces of the foe are come so nigh
That he will let the passage of the river,
So unawares you will be forced to fight.   45
But know, O King, and you thrice valiant lords,
Few blows will serve. I ask but only this:
That with your power you march into the field,
For now is all the army resolute
To leave the traitor helpless in the fight   50
And fly to me as to their rightful prince.
Some horsemen have already led the way
And vow the like for their companions;
The host is full of tumult and of fear.
Then as you come to plant me in my seat   55
And to enlarge your fame in Africa,
Now, now or never, bravely execute
Your resolution sound and honourable,
And end this war together with his life,
That doth usurp the crown with tyranny.   60
Sebastian. Captains, you hear the reasons of the King,
Which so effectually have pierced mine ears
That I am fully resolute to fight,
And who refuseth now to follow me,
Let him be ever counted cowardly.   65

---

42. Larissa] *Yoklavich;* Tarissa *Q.*

---

what Muly Mahamet feared most, so he, 'a subtile fellow, ambitious, and deceitfull
. . . began with a craftie tale to tel [Sebastian] that many Moores horse men had
fled unto him from Abdelmelec, & that the rest of the armie went about to do the
same . . . He added also other arguments making for his purpose, by the which hee dis-
swaded the Portugall from going to Larissa, and to saie the truth, it had otherwise bene
an harde matter for him to have gon forward, seeing his enimy was so neere' (sig. U3r,
U4r).

40. *forslow*] to be slow or dilatory (*OED v* 1); cf. *3 Henry VI*, 'Forslow no longer,
make we hence amain' (2.3.56).

42. *Larissa*] The Roman town of Lixus, now Larache, on the west coast of Morocco,
forty miles west of Alcazar. A 1574 document preserved in the *State Papers Domestic*
names 'the port of Allarache and other portes within the Streates, which serve for the
trade of Fesse for saill of clothes' among the Barbary ports 'which the Queenes subjects use to trafick' (Castries, 1: 132–3).

44. *let*] hinder, prevent (*OED v* 2).

Avero. Shame be his share that flies when kings do fight,
Avero lays his life before your feet.
Stukeley. For my part, lords, I cannot sell my blood
Dearer than in the company of kings.
                              Exeunt. Manet MULY MAHAMET.
Muly Mahamet. Now have I set these Portugals awork   70
To hew a way for me unto the crown [. . .]
Or with your weapons here to dig your graves.
You bastards of the Night and Erebus,
Fiends, furies, hags that fight in beds of steel,
Range through this army with your iron whips,   75
Drive forward to this deed this Christian crew,
And let me triumph in the tragedy,
Though it be sealed and honoured with the blood,
Both of the Portugal and barbarous Moor.
Ride, Nemesis, ride in thy fiery cart,   80
And sprinkle gore amongst these men of war,
That either party eager of revenge
May honour thee with sacrifice of death;
And having bathed thy chariot wheels in blood,
Descend and take to thy tormenting hell   85
The mangled body of that traitor king
That scorns the power and force of Portugal.
Then let the earth discover to his ghost,
Such tortures as usurpers feel below,
Racked let him be in proud Ixion's wheel,   90

---

69. SD.] *Q, Bullen; Exeunt all except the Moor Dyce².* 73. bastards] *Dyce²*; dastards *Q.* 74. furies] *Dyce²*; Fairies *Q, Bullen.* 78. the blood] *Dyce²*; my blood *Q.*

70–97.] In what was to be his final essay, Swinburne (p. 8) wrote 'the soliloquy which closes the fourth act is matchless, I should hope, for drivel of desperation and platitude of bombast, in all the dramatic memorials of hopeless impotence'.

72.] Some text is probably missing before this line. Deleting it would restore some sense to the passage.

73. *bastards of the Night*] 'Peele is apparently alluding to the monstrous issue of *Nox*, the sister of Erebus, by whom she became the mother of various offspring' (Yoklavich, p. 366); see also n. 2.Prol.21.

74. *furies*] Of Q's 'Fairies', Bullen notes, 'Dyce reads "furies"–perhaps rightly, but we often find "fairy" when we should expect "fury"'. How 'often' this occurs is uncertain, but this text is so full of furies and so seemingly bereft of fairies that Dyce must be correct.

beds of steel] See n. 2.Prol.17–18.

90. *Ixion's wheel*] Ixion is the first of four criminals named in this passage who were famous for their punishments in the underworld, as told in Book 4 of *Metamorphoses.* He tried to seduce Hera, so Zeus chained him to a wheel; he is 'always behind himself, always ahead' (4.461); see n. 2.Prol.26–9.

Pined let him be with Tantalus' endless thirst,
Pray let him be to Tityus' greedy bird,
Wearied with Sisyphus' immortal toil;
And lastly for revenge, for deep revenge,
Whereof thou goddess and deviser art,   95
Damned let him be, damned and condemned to bear
All torments, tortures, plagues and pains of hell.

                                                        Exit.

92. Tityus'] *Dyce¹; Tisons Q; Titan's Yoklavich.*

---

91. *Pined*] afflicted with pain (pine *OED* v 1); cf. *Knight of the Burning Pestle*, 'Here be these pinèd wretches' (3.1.432).

Tantalus] The father of Niobe, Tantalus stole nectar and ambrosia from the gods; his punishment was to be placed where he 'can never catch the water, never grasp / The overhanging branches' (*Metamorphoses*, 4.458–9).

92. *Tityus*] the giant slain by Apollo and Artemis for his attempted rape of their mother, Leto. He 'lies stretched across nine acres and provides / His vitals for the vultures' (*Metamorphoses*, 4.457–8). Greg's view (p. 116) that Q's 'Tisons' was meant to be 'Titans', since it is closer to it than to 'Tityus', is doubtful.

93. *Sisyphus*] amongst the various misdeeds ascribed to Sisyphus is his telling Asopus that his daughter Aegina was having a liaison with Zeus. As punishment, he 'chases and heaves the boulder doomed to roll / For ever back' (*Metamorphoses*, 4.460).

ACT 5

[5.Prol.]

Enter the PRESENTER *before the last dumb show, and speaketh.*

Presenter. Ill be to him that so much ill bethinks,
  And ill betide this foul ambitious Moor
  Whose wily trains with smoothest course of speech
  Hath tied and tangled in a dangerous war,
  The fierce and manly King of Portugal.   5

            Lightning and thunder.

Now throw the heavens forth their lightning flames,
And thunder over Afric's fatal fields,
Blood will have blood, foul murder 'scape no scourge.

  Enter Fame *like an Angel, and hangs the crowns upon a tree.*

At last descendeth Fame, as Iris
To finish fainting Dido's dying life;   10
Fame from her stately bower doth descend
And on the tree as fruit new ripe to fall,
Placeth the crowns of these unhappy kings,
That erst she kept in eye of all the world.

            Here the blazing star.

Now fiery stars and streaming comets blaze,   15
That threat the earth and princes of the same.

            Fireworks.

Act 5] *This ed.*; Actus V *Dyce¹*; Act V *Dyce²*; *not in* Q.   5. Prol.] *This ed.; not in* Q.
SH.] *This ed.; not in* Q.   4. Hath] Q; Have *Dyce¹*.

OSD.] There is no surviving fragment of the Plot for the Act 5 dumb show, but Q's
stage directions provide some indication.
  9. *Fame*] *Fama*, usually translated as 'Rumour', as in the *Metamorphoses*
(12.39–63) and the *Aeneid* (4.171–90); cf. *Titus Andronicus*, 'The Emperor's court is
like the house of Fame / The palace full of tongues, of eyes and ears' (2.1.127–8).
  as Iris] This line is short a syllable in a speech that is otherwise metrically regular;
'as Iris did' or 'went' was probably intended. In the *Aeneid*, Juno, unhappy that Dido
should suffer a lingering death, 'Sent Iris down, to free her from the strife / Of lab'ring
nature, and dissolve her life' (4.997–8); see n. 2.1.3.

Fire, fire about the axle-tree of heaven,
Whirls round, and from the foot of Cassiope
In fatal hour consumes these fatal crowns.

One falls.

Down falls the diadem of Portugal,   20

The other falls.

The crown of Barbary, and kingdoms fall.
Ay me, that kingdoms may not stable stand.
And now approaching near the dismal day,
The bloody day wherein the battles join,
Monday the fourth of August seventy-eight.   25
The sun shines wholly on the parchèd earth,
The brightest planet in the highest heaven.
The heathens, eager bent against their foe,
Give onset with great ordnance to the war;
The Christians with great noise of cannon shot,   30
Send angry onsets to the enemy.
Give ear and hear how war begins his song,
With dreadful clamours, noise and trumpets' sound.

Exit.

---

21. crown of Barbary, and] *This ed.;* crownes of Barbary and *Q.*

---

18. *Cassiope*] a mythical queen of Ethiopia, who boasted that 'she excelled the
Nereids in beauty, [and] for this she was put among the constellations, seated in a chair
... as the sky turns, she seems to be carried along lying on her back' (Hyginus, *Poetica
Astronomica*, trans. Mary Grant, Lawrence, Kansas, 1960, p. 195).

21. *crown...fall*] *Q* shows 'crownes', but the stage directions have only two
crowns in the dumb show, so it follows that the Presenter should speak of the
'diadem' of Portugal and the 'crown of Barbary'. The placing of *The other falls*
makes the passage seem more difficult than it is, for there is no reason for the Presenter to stop speaking: the diadem and crown are part of a single thought. I have
inserted a comma after 'Barbary'; the sense might be improved if the Presenter pauses
there.

29. *onset*] attack, assault; cf. Heywood, *Four Prentices*, 'Give a brave onset,
shivering all their pikes' (sig. K2r).

great ordnance] One of the great ironies of this battle is that the ordnance of the
'heathens' was supplied by England, in exchange for Moroccan saltpetre, the chief
ingredient of gunpowder (see p. 14). After the battle, Bishop Philip Sega, the Pope's
Nuncio in Spain, wrote of Queen Elizabeth, 'there is no evil that is not devised by that
woman, who it is perfectly plain, succoured Mulocco [Abdelmelec] with arms and especially with artillery' (*CSP Rom.* (1572–78), p. 495).

[5.1]

> *Alarums within, let the chambers be discharged,*
> *then enter to the battle, and the Moors fly.*
> *Skirmish still, then enter* ABDELMELEC *in his chair,*
> ZAREO *and their train.*

Abdelmelec. Say on, Zareo, tell me all the news,
Tell me what fury rangeth in our camp
That hath enforced our Moors to turn their backs.
Zareo, say, what chance did bode this ill,
What ill enforced this dastard cowardice?   5
Zareo. My lord, such chance as wilful war affords
Such chances and misfortunes as attend
On him, the god of battle and of arms.
My lord, when with our ordnance fierce we sent [. . .]
Our Moors with smaller shot as thick as hail [. . .]   10
Follows apace to charge the Portugal.
The valiant Duke, the devil of Avero,
The bane of Barbary, fraughted full of ire
Breaks through the ranks, and with five hundred horse,
All men at arms, forward and full of might,   15
Assaults the middle wing, and puts to flight
Eight thousand harquebus that served on foot
And twenty thousand Moors with spear and shield:
And therewithal the honour of the day.
Abdelmelec. Ah, Abdelmelec, dost thou live to hear   20
This bitter process of this first attempt?
Labour, my lords, to renew our force
Of fainting Moors, and fight it to the last.
My horse, Zareo! O the goal is lost,
The goal is lost. Thou King of Portugal,   25
Thrice happy chance it is for thee and thine
That heaven abates my strength and calls me hence.
My sight doth fail, my soul, my feeble soul

5.1] *This ed.;* Scene I *Dyce²; not in* Q.   OSD.] *Q, Bullen;* the Moors, who form
Abdelmelec's army, fly *Dyce².*   Zareo] *Q, Bullen;* Argerd Zareo *Dyce².*   17. harque-
bus] *This ed.;* Harquebush *Q;* harquebuze *Dyce¹.*   27. heaven] *Dyce¹;* heavens *Q,*
Bullen.

5.1.] Act 5 is a single battle scene; the action is continuous.
OSD. chambers be discharged] See p. 24.
9–19.] This speech is seriously corrupt; some text must be missing here, after l. 10
and possibly after l. 17.
13. *fraughted*] loaded, laden (fraught *OED ppl* 1).

Shall be released from prison on this earth,
Farewell, vain world, for I have played my part.   30

Dies.

A long skirmish, and then enter [Abdelmelec's] brother,
MULY MAHAMET SETH.

Muly Mahamet Seth. Brave Abdelmelec, thou thrice noble lord,
Not such a wound was given to Barbary
Had twenty hosts of men been put to sword,
As death, pale death with fatal shaft, hath given.
Lo, dead is he, my brother and my king,   35
Whom I might have revived with news I bring.
Zareo. His honours and his types he hath resigned
Unto the world, and of a manly man,
Lo, in a twinkling a senseless stock we see.
Muly Mahamet Seth. You trusty soldiers of this warlike King,   40
Be counselled now by us in this advice:
Let not his death be bruited in the camp,
Lest with the sudden sorrow of the news
The army wholly be discomfited.
My lord Zareo, thus I comfort you: 45
Our Moors have bravely borne themselves in fight,
Likely to get the honour of the day,
If aught may gotten be where loss is such.
Therefore in this apparel as he died
My noble brother will we here advance,   50
And set him in his chair with cunning props,
That our Barbarians may behold their king
And think he doth repose him in his tent.
Zareo. Right politic and good is your advice.

---

30 SD. *Dies*] *Dyce²*; He   dyeth   *Q*; He   dieth   *Bullen.* 30 SD.   *enter*
[Abdelmelec's] brother] *This ed.; enter his brother Q, Bullen; enter Muly Mahamet*
Seth *Dyce².*

37. *types*] high titles, dignities (tipe *OED sb* 1); cf. *3 Henry VI*, 'Thy father bears
the type of King of Naples / Of both the Sicils, and Jerusalem' (1.4.122–3).
39. *stock*] a log, block of wood (*OED sb* 1b).
42. *bruited*] reported; cf. *2 Henry IV*, where the death of Hotspur, 'Being bruited
once, took fire and heat away / From the best-tempered courage in his troops'
(1.1.114–15).
53.] 'The litter being shut, they placed at the doore a wittie yoong childe, who being
instructed what he had to doe, making shewe to speake unto him, and receive his
answer, tolde them his pleasure was they should passe forward' (*Uniting*, pp. 47–8);
see also p. 31.

Muly Mahamet Seth. Go then to see it speedily performed.   55
    Brave lord, if Barbary recover this,
    Thy soul with joy will sit and see the sight.
                                                          Exeunt.

        Alarums. Enter to the battle, and the Christians fly.
        The DUKE OF AVERO *slain. Enter* SEBASTIAN *and* STUKELEY.

Sebastian. See'st thou not, Stukeley, O Stukeley, see'st thou not
    The great dishonour done to Christendom?
    Our cheerful onset crossed in springing hope,   60
    The brave and mighty prince, Duke of Avero
    Slain in my sight; now joy betide his ghost,
    For like a lion did he bear himself.
    Our battles are all now disorderèd,
    And by our horses' strange retiring back,   65
    Our middle wing of footmen overrode.
    Stukeley, alas, I see my oversight.
    False-hearted Mahamet, now to my cost
    I see thy treachery, warned to beware
    A face so full of fraud and villainy.   70

        Alarums within, and [as] they run out, two [soldiers] set upon
        STUKELEY, *and he driveth them in. [Exit* SEBASTIAN].

        Then enter the Moor and his BOY, *flying.*

Muly Mahamet. Villain, a horse!
Boy. O, my lord, if you return you die.
Muly Mahamet. Villain, I say, give me a horse to fly,
    To swim the river, villain, and to fly.
                                                      Exit BOY.

---

55 SH.] *Dyce²*, *Yoklavich; no new speaker Q.*   57 SD. *Alarums*] *Q, Bullen;* Alarums
within *Dyce².*   70 SD.] *This ed.;* Alarums within, and they runne out, and two set
upon Stukley, and he driveth them in *Q.*

---

55 SH.] Q has no speech heading, but the next three lines obviously belong to Muly
Mahamet Seth.
    see it speedily performed] Dyce² inserts a stage direction here, 'The body of
Abdelmelec is propped up in his chair'.
    57 SD.] If the direction is taken literally, then Avero's body is left on stage, as occurs
with Stukeley's body at 5.1.180. The carrying off of bodies is often unaccounted for in
plays of this period: two of many examples that could be cited are Rutland in *3 Henry
VI* (QF, 1.3.52) and the King at the end of *Richard III* (QF, 5.8 OSD).
    70 SD.] Q's stage direction has Stukeley and Sebastian running off *before* 'two set
upon Stukeley'. Stukeley's assailants may be the two Italians of the next sequence, but
one cannot be sure (see Appendix I).

Where shall I find some unfrequented place,   75
Some uncouth walk where I may curse my fill:
My stars, my dam, my planets and my nurse,
The fire, the air, the water, and the earth,
All causes that have thus conspired in one
To nourish and preserve me to this shame?   80
Thou that wert at my birth predominate,
Thou fatal star, what planet ere thou be,
Spit out thy poison bad, and all the ill
That fortune, fate or heaven may bode a man.
Thou nurse infortunate, guilty of all,   85
Thou mother of my life that brought'st me forth,
Cursed mayst thou be for such a cursèd son,
Cursed be thy son with every curse thou hast.
Ye elements of whom consists this clay,
This mass of flesh, this cursèd crazèd corpse,   90
Destroy, dissolve, disturb and dissipate
What water, earth, and air congealed.

                    Alarums and enter the BOY.

Boy. O my lord,
These ruthless Moors pursue you at the heels
And come amain to put you to the sword.   95
Muly Mahamet. A horse, a horse, villain, a horse
That I may take the river straight and fly.
Boy. Here is a horse, my lord,
As swiftly paced as Pegasus.
Mount thee thereon, and save thyself by flight.   100
Muly Mahamet. Mount me I will,
But may I never pass the river till I be
Revenged upon thy soul, accursèd Abdelmelec,
If not on earth, yet when we meet in hell,
Before grim Minos, Rhadamanth and Aeacus.   105
The combat will I crave upon thy ghost,

---

93. my lord / These] *subst. Dyce¹*; my Lord, these *Q.*   105. Minos, Rhadamanth and
Aeacus] *Dyce¹*; Minos, Rodamant, and Eocus *Q.*

85. *infortunate*] This form of 'unfortunate' was common in early modern usage.
93–4. *O my Lord / These*] See n. 1.2.8.
96. *a horse*] Maurice Pope sees this sequence as 'dramatic precedent' for the famous
line from *Richard III* ('My Kingdom for a Horse', *N&Q* 41 (1994): 476). The remainder of the scene has short and long lines, but any attempt to alter *Q*'s lineation creates
a problem elsewhere.
105. *Minos, Rhadamanth and Aeacus*] the judges of the dead in the underworld; cf.
Spanish Tragedy, 'Not far from hence amidst ten thousand souls / Sat Minos, Aeacus,
and Rhadamanth' (1.1.32–3).

And drag thee thorough the loathsome pools
Of Lethe, Styx and fiery Phlethegon.
                                        [*Exeunt.*]

Alarums. Enter STUKELEY *with two* ITALIANS.

First Italian. Stand, traitor, stand ambitious Englishman,
Proud Stukeley stand, and stir not ere thou die.   110
Thy forwardness to follow wrongful arms,
And leave our famous expedition erst
Intended by his Holiness for Ireland,
Foully hath here betrayed and tied us all
To ruthless fury of our heathen foe,   115
For which as we are sure to die,
Thou shalt pay satisfaction with thy blood.
Stukeley. Avaunt, base villains, twit ye me with shame
Or infamy of this injurious war,
When he that is the judge of right and wrong   120
Determines battle as him pleaseth best?
But since my stars bode me this tragic end
That I must perish by these barbarous Moors,
Whose weapons have made passage for my soul
That breaks from out the prison of my breast,   125
Ye proud malicious dogs of Italy,
Strike on, strike down this body to the earth
Whose mounting mind stoops to no feeble stroke.
                                        Stab him.
Second Italian. Why suffer we this English man to live?
Villain, bleed on, thy blood in channels run   130
And meet with those whom thou to death hast done.
                                Exeunt [*two* ITALIANS].
Stukeley. Thus Stukeley, slain with many a deadly stab,
Dies in these desert fields of Africa.

---

108. Lethe, Styx and fiery Phlethegon] *Dyce¹*; Lethes, Stikes, and fiery Phlegiton *Q*.
108 SD.] *Dyce²*; Exit *Q*. Alarums . . . Italians] *Q*; Alarums within: re-enter Stukeley
wounded, followed by Hercules and Jonas *Dyce²*; Alarums. Enter Stukeley with two
Italians, Hercules and Jonas *Bullen*. 109 SH.] *This ed.*; Herc. *Q, Dyce¹*; Italian
Yoklavich. 129 SH.] *Yoklavich*; Jonas *Q*; Jon. *Dyce¹*. 131 SD.] *Yoklavich*; Exeunt
Q; Exeunt Herc. and Jonas *Dyce¹*; Exeunt Hercules and Jonas *Dyce²*.

---

108. *Lethe, Styx and fiery Phlethegon*] the three rivers of Hades. Lethe was the river
of oblivion – those who drank from it forgot their former lives. Styx was the main
passage to and through the underworld, and Phlegethon was the river of flames; cf.
Faustus: 'Now, by the kingdoms of infernal rule / Of Styx, Acheron, and the fiery lake
/ Of ever-burning Phlegethon, I swear' (8.47–9).
108 SD. *two* ITALIANS] See Appendix I.

Hark, friends, and with the story of my life
Let me beguile the torment of my death.   135
In England's London, lordings, was I born,
On that brave bridge, the bar that thwarts the Thames.
My golden days, my younger careless years,
Were when I touched the height of Fortune's wheel,
And lived in affluence of wealth and ease.   140
Thus in my country carried long aloft,
A discontented humour drave me thence
To cross the seas to Ireland, then to Spain;
There had I welcome and right royal pay
Of Philip, whom some call the Catholic king.   145
There did Tom Stukeley glitter all in gold,
Mounted upon his jennet white as snow,
Shining as Phoebus in King Philip's court;
There like a lord famous Don Stukeley lived,
For so they called me in the court of Spain,   150
Till for a blow I gave a bishop's man,
A strife 'gan rise between his lord and me,
For which we both were banished by the King.
From thence, to Rome rides Stukeley all aflaunt,
Received with royal welcomes of the Pope.   155
There was I graced by Gregory the Great,
That then created me Marquess of Ireland.
Short be my tale, because my life is short:
The coast of Italy and Rome I left,
Then was I made lieutenant general   160
Of those small forces that for Ireland went,
And with my companies embarked at Ostia.

---

162. Ostia] *Dyce¹, Yoklavich*; Austria *Q*.

---

136. *In England's London*] Stukeley was from Devonshire; see p. 1.

151. *blow . . . man*] see Appendix II.

154. *aflaunt*] 'in a flaunting state or position' (*OED adv*); cf. Puttenham, *The Arte of English Poesie* (London, 1589, p. 250), 'for a courtier to know how to weare a fether, and set his cappe a flaunt'.

156. *Gregory the Great*] Peele's second attempt at naming the correct Pope is more wildly off than the first (2.4.139). Gregory I, usually named 'the Great', lived c. 540–604.

160. *lieutenant general*] a 'general lieutenant', someone with wide-ranging authority; see Edelman, *Military*, p. 204.

162. *Ostia*] Obviously the basis of the compositor's 'Austria', but Ostia was not in fact Stukeley's embarkation point. On 19 February 1578, Sir Amias Paulet, the English ambassador to France, wrote to Lord Burghley, 'I am credibly infourmid that Stukeley was still at Civita Vechia on the xxviiiᵗʰ of the laste, where there had bene some mutinie emongst his souldiours' (Castries, 1: 289); on 4 March, Bernardino de Mendoza, Philip

My sails I spread, and with these men of war
In fatal hour at Lisbon we arrived.
From thence to this, to this hard exigent   165
Was Stukeley driven to fight or else to die,
Dared to the field, that never could endure
To hear god Mars his drum, but he must march.
Ah sweet Sebastian, hadst thou been well advised
Thou mightst have managed arms successfully,   170
But from our cradles we were markèd all
And destinate to die in Afric here.
Stukeley, the story of thy life is told,
Here breathe thy last and bid thy friends farewell.
And if thy country's kindness be so much,   175
Then let thy country kindly ring thy knell.
Now go, and in that bed of honour die
Where brave Sebastian's breathless corse doth lie.
Here endeth Fortune's rule, and bitter rage,
Here ends Tom Stukeley's pilgrimage.   180
                                                              Dies.

        Enter MULY MAHAMET SETH, [ZAREO] *and train,*
                  with drums and trumpets.

Muly Mahamet Seth. Retreat is sounded through our camp, and now
From battle's fury cease, our conquering Moors.
Pay thanks to heaven with sacrificing fire,
Alcazar and ye towns of Barbary.   [*Turns to Abdelmelec's body*]
Now hast thou sat as in a trance and seen,   185
To thy soul's joy and honour of thy house,
The trophies and the triumphs of thy men,
Great Abdelmelec and the god of kings
Hath made thy war successful by thy right [. . .]

---

180 SD. *Dies*] *Dyce²*; He dyeth *Q; He dieth Bullen.*   180 SD.] *subst. Q.*   ZAREO]
This ed.; Argerd Zareo *Dyce².*   184 SD.] *This ed.; not in Q.*   185. sat] *conj. Bullen*;
sit *Q.*   187. trophies] *Dyce¹*; trophes *Q.*

II's ambassador to England, told his king that Queen Elizabeth 'is much alarmed at
news from Florence that Stukeley had left Civita Vecchia with six hundred men in a
galleon' (*CSP Spn.* (1568–79), p. 561).
    172. *destinate*] ordained, destined (*OED ppl*); cf. *The London Prodigal*, 'That a
guilty conscience / May bring him to this destinate repentance' (sig. A4v).
    180 SD.] See n. 5.1.57 SD.
    185.] Muly Mahamet Seth must be addressing Abdelmelec's lifeless body here.
Bullen's 'hast thou sat' instead of *Q*'s 'sit' slightly improves the sense, but the speech is
apparently so corrupt that no coherent reading is possible.
    188. *god of kings*] Amurath (see 1.1.35–6).

His friends whom death and fates hath ta'en from thee.   190
Lo, this was he that was the people's pride,
And cheerful sunshine to his subjects all.
Now have him hence, that royally he may
Be buried and embalmèd as is meet.
Zareo, have you through the camp proclaimed   195
As erst we gave in charge?
Zareo. We have, my lord, and rich rewards proposed
For them that find the body of the King.
For by those guards that had him in their charge,
We understand that he was done to death,   200
And for his search two prisoners, Portugals,
Are set at large to find their royal king.
Muly Mahamet Seth. But of the trait'rous Moor you hear no news,
That fled the field and sought to swim the ford?
Zareo. Not yet, my lord, but doubtless God will tell   205
And with his finger point out where he haunts.
Muly Mahamet Seth. So let it rest, and on this earth bestow
This princely corse, till further for his funerals
We provide.
Zareo. From him to thee as true succeeding prince,   210
With all allegiance, and with honour's types,
In name of all thy people and thy land,
We give this kingly crown and diadem.
Muly Mahamet Seth. We thank you all, and as my lawful right,
With God's defence and yours shall I it keep.   215

    Enter two PORTUGALS *with the body of* [*King* SEBASTIAN].

---

199. guards] *Dyce²*; gard Q.   215. God's] *Dyce¹*; Gods Q.   shall I it keep] *Dyce²*;
shall I keepe Q.   215 SD.] *Dyce²*; Enter two Portugals with the bodie of the king Q.

190.] 'His' appears to have no antecedent; as *Dyce²* notes, 'something is wanting
before this line'. Indeed, something is wanting after it as well: the transition from
addressing Abdelmelec's body to a tribute, addressed to Abdelmelec's followers – 'Lo,
this was he' – is very abrupt.

193. *have him hence*] apparently a command to carry off Abdelmelec's body, but Q
has no stage direction, and there is a similar instruction at ll. 207–8.

204. *sought to swim the ford*] 'Muley Mahamet seeking to save himselfe by flight,
as he would have passed over at the foord of the river of Larissa which is myrie and
moorish, was cast out of his saddle by his horse that strived and struggeled to get out
of the durt, and beeing unskilfull to swimme, was drowned and perished in the river'
(Polemon, sig. X4r). Polemon's 'river of Larissa' is wad Loukkas, or 'Luccus', as in Leo
Africanus (Brown, p. 495).

205. *God*] See n. 4.1.69.

208. *funerals*] often denotes the singular; cf. *Julius Caesar*, 'His funerals shall not
be in our camp' (5.2.104).

211. *types*] See n. 5.1.37.

215. *God's*] See n. 4.1.69.

Portuguese Soldier. As gave your grace in charge, right royal prince,
    The fields and sandy plains we have surveyed,
    And even among the thickest of his lords,
    The noble King of Portugal we found
    Wrapped in his colours coldly on the earth,   220
    And done to death with many a mortal wound.
Muly Mahamet Seth. Lo, here, my lords, this is the earth and clay
    Of him that erst was mighty King of Portugal.
    There let him lie, and you for this be free
    To make return from hence to Christendom.   225

       Enter two [SOLDIERS] *bringing in the Moor.*

Soldier. Long live the mighty King of Barbary.
Muly Mahamet Seth. Welcome, my friend, what body hast thou there?
Soldier. The body of the ambitious enemy,
    That squandered all this blood in Africa,
    Whose malice sent so many souls to hell,   230
    The traitor Muly Mahamet do I bring,
    And for thy slave I throw him at thy feet.
Muly Mahamet Seth. Zareo, give this man a rich reward,
    And thankèd be the god of just revenge
    That he hath given our foe into our hands,   235
    Beastly, unarmed, slavish, full of shame.
    But say, how came this traitor to his end?
Soldier. Seeking to save his life by shameful flight,
    He mounteth on a hot Barbarian horse,
    And so in purpose to have past the stream,   240
    His headstrong steed throws him from out his seat,
    Where diving oft for lack of skill to swim,
    It was my chance alone to see him drowned,
    Whom by the heels I dragged from out the pool
    And hither have him brought thus filed with mud.   245
Muly Mahamet Seth. A death too good for such a damnèd wretch.
    But since our rage and rigour of revenge
    By violence of his end prevented is,
    That all the world may learn by him to avoid
    To hale on princes to injurious war,   250

---

216 SH.] *This ed.;* Port. *Q;* First Port. *Dyce²*.   225 SD.] *This ed.;* Enter two bringing in the Moore *Q;* Enter two Peasants bringing in the body of the Moor *Dyce²*.   226
SH.] *This ed.;* One *Q,* First Peas. *Dyce²*.

---

225 SD.] Dyce has two peasants bringing in the body; one can only wonder from
where they may have come. It is most unlikely that, with soldiers available, two actors
would don peasant costumes just for this entrance.
245. *filed*] defiled, the shorter form being common in the sixteenth century; cf. *Apius
and Virginia* (*Q,* 1575), 'Or should my Virgins name be filde' (sig. A3r).

His skin we will be parted from his flesh,
And being stiffened out and stuffed with straw [. . .]
So to deter and fear the lookers on
From any such fool fact or bad attempt.
Away with him.   255
And now, my lords, for this Christian king:
My lord Zareo, let it be your charge,
To see the soldiers tread a solemn march,
Trailing their pikes and ensigns on the ground,
So to perform the prince's funerals.   260
                                                    [*Exeunt*].

Here endeth the tragical battle of Alcazar

260 SD.] *This ed.; not in Q.*

___

252. *stuffed with straw*] 'But as for the bodie of Muley Mahamet, the newe king his uncle commaunded the skinne to be pulled off (because he had beene the author of so many slaughters) and to be salted, and then stuffed with strawe, and to be carried about thorough out all provinces of his kingdome, for to deterre all other for attempting the like at anie time after' (Polemon, sig. Y2r). The compositor must have missed a line or lines following this one, describing how the stuffed body was to be displayed (Bradley, p. 167). This idea was not original to Muly Ahmed al-Monsour: Earle Nestor Martiningo's 'True Report' of the siege of Famagusta in 1571 reveals that, when the city fell to the Turks, the body of the Venetian general, 'that woorthy and noble Bragadino', was 'taken and filled with strawe [and] was commanded foorthwith to be hanged upon the bowsprit of a foist [a small galley], and too be caried alongst the coast of Syria by the sea side' (Hakluyt, 5: 47).
254. *fact*] deed, exploit (*OED sb* 1b).
259.] Muly Mahamet Seth is ordering his men to trail their pikes in 'the funerall posture' with the head, not the butt, resting on the ground; see Edward Davies, *The Art of War and Englands Traynings* (London, 1619, p. 198); Edelman, *Military*, pp. 253–4.
260. *the prince's funerals*] It might seem unusual that the play does not end with a couplet, but there is no final couplet in either *Hamlet* or *Coriolanus*, two plays that close, as this one does, with an order for a military funeral.

*The Famous History of the Life and Death
of Captain Thomas Stukeley*

EDITIONS AND TEXTUAL
CONVENTIONS

This edition relies on Judith C. Levinson's Malone Society reprint of the 1605 quarto.[1] Copies of the original quarto are more plentiful than for *Alcazar*, and Levinson has collated all but one without noting any significant variation. References to the Malone reprint are indicated in the textual collation by *Q*; Levinson's own suggested emendations, appearing in her list of 'Irregular and Doubtful Readings' (pp. xi–xvii), are indicated by *Levinson*.

The only modern edition to precede this one is by Richard Simpson, in *The School of Shakspere*, v. 1, 1878. Simpson died before the work was completed, and J. W. M. Gibbs was responsible for the final revision. According to F. J. Furnivall's Preface, some of the notes are Gibbs's, although these are not identified. This text has many silent emendations, often unnecessary, and almost invariably fails to emend where *Q* is clearly nonsensical.

J. Q. Adams offers a short list of suggested readings in his 1916 essay.[2] These are indicated by *Adams* in the textual collation.

Anyone comparing this edition with a quarto facsimile or with Simpson's text will see some stark differences, other than the usual ones of modern spelling and typography. Along with changing the order of the final scenes[3] and placing the alternative Irish scene at the end, I have radically altered the lineation of many passages in Scenes 1–6 and Scene 13. As noted, there are numerous lines that could be either prose or verse, since they neither start with a capital letter nor go to the right margin.[4] Simpson followed what Stephen Orgel describes as the standard assumption held by editors of Shakespearian and, by inference, other texts: 'verse is better than prose, Shakespeare is the best poet, therefore anything that can be made to look like verse should be'.[5] I have gone in the opposite direction: 'if it looks anything like prose, it probably is'.

Q has no act or scene divisions; what constitutes an act in this text is so problematic that I have simply numbered the scenes.

NOTES

1 London, 1975. Levinson's edition of Q was preceded by a facsimile edition in Farmer's *Tudor Facsimile Texts*, London, 1911. Owing to the darkness of the printing, it is much less easy to read.
2 Adams, p. 129; see pp. 36–8.
3 See pp. 45–8.
4 See pp. 40–1.
5 Stephen Orgel, *The Authentic Shakespeare and Other Problems of the Early Modern Stage*, London, 2002, p. 38.

LIST OF CHARACTERS

First Appearing in London

Sir Thomas CURTIS, *an Alderman of London.*
LADY (Bess) CURTIS, *his wife.*
NELL Curtis, *his daughter.*
Thomas STUKELEY.
VERNON, *his friend.*
OLD STUKELEY, *Thomas's father.*
Master NEWTON, *Old Stukeley's friend.*
Tom Stukeley's PAGE.
Arthur CROSS the mercer.
John SPARING the vintner.
William SHARP the cutler.
BLUNT the buckler-maker.
Sir Thomas Curtis's CASHIER.
George HAZARD, *a tennis-keeper.*
Geoffrey BLURT, *Bailiff of Finsbury.*
Henry CRACK the fencer.
Captain Jack HARBERT.
HAMDON, *friend to Vernon.*
RIDLEY, *friend to Vernon.*
Another CAPTAIN.
STUKELEY'S LIEUTENANT.
ENSIGN.
Soldiers and Drummer.

First Appearing in Ireland

Shane O'NEILL.
Neil MACKENER, *O'Neill's Secretary.*
Rory O'HANLON.
Captain GAINSFORD.
HARBERT'S LIEUTENANT.
Harbert's Page.
ALEXANDER OGE.
MacGilliam BUSKE.
SOLDIERS.
Ensign.

First Appearing in Spain or Portugal

Hernando, GOVERNOR of Cales (Cadiz).
GOVERNOR'S LADY.
ATTENDANT.
PROVOST.
KING PHILIP II of Spain.
Lord ALVA.
Sancto DAVILA.
BOTELLIO, Ambassador from Portugal to the King of Spain.
CARDINAL Henry, great-uncle to King Sebastian.
VALDES, Marshal to the King of Spain.
King SEBASTIAN of Portugal.
Don ANTONIO, Prior of Crato, cousin to King Sebastian.
LANTADO.
SHIP'S MASTER.
King's NUNCIO.
Officers, Attendants.

First Appearing in Morocco

CHORUS.
ABDELMELEC, rightful King of Morocco.
MULY HAMET, his brother.
MULY MAHAMET, the Moor.
CALIPOLIS, his wife.
MESSENGER from King Sebastian.
Duke of AVERO.
SOLDIERS.
Attendants.

CAPTAIN THOMAS STUKELEY

Scene 1

[*Enter Sir Thomas* CURTIS, LADY CURTIS, NELL *Curtis,*
VERNON *and* STUKELEY.]

Curtis. Proceed, son Vernon, on with your discourse.
Vernon. Sir Thomas Curtis, spare that name of son.
  I must confess I should have been your son
  And had thereto your wife's and your consent.
Curtis. And had, son Vernon? Ay, and so have still!   5
  (*Roundly off*) Bones a dod, man, if I be a knight,
  Sir Thomas Curtis and an alderman,
  They that deny my daughter is not yours,
  By yea and nay, I think them not my friends.
  Passion of me, man, not my daughter yours?   10
  What say you, wife?
Lady Curtis.   Husband, what should I say?
  Is it not known through London? Do not our friends
  Daily expect the marriage of our child
  To Master Vernon here? And ask ye me,
  'What say you wife'?
Curtis.   Why heard ye not his words?   15

Scene 1] *This ed.;* Sc. i. *Levinson; not in Q.* OSD.] *This ed.; not in Q.* 6. SD.] *At
rt mgn l. 8 Q.* 8. deny] *This ed.;* say deny *Q.* 11. SH.] *This ed; Q has* Wife *Sc. 1;*
Moth., Mother *Sc. 3;* Lady *Sc. 5.*

Scene 1] The action of this first scene takes place at Sir Thomas Curtis's house in
London.
  6. SD. Roundly off] Bluntly, without mincing words (*OED adv* 3); cf. Malvolio in
Twelfth Night, 'Sir Toby, I must be round with you' (2.3.91).
  Bones a dod] this expression and 'bones *of* dod', mild forms of 'God's bones', are
frequently used by Curtis, and are very similar to those employed by Hobson in
Heywood's 2 *If You Know Not Me, You Know Nobody*; see p. 39.
  8. *deny*] Q reads 'say deny'; one of the words was almost certainly crossed out.
'Deny' fits the metre, and double negatives were not unusual at this time (Abbott,
p. 295); cf. *Richard III*, 'You may deny that you were not the mean / Of my Lord Hast-
ings' late imprisonment' (1.3.90–1).
  daughter] Documents of the time suggest that Stukeley's wife was the alderman's
granddaughter or niece; see p. 2.
  10. *Passion of me*] a common oath, also found in Middleton's *A Trick to Catch the
Old One* (2.1.139; 3.3.97) and *A Mad World My Masters* (2.1.24; 5.2.41); see p. 39.

He must confess he should have been our son
And thereto had both your consent and mine?
Have you denied him since? Passion of me,
Bess and son both, these speeches make me muse.
Not have our daughter!   20
Lady Curtis. Husband, husband, perhaps his mind is changed
Or our girl's portion is not great enough,
And therefore now he seeks to break it off.
Curtis. Sits the wind there, wife? Ha, think ye so?
By yea and nay then, wife, he deals not well.   25
Come roundly, roundly come, what is the matter?
Passion of me, break off, and for no cause? Ha?
Vernon. Sir Thomas, patience but yourself awhile
And you shall see that mere necessity
Breaks off our match.
Curtis.   On, then, a' God's name.   30
Vernon. I doubt not, but by marriage of your child,
You seek such comforts as the sacred state
Yields you as parents, us as children?
Curtis. What else, son Vernon?
Vernon. And those high blessings no way are attained   35
But by the mutual sympathising love,
That as combining hands, so should the hearts
Of either party. Else it cannot be.
Curtis. All this is true, son Vernon.
Vernon. Now then, Sir Thomas, you cannot expect   40
These comforts by our match on neither part,
If you give me her hand and not her heart.
The one I know you may, compulsively,
The other never but unwillingly.
Curtis. Bones of dod, man, how? What have we here?   45
Her hand and not her heart? Nell, come hither, Nell.
Passion of me, wench, how comes this to pass?
We 'point ye one, you love another, ha?
Lady Curtis. May this be so, maid, ha? Why speak ye not?
Vernon. Madam, and good Sir Thomas, be not rough   50
With your fair daughter. What her bashfulness
Conceals from you, favour me to disclose.

35. SH.] *Simpson; no new speaker Q.*   41. match] *Simpson; matches Q.*

28. *patience*] exercise patience (*OED v* 1).
43. *compulsively*] by compulsion (*OED adv* 1, earliest cit.).
46. *Nell*] Stukeley's wife was Anne Curtis, not Helen or Nell (see p. 2). This editon uses 'Nell' in speech headings, as that is what the audience would know her by.
52. *favour me*] allow me; cf. Fletcher's *Honest Man's Fortune*, 'I pray then favour me / To inform your lady' (4.1.188–9).

    See ye this gentleman here, Master Stukeley?
Curtis. O, Master Stukeley, a courteous gentleman. What of him?
Vernon. He is the substance of my shadowed love,   55
    I but a cipher, in respect of him.
    You give me your consent, but he gains hers,
    You wed me to her hand, he hath her heart.
    O what a wrong in you were this to her,
    Being your child and hope of after joy.   60
    O what a wrong in me were this to him,
    Being my friend, my dear esteemèd friend,
    To rob her of her heart's best happiness,
    Him of the good his gracious fortune gives,
    If I should hinder him, or you keep her   65
    From this right match, which reason doth prefer.
Curtis. Bones a dod, Nell, how? Love Master Stukeley?
Lady Curtis. A handsome proper man, but how now, daughter?
    Must maids be choosers?
Stukeley. Madam, and kind Sir Thomas, look on me   70
    Not with disdainful looks, or base contempt.
    I am a gentleman and well derived,
    Equal, I may say, in all true respects,
    With higher fortune than I aim at now.
    But since your daughter's virtues and firm love   75
    In each of us hath made resolvèd choice,
    Since my dear friend to me hath yielded up
    What right he might prefer to your fair child
    In true regard of our so mutual love,
    So you yourselves make perfect those fair hopes,   80
    That by contracted marriage you expect
    Where either party resteth fully pleased.
Nell. Upon my knees, dear parents, I entreat it,
    And count it not in me immodesty
    To love the man, whom heaven appointed for me.   85
    Your choice I must commend, but mine much more,
    Bearing the seal of firm affection.
    His virtues in the public world's repute
    Deserveth one more worthy than myself.
    Since Master Vernon then prefers his friend   90
    Before himself, and in so just a case,
    Let me entreat that reason may take place.

83. SH.] *This ed.; Q has* Hel. *Sc.* 1, Bride *Sc.* 3, Wife *Sc.* 6.

Vernon. To further it, thus frankly I begin:
Here, dear Tom Stukeley, all the right I have
In fair Nell Curtis, I resign to thee.   95
Be but her parents pleased so well as I,
God give you joy as man and wife, say I.
Stukeley. What says Sir Thomas? Shall I call him father,
And, madam, you my mother?
Curtis.   Soft and fair, sir.
Come hither, wife. Stukeley is a gallant man,   100
And one here in our city much beloved.
Lady Curtis. Nay, husband, both in court and country too,
A gentleman well born, and as I hear,
His father's heir. The match were not amiss,
Since Nell is so affected to him, and beside,   105
You see that Master Vernon leaves her quite.
Curtis. Passion of me, wife, but I heard last day,
He's very wild, a quarreller, a fighter,
Ay, and I doubt a spend-good too.
Lady Curtis. That is but youthfulness – marriage will tame him.   110
Young gentlemen will run their course awhile
And yet be ne'er the worse.
Curtis.   Say ye so, wife?
Well, son Vernon (should have been) and Master Stukeley,
Come, we will dine together, and talk more
Concerning this new motion. Well, Nell, well,   115
You cannot choose a man, not you? By yea and nay,
I grow in good opinion of him. Come, no more ado,
We will to dinner, and be merry too.
Stukeley. I feel thee coming, fortune; if it prove,
Blest be the wooing speeds so soon of love.   120
                                                                Exeunt.

---

99. *Soft and fair*] 'take it easy', or similar; a common expression; cf. *Night of the Burning Pestle*, 'Remove and march, soft and fair, gentlemen, soft and fair' (5.1.133–4).

104. *father's heir*] Thomas, as the third son of Sir Hugh Stukeley, was not his heir; see p. 1.

109. *spend-good*] spendthrift; cf. Heywood's 2 *If You Know Not Me*, 'Where be these varlets, bones a me, at Taverne? / Knaves, villaines, spend goods' (sig. A4v); see p. 39.

Scene 2

Enter [OLD] STUKELEY, *and Master* NEWTON, *a citizen.*

Old Stukeley. By'r Lady we have sitten well, my host.
'Tis one o'clock, my watch says, what says your clock?
Newton. Much there about, sir.
Is it your pleasure we prepare your lodging?
Old Stukeley. What else, sir? Nay, I will not change mine host.   5
Good Master Newton, I'll be bold with you,
Mine old friend and acquaintance and companion,
Whoever else be here I must be one;
You shall not drive me from you, that you shall not.
Newton. My very worshipful and loving friend,   10
Master Stukeley, you are right welcome to my house,
And be as bold here as you were at home.
Will you abroad so soon, sir, after dinner?
Old Stukeley. Yes, sir, about a little businesses.
Newton. Beshrew me, sir, you have come far today;   15
I pray you rest yourself this afternoon.
Your bed shall be made ready if you please,
And take tomorrow for your businesses.
Old Stukeley. O sir, I thank you, but it shall not need.
I thank God, sir, I am as fresh and lusty   20
As when I set this morning from mine inn.
Tut, forty miles, 'tis nothing before noon,
Now in mid-April and the ways so fair.
Newton. I am younger than yourself by twenty years,
And by'r lady would not undertake it.   25
Old Stukeley. Ho, twenty years ago I have ridden from
This town to my house and ne'er drawn bit,
But, Master Newton, those days and I be parted.
Well, sir, I'll to the Temple to see my son.

Scene 2] *This ed.; Sc. ii. Levinson; not in Q.* OSD. [OLD] STUKELEY] *This ed.;*
maister stukly *Q.* 1. By'r Lady] *This ed.;* Ber Lady *Q;* Be'r Lady *Simpson* (& 1.25.)
27. drawn] *This ed.;* draw *Q;* drew *conj. Levinson.*

Scene 2] As often occurs in plays written for the Elizabethan platform stage, this
scene changes locale as it proceeds. The action begins at Master Newton's house and
ends at the door of Stukeley's rooms at the Inns of Court.
14. *businesses*] common in early modern plays, although not with the singular
article. It is retained here to comply with Newton's unexceptional use of the word
four lines later.
29. *Temple*] the Middle or Inner Temple, one of the Inns of Court. There is no record
of the historical Stukeley having been a student there.

When saw you that unthrifty boy, Tom Stukeley?   30
Newton. He was not here since you were last in town,
      But the other day I saw him come up Fleet Street
      With the Lord Windsor and Lord Aberganny,
      An Irish lord or two in company.
      I promise you he is a gallant man.   35
Old Stukeley. I had as lief you had seen him in the Temple Walk,
      Conferring with some learned counsellor,
      Or at the moot upon a case in law.
Newton. Sir, so you may, I doubt not, on occasion.
Old Stukeley. I promise you I doubt it, Master Newton,   40
      I hear some things that pleaseth me but a little.
      It is not my allowance serves the turn
      To maintain company with noblemen.
Newton. Why, sir, it shows he bears a gallant mind.
      I' faith he is a gallant sprightly youth,   45
      Of a fine mettle and an active spirit.
Old Stukeley. God make him honest, sir, and give him grace.
Newton. My wife expects your company at supper.
Old Stukeley. Yes, sir, God willing.
Newton. And if your son be at leisure, I pray you bring him.   50
Old Stukeley. I thank you, sir.

                                        [*Exit* NEWTON]

      I hear his courage very much commended,
      But too licentious, that is all I fear.

---

51. sir. / I hear] *Simpson;* Sir, I her Q.   SD.] *This ed.; not in Q.*

30. *unthrifty*] cf. Bolingbroke in *Richard II*, 'Can no man tell of my unthrifty son?'
(5.3.1).
33. *Lord Windsor and Lord Aberganny*] Frederick, fourth Lord Windsor (b. 1558),
would be a fitting companion for the fictional law student Stukeley. He was
admitted to the Middle Temple on 20 February 1580, and, according to Arthur Collins'
Historical Collections of the Noble Family of Windsor (London, 1754, p. 69), he
'shewed himself, from his youth, a nobleman of spirit and honour, being in 23 Eliz.
[1581] among the gallants of that age, expert in justings, barriers, and turney'. Edward
Neville, eighth Lord Abergavenny, was MP for Windsor for a time, and later patron of
Lord Abergavenny's Men, a company about which little is known except that it performed in Coventry, 1609–10; see G. E. Cokayne, *The Complete Peerage of England
Scotland and Ireland,* ed. Vicary Gibbs, 12 v., London, 1910, 1: 33–7; 12: 798–9; P.
W. Hasler, ed., *The House of Commons, 1558–1603,* 3 v., London, 1981, 3: 122; John
Tucker Murray, *English Dramatic Companies, 1558–1642,* 2 v., New York, 1963, 2:
19.
36. *Temple Walk*] probably the King's Bench Walk, by the Inner Temple Library.
38. *moot*] a hypothetical case argued by law students for practice (*OED sb¹* 4).
51. SD.] Newton is not heard from or spoken to for the rest of the scene, and Old
Stukeley's speech works well as a soliloquy.

But that he doth accommodate with the best
In that he shows himself a gentleman,   55
And though perhaps he shall not know so much,
I do not much mislike that humour in him.
A gentleman of blood and quality,
To sort himself amongst the noblest spirits,
Shows the true sparks of honourable worth   60
And rightly shows in this he is mine own.
For when I was of young Tom Stukeley's years,
And of the Inns of Court as he is now,
I would be conversant still with the best,
The bravest spirits, that were about the town.   65
But soft, this is his chamber as I take it.

He knocks. Enter the PAGE.

Page. Who calls there? God's me, my master's father! Now my master,
he's at the tabling house too. What the devil makes this old crackle-
breech here now? How the pox stumbled he hither? [*To Old Stukeley*] God save your worship.   70
Old Stukeley. How now, boy? Where's your master?
Page. He is not come from dinner, sir.
Old Stukeley. How? Not from dinner? 'Tis past dinner time in the hall
an hour ago. Hark ye, sirrah, tell me true, is he in commons? Tell
me not a lie now.   75
Page. (*Aside*) What shall I do? I am in a pitiful case. A pox on him for
an old scant-pouch! If he take me with a lie now, by this flesh and
blood, he'll whip me most perniciously. If I should say he is in
commons and he prove it not so, by this light he'll pepper me.
Faith, I'll tell truth.   80
Old Stukeley. Sirrah, why speak you not?
Page. I think he be not in commons, sir.
Old Stukeley. Where dines he?
Page. At Palmer's ordinary.

69. SD.] *This ed.; not in* Q.   76. SD. Aside] *placed above l.* Q.   77. scant-pouch]
This ed.; Scand-pouch Q.

---

54. *accommodate*] fits, equips himself (*OED v* 11).
67. *God's me*] 'God save me', cf. *1 Henry IV*, 'God's me, my horse!' (2.3.91).
68. *tabling house*] 'tables' was another name for backgammon (table *OED sb* 11).
68–9. *crackle-breech*] a seemingly unique expression, presumably akin to 'old fart'.
73. *dinner time in the hall*] Dinner was taken at about noon in Elizabethan England;
the 'hall' would be the main hall of the Temple.
74. *commons*] i.e. the common table at the Middle or Inner Temple.
77. *scant-pouch*] scant-purse, miser; another interesting expression from the Page.
84. *ordinary*] an eating-house or tavern where public meals are provided at a fixed
price (*OED sb* 14b). In *The Gull's Hornbook*, Dekker advises 'How a young gallant
should behave himself in an ordinary: First having diligently enquired out an ordinary

Old Stukeley. Your master is an ordinary student!   85
Page. Indeed sir, he studies very extraordinarily.
Old Stukeley. And you the rope-ripe ordinarily.
    I sent him money to provide him books.
Page. [*Aside*] See, see, the devil owed my master a shame and now he
    has paid him: he had ne'er so much grace as to buy him a key to   90
    his study door. If he have e'er a book there, but old hacked swords,
    as foxes, bilboes and horn-bucklers, I am an infidel. I cannot tell
    what to do. I'll devise some 'scuse.
Old Stukeley. Sirrah, hear ye me. Give me the key of his study.
Page. Sir, he ever carries it about him.   95
Old Stukeley. How? Let me see, methinks the door stands open.
Page. [*Aside*] A plague on't, he hath found it. [*To Old Stukeley*] I was
    not 'ware, sir, belike he had thought it he had locked it and turned
    the key too short. (*Aside*) Now we shall see this old cutter play his
    part, for in faith he's furnished with all kind of weapons.   100
Old Stukeley. What, be these my son's books? I promise you, a study
    richly furnished! Well said, Tom Stukeley. (*Laying out all his tools*)
    Here, gallows-clapper, here. Be these your master's books? For Lit-
    tleton, Stamford and Brooke here's long sword, short sword, and

---

89. owed] *This ed.;* ought *Q.* SD. *Aside*] *This ed; not in Q.* 92. horn-bucklers]
conj. Levinson; Horne-Buckles *Q.* 96. How? Let me see] *subst. Simpson;* how let me
see *Q.* 97. SD. *Aside*] *This ed; not in Q.* SD. *To Old Stukeley*] *This ed.; not in Q.*

---

of the largest reckoning whither most of your courtly gallants do resort, let it be your
use to repair thither some half-hour after eleven, for then you shall find most of your
fashion-mongers planted in the room waiting for meat' (p. 93).
    87. *rope-ripe*] one ripe for the gallows (*OED sb*); cf. *The Maid's Metamorphosis*,
'How the divel stumbled this case of rope-ripes in–into my way?' (sig. C3v).
    92. *foxes, bilboes and horn-bucklers*] Both the fox and the bilbo are types of sword.
The former might derive from an armourer of Passau, who stamped his product with
a wolf, mistaken for a fox, or later changed to resemble one; the bilbo took its name
from Bilbao, the city of manufacture, and was highly regarded for its temper and elas-
ticity (Edelman, *Military*, p. 51). 'Horn-bucklers' (if that is what *Q* is meant to read)
is more difficult, since bucklers (small shields) were made of wood. But 'horn', in bib-
lical use, was 'an emblem of power and might, a means of defence or resistance' (*OED
sb* 8), and was hence associated with shields, as in Psalms (18.2), 'The Lord is . . . my
buckler, and the horn of my salvation'. In *2 Henry VI*, Shakespeare gives the name
Peter Horner to an armourer who fights a drunken duel with his apprentice (see n.
5.14. SD), although in Stow's *Survey* his name is William Catur (Hattaway, p. 77).
    99. *cutter*] One over-ready to resort to weapons, a bully; a cutthroat, highway-
robber (*OED sb¹* 3a). Cuthbert Cutter is a thief in *The Famous Victories of Henry V*.
    103. *gallows-clapper*] one fit to be hanged, a gallows-bird (*OED*).
    103–4. *Littleton, Stamford and Brooke*] three essential authorities for any serious
student of the law. Sir Thomas Littleton (1422–81) was the author of *Tenures*, a major
work on property law; Sir William Stamford, or Stanford (1509–58), was a judge and
prosecutor, and wrote several legal texts; Sir Robert Brooke (d. 1558) wrote *La
Graunde Abridgement*, a comprehensive record of cases that established important
precedents.

buckler, but all's for the bar? Yet I had meant to have made my   105
son a barrister, not a barrater, but I see he means not to trouble
the law. I pray God the law trouble not him. Sirrah halter-sack!
Page. Sir?
Old Stukeley. Where is this towardly youth, your master? This lawyer,
this lawyer, I would fain see him, his learned mastership. Where is   110
he?
Page. It will not be long before he comes, sir. (OLD STUKELEY *goes*
again to the study.) If he be not cursed in his mother's belly, he'll
keep him out of the way; I would I were with him too, for I shall
have a basting worse then a hanging.   115
Old Stukeley. If he have so much as a candlestick, I am a traitor, but
an old hilt of a broken sword to set his light in. Not a standish, as
I am a man, but the bottom of a Temple pot, with a little old
sarsenet on it. Here's a fellow like to prove a lawyer, if sword and
buckler hold.   120

> Enter STUKELEY *at the further end of the stage.*

Stukeley. Boy, has Dick Blackstone sent home my new buckler? Rogue,
why stirs thou not?
Page. What a gaping keep you? A pox on't, my old master is here:
you'll ha't i' faith.
Stukeley. How long has he been here, rogue?   125
Page. This two hours.
Stukeley. Zounds, he has been taking an inventory of my household
stuff: all my bravery lies about the floor.
Old Stukeley. O, thou graceless boy, how dost thou bestow thy time?

> [STUKELEY] *kneels down*

Stukeley. Your blessing, good father.   130
Old Stukeley. O thou unblessed boy, thou wild, lewd, unthrift!

---

115. basting] *This ed.;* baiting *Q.*   116. candlestick] *This ed.;* candstick *Q.*   119.
on it] *This ed.;* in it *Q.*   129. SD.] *This ed.;* He kneels down *Q.*

---

106. *barrater*] quarreller (*OED sb* 5).

107. *halter-sack*] another expression for one who warrants hanging (*OED*); cf.
Pestle, 'If he were my son, I would hang him up by the heels, and flay him and salt
him, whoreson haltersack' (1.1.337–8).

115. *basting*] beating, cudgelling; cf. *Comedy of Errors,* 'Lest it make you choleric
and purchase me another dry basting' (2.2.62–3). *Q* has 'baiting', but even figuratively
the Page would not be 'baited', i.e. bitten by dogs, as in bear-baiting.

117. *standish*] a writing stand (*OED*); cf. Fletcher's *The Woman Hater,* 'Secretary,
fetch the gowne I use to read petitions in, and the standish I answer French Letters
with' (5.1.8–9).

119. *sarsenet on it*] sarsenet, a fine silk, would be 'on' (not *Q*'s 'in') the bottom of
the (upturned) pot.

Stukeley. How does my mother, sir, and all in Hampshire?
Old Stukeley. The worse to hear of thy demeanour here.
Stukeley. I am glad to hear of their good health; God continue it.
Old Stukeley. Thou graceless rake-hell! And is all my cost   135
    This five years' space here for thy maintenance,
    Spent in this sort, thou lewd misordered villain?
Stukeley. Sir, I am glad to see you look so well,
    I promise you it joys me at the heart.
    Boy, bring the chair and let my father sit,   140
    And if old Master Provey be within,
    I'll call him, sir, to bear you company.
Old Stukeley. Ay, ay, thou car'st not how thou stop'st my mouth,
    So that thou hear'st not of thy villainy.
    It is no marvel, though you write so oft   145
    For several sums to furnish you with books,
    Believe me, sir, your study's richly furnished.
Stukeley. This villain boy ne'er dresses up the chamber.
    I pray thee put these things out of the way.
Old Stukeley. I would I could cast thee out of the way,   150
    And so I should not see my shameless son.
    Be these the books, sir, that you look upon?
Stukeley. Father, this is as right a fox as e'er you saw, and has been as
    soundly tried as any blade in England.
Old Stukeley. I trust you'll make me account, sir, of my money?   155
Stukeley. Indeed, sir, he does rascand very fast in the hilts, and is a little
    crooked at the point.
Old Stukeley. Tom Stukeley, what a shame is this for thee,
    To see so many of thy countrymen,

---

141. Provey] *This ed.;* Provye *Q.*   153. this is] *Simpson;* this *Q.*   156. SH.]
Simpson; no new speaker Q.

132. *Hampshire*] Stukeley was from Devonshire; cf. *Alcazar* (5.1.136), where he
says he was born in London.

136. *five years' space*] the average age of entry to the Inns of Court was eighteen
(Simpson, p. 168), making this fictional Stukeley about twenty-three years old, consistent with his characterisation. The historical Stukeley was about forty when he married
and over fifty when he died at Alcazar.

156. *he does rascand very fast*] Commentators, including this one, have struggled
with Q's 'rascand'. Levinson offers *rescide*, to cut (*OED v*), which would not apply to
a sword's hilts; Simpson suggests 'shake', from the OE *raescian*; but hilts would not do
this 'fast', i.e. quickly (*OED adv* 6a). As many Elizabethan fencing terms were Italian
or Spanish, perhaps 'rascand' is a compositor's guess at *raschiare* or *rascar*, 'to scratch',
the idea being 'the hilts are scratched too easily'. This sits well with the weapon being
'a little crooked at the point' – his father having demanded an account of the money
spent, Stukeley is now saying it was a cheap sword.

hilts] often written in the plural while retaining the singular sense.

Of whom the world did ne'er expect thy hopes,   160
So forward and so towardly to the law,
And thou whose infancy did flatter me
With expectation of so many goods,
To prove a very changeling, and to follow
These ruffianly and wild disordered courses.   165
Stukeley. Nay, hark you, father, I pray you be content. I have done my
    goodwill, but it will not do. John a-Nokes and John a-Styles and I
    cannot cotton. O, this law French is worse than buttered mackerel,
    full of bones, full of bones, it sticks here, it will not down. *Aurum*
    potabile will not get it down. My grandfather bestowed as much of   170
    you as you have done of me, but of my conscience you were as I am:
    a true man to the house, you took nothing away with you.
Old Stukeley. O had thy grandsire been as kind to me
    As I have been to thee, thou wild lewd unthrift,
    I had done well.   175
Stukeley. Nay so you do, God be thanked. But hark you, father, there
    is a nearer way to the wood than all this, a nearer cut than scratch-
    ing for things out of a standish all a man's life, which I have found
    out. And if you will stick to me, I doubt not but you shall think I
    have bestowed my time well, and this it is: I am in possibility to   180
    marry alderman Curtis's daughter. Now, father, if you will open
    the bag of your affection and speak but a few good words for me
    to the old alderman, she's mine, horse and foot.
Old Stukeley. But with what colour can I speak for thee,
    Being so lewd and prodigal a spendthrift,   185
    A common quarreller, with shame I speak it,
    That I dare scarcely own thee with my credit?
Stukeley. Peace, good father, no more of that. Stick to me once. If you
    will but tickle the old fellow in the ear, look you, with a certain
    word called a jointure; ha, that same jointure, and a proper man   190

---

162. infancy] *This ed.; infancies Q.*

---

167. *John a-Nokes and John a-Styles*] stock names given as examples in legal discourse, counterparts of the American 'John Doe'.

168. *cotton*] 'get on' (*OED v¹* 5, earliest cit.).

law French] an old form of Norman French; the basis of many legal expressions still
in use, e.g. 'escheat', 'tort'.

169. *Aurum potabile*] 'drinkable gold', gold held in a state of minute subdivision in
some volatile oil, formerly in repute as a cordial (*OED*); cf. *Volpone* ''Tis *aurum pal-*
pabile, if not *potabile*' (1.4.73).

183. *horse and foot*] lit. 'both cavalry and infantry', fig. 'including everything'; cf.
Dekker, *Whore of Babylon*, 'your captaine and brave man is cal'd to the last reckoning, and is overthrown horse and foot' (2.1.89–91).

190. *jointure*] property held jointly by husband and wife, as a provision for the latter
in the event of her widowhood (*OED sb* 4a).

withal as I am, will draw you on a wench, as a squirrel's skin will
draw on a Spanish shoe.
Old Stukeley. Now afore God, Tom Stukeley, thy riots
Are so notorious in the city,
As I am much afraid the alderman   195
Will not be wrought to yield unto the match.
Stukeley. Ay, father, this is certain, but all that's nothing. I have the
wench's goodwill, and he must yield, 'spite of his heart. She's worth
forty thousand pound. O father, this is the right philosopher's
stone! True multiplication, I have found it!   200
Old Stukeley. Well, sirrah, come and go with me to supper,
Whither I'll send for a friend or two of mine
And take their better counsels in the matter.
Stukeley. I pray you let it be so. Sirrah boy, lock the door, and bring
my sword.   205
Page. I will, sir.

[*Exeunt*]

Scene 3

Enter at one door CROSS *the mercer, at another* [SPARING]
the vintner.

Cross. I ne'er heard such a murmur of a marriage,
Yet for my life I cannot meet a man
That soundly can report the certainty.
Sparing. I cannot meet a man in any place,
But still he hath this marriage in his mouth.   5
'This day', says one, 'tomorrow', says another,
Another says ''tis past', and he was there,
Another tells me that upon his knowledge
It is not yet this three days at the least.
I think the world is set a-madding, I.   10
Cross. What, Master Sparing the vintner? I pray God, sir, your smell
be as good as your taste.

206. SD.] *Simpson; not in Q.*

Scene 3] *This ed.;* Sc. iii. *Levinson; not in Q.*   OSD. SPARING.] *This ed.;* Spring Q
(Sc. 3).   4. SH.] *This ed.;* Spring Q *(Sc. 3).*

191. *squirrel's skin*] 'This figure of the shoeing horn is common in old ballads, &c.'
(Simpson).

Scene 3] The action takes place outside Sir Thomas Curtis's house.
OSD SPARING] In Q and the Simpson edition, the vintner starts off as Spring, but
changes to Sparing in Scene 5. I have used the Scene 5 name, for the sake of a pun at
5.42.

Sparing. Master Cross the mercer, is't even so, you have something in
the wind? I believe you have been brought to the book as well as
your neighbours. [*Aside*] Upon my life, he comes upon the same   15
business that I do, and perhaps he can tell me how the world goes
here. Well met, Master Cross.
Cross. What, Master Sparing, whither away?
Sparing. I was about to ask you as much. Come, I know you are hear-
kening to Alderman Curtis here.   20
Cross. O, you would fain have some company, I feel you! Go to, Tom
Stukeley shall have the wench, and helter-skelter the alderman's
bags shall pay for all.
Sparing. Art thou a true prophet?
Cross. I was a'dreamt tonight that he paid me all in double pistolets.   25
Sparing. I would I had mine in plain testerns.
Cross. Tut, beggarly payment, hang it.

    Enter SHARP *the cutler, and* BLUNT *the buckler-maker.*

What, more of the same covey, all birds of a feather.
Sparing. Sharp the cutler of Fleet Street, methinks, and Blunt of the
Strand, the buckler-maker.   30
Cross. Have at him, Blunt and Sharp, for sword and buckler, we are
for him.
Sharp. Well met, Master Sparing.
Sparing. So are you, Master Sharp.
Cross. What, Master Blunt, shall we lie at ward?   35
                                  Putting out his hand.
Blunt. I pray God we may, sir, to save ourselves by this marriage.
Sparing. Stay, here comes Tom Stukeley, and Jack Harbert.

    Enter STUKELEY *and* HARBERT *in their hose and doublets.*

Cross. What's the matter?
Stukeley. To speak it publicly, in such a presence,

15. SD. *Aside.*] *This ed.; not in Q.*   31. at him, Blunt] *This ed.; at him at Blunt Q.*

---

    25. *tonight*] last night; cf. *Romeo and Juliet*, 'I dreamt a dream tonight' (1.4.50).
pistolets] Spanish gold coins; cf. *Alchemist*, 'furnish'd with pistolets, and pieces of eight'
(3.3.15).
    26. *testerns*] coins worth about sixpence, from the 'teston' of Henry VIII's time as
debased and depreciated (tester *OED sb* 3); cf. Cooke's *Greene's Tu Quoque* 'A testerne
or a shilling to a servant that brings you a glasse of beere, bindes his hands to his lippes'
(sig. D3v).
    27. SD. BLUNT] As with the vintner (see n. 3.OSD) the buckler-maker has two
names. He starts off as Blunt, but with the subsequent introduction of a Constable
named 'Blurt' in Scene 5 (see n. 5.14 SD), he changes to 'Thump', possibly to avoid
confusion, with the correction not being made in the printer's copy (Wiggins, 'Things',
pp. 16–17). I adopt Scene 3's Blunt to retain the joke in 'have at him, Blunt and Sharp'
(3.31); there is no word-play on 'Thump'.
    35. *lie at ward*] remain on guard (lie *OED v¹* 4).

'He hath undone his daughter by the marriage'!   40
You are a most disgraceful idiot,
The greatest injury ere crossed my spirit
Could not have drawn so base a wrong from me.
Harbert. I spake it but in mirth, but since your snuff
Is so soon lighted, let it quench again.   45
Are you so tetchy, Stukeley, with a pox?
Stukeley. You are a slave thus to abuse me, Harbert.
Harbert. You are a vain fool, Stukeley, so to call me.
Stukeley. Enforce me not, I prithee, at this time.
Harbert. Enforce you, 's blood, you will not be enforced.   50
Stukeley. Harbert, your blood's too hot.
Harbert. You have brought me into the air to cool it then.
Stukeley. Thou hast almost tempted me beyond my strength.
Harbert. If I wished that, I would be your evil spirit.
Cross. Here's sword and buckler by me. Call for clubs.   55
Sparing. So we may beat out the brains of our business.
Sharp. We come in an ill time.
Blunt. So I fear.
Cross. How now, Sharp, is your edge taken off?
Sharp. I am blunted with my neighbour, in faith.   60
Stukeley. Thou cam'st on purpose, Harbert, to disgrace me.
Harbert. Sirrah, your mother's son lies in his throat.
Stukeley. I pray thee stand not thus.
Harbert. To underprop your choler lest it fall.
Stukeley. Thou hast found a time to triumph on my courage when I   65
am gyved. Durst thou else have said thus much?
Harbert. When will ye be unfettered?
Stukeley. Where'er I meet you next, I'll have you by the ears.
Harbert. Stukeley, you shall not. I'll keep you from my ears by the
length of my rapier.   70
Stukeley. Say no more.

Enter CURTIS, [LADY CURTIS, NELL] *and the rest.*

46. tetchy] *Simpson;* tetche *Q.* 71. SD.] *This ed.;* Enter Curteis, Mother Bride, and the rest *Q.*

46. *tetchy*] petulant, short-tempered; cf. *Richard III*, 'Tetchy and wayward was thy infancy' (4.4.169).
55. *Call for clubs*] the common rallying cry to apprentices, either to put down a civil disturbance or to start one; cf. the Mayor of London in *1 Henry VI*, 'I'll call for clubs if you will not away' (1.4.82).
64.] Text may be missing here, as Harbert appears to be answering a question. Perhaps the previous line was meant to be 'I pray thee, why stand'st thou thus?'
66. *gyved*] shackled (*OED* ppl); cf. Webster, *Appius and Virginia* (1624), 'Appius, and Marcus Clodius in prison, fettered and gyved' (5.1.2 SD); *Romeo and Juliet*, 'Like a poor prisoner in his twisted gyves' (2.1.224).

Nell. Where is my husband, where is Master Stukeley? Alas my heart,
    upon my wedding to fall out thus.
Lady Curtis. For God's love, good son Stukeley and Master Harbert,
    pacify yourself.   75
Curtis. Fie, Tom! Fie, fie! Bones a dod, man, what coil is here? What
    mean you, sir, why rise you from the table?
Stukeley. We rise for nothing but to talk a little.
    (*Aside*) Harbert, look to it, by this blessèd day
    I'll be with you.   80
Harbert. I would the day were come,
    But you take day still with your creditors.
Sparing. I do not like that.
Cross. What dost thou mean?
Sparing. That he should take longer day with his creditors.   85
Lady Curtis. For God's love, good son Stukeley, be content.
Curtis. God's blest, Captain Harbert, bones of dod man, be content.
Harbert. We are good friends with all my heart.
    The dining room, sir, growing somewhat hot,
    We stepped out hither but to take the air.   90
Nell. I pray thee, good sweetheart, be not so angry,
    And, Captain Harbert, let me tell you this:
    Knowing the disposition of your friend,
    You might have spared the speeches that you used.
Harbert. If they have any way displeased you, I am very sorry. But let   95
    him take them how he will, I care not.
Stukeley. Harbert, I'll make you eat your words.
Curtis. God's me blest, let's to dinner again, all's well, all's well. Come,
    come, come!
Lady Curtis. Come, Master Harbert, you shall be my prisoner.   100
    Daughter, take you your husband by the hand,
    And let us in to dinner.
    [*Exeunt* STUKELEY, NELL, CURTIS, LADY CURTIS, HARBERT.]
Cross. Here's a wedding indeed! I perceive by this that we come in ill
    season for our money.
Sparing. I would I had my debt before Harbert and he meet.   105
Sharp. Why so, Master Sparing?
Sparing. Because if they two meet, I fear one of them pays for it. They
    are two tall gentlemen as England yields.

---

78. SH.] *before previous sentence in* Q.   102. SD.] *This ed.;* Exit Q.

---

   76. *coil*] commotion, turmoil; cf. *Comedy of Errors*, 'What a coil is there, Dromio?'
(3.1.48).
   82. *take day*] have a business appointment (take *OED v* 67).
   87. *God's blest*] short for 'by God's blessèd mother', a common expression.

Blunt. Well, let's away for this, and come tomorrow the sooner.
Cross. Content.   110

                              [*Exeunt.*]

                              Scene 4

            Enter VERNON, *with* HAMDON *and* RIDLEY, *two of*
                            his friends.

Hamdon. If not at our requests, yet, gentle friend,
    For your own safety, change your former mind.
    Have you not wealth? Why should you leave the land?
Ridley. Are you not here of credit in the city?
    Why should you then betray your forward hopes   5
    Upon a wilful and uncertain humour?
Vernon. I know that my estate is sound and good,
    As on the one side strengthened with rich friends,
    And on the other well establishèd
    By the assistance of a private stock.   10
    Yet what is this, or all external pomp
    That otherwise is incident to men,
    If the mind want that comfort it should have?
    Believe me, gentlemen, it is as music
    To men in prison, or as dainty meat   15
    Brought to a sick man, whose afflicting pain
    Hath neither left him appetite nor taste.
Hamdon. How springs this discontent? Wherein lies
    This gall of conscience that disturbs you so?
Ridley. We are your friends. Show us your inward grief,   20
    And we will either find a remedy
    Or, sharing every one a part of it,
    So lessen it, and it shall lose his force.
Hamdon. Is it for sorrow you forsook your bride,
    And gave your interest to another man?   25
Ridley. You hit the nail upon the head; 'tis that
    And nothing else that breeds this discontent.
Vernon. Be not deceived. I did it by advice,
    Nor do I any way repent me of it.

110. SD.] *Simpson; not in Q.*

Scene 4] *This ed.;* Sc. iv. *Levinson; not in Q.*   23. lose] *Simpson;* loose *Q.*   24. Is it]
Simpson; In it *Q.*

Scene 4] The action continues in London.
16. *afflicting*] painful, distressing (*OED a,* earliest cit.).

She loved not me, albeit I honoured her,   30
And such a match, what were it but to join
Fire and water? Marriage is no toy
To be desirèd where there is dislike,
And therefore weighing his deserts with mine,
Her love to him, and his to her again,   35
I rather chose to benefit my friend,
Whereby two might be pleased, than greedily
Assuming what I might, displease all three.
Hamdon. What then hath weaned you from your country's love?
Vernon. Nor that, nor anything. I know not what.   40
Yet whilst I breathe this native air of mine,
Methinks I suck in poison to my heart,
And whilst I tread upon this English earth,
It is as if I set my careless feet
Upon a bank, where underneath is hid   45
A bed of crawling serpents. Any place
But only here, methinks, would make me happy,
Say 'twere the meanest cottage in the world.
But here I am accursed, and here I live
As one deprivèd both of soul and sense,   50
Which strange conceit from whence it should proceed,
I cannot utter, other than from this:
That I am fired with a desire to travel
And see the fashions, state and qualities
Of other countries. Therefore, if you love me,   55
Offer no further to resist in me
The settled resolution of my mind.
Ridley. Yet since you needs will leave us and the realm,
Go not to Ireland. The country's rude
And full of tumult and rebellious strife.   60
Rather make choice of Italy or France.
Vernon. My word is passed unto a gentleman,
With whom I will not break: and here he comes.

Enter HARBERT *and another* CAPTAIN.

---

62. passed] *This ed.; past Q.*

61. *choice of Italy or France*] an indication that this play is Henslowe's *Stewtly* of November 1596 (see pp. 34–8). Ireland was indeed 'full of tumult and rebellious strife' at that time, but, after retaking Fort Crozen in Brittany in late 1594, the English withdrew completely from France for the remainder of Elizabeth's reign, except for a small force sent to Picardy in October of 1596. English forces were never committed to Italy during Tudor times, so the distinction made by Ridley fits a play written 1595–96 (see R. B. Wernham, *After the Armada: Elizabethan England and the Struggle for Western Europe*, Oxford, 1984, pp. 557–8).

Harbert. Sir, as I told you, even at dinner time,
    His fury was so great, as he must needs   65
    Rise from the table to confer with me
    About my speeches, which I did maintain,
    And sure if place had served, we there had fought.
Captain. I would I could devise to make you friends,
    The rather for I hear he is appointed   70
    To have a charge in this our Irish expedition.
Harbert. It is no matter, Harbert fears him not.
    I make as little reckoning of my blood
    As he of his, and will at any time,
    Or when he dares, meet him upon that quarrel.   75
Vernon. Captain, well met.
Harbert. Master Vernon, we stay for you.
    Our horses half an hour ago were ready
    And we had backed them, but we lacked your company.
Vernon. Some conference with these gentlemen my friends   80
    Made me neglect mine hour. But when you please,
    I now am ready to attend on you.
Harbert. It is well done. We will away forthwith;
    Saint Albans, though the day were further spent,
    We may well reach to bed tonight.   85
Vernon. Kind friends, I now must bid ye both farewell.
Hamdon. Nay, we will see you mounted ere we part.

                                           Exeunt.

Scene 5

Enter CURTIS *and his* CASHIER.

Curtis. Sirrah, what men are those that stay without?
Cashier. Some that would speak with Master Stukeley, sir.
Curtis. Know'st what their business is, or whence they come?
Cashier. Tradesmen they are, and of the city, sir,
    But what their business is I cannot tell.   5

---

72. SH.] *This ed.;* Ham. *Q;* Harb. *Simpson.*

Scene 5] *This ed.;* Sc. v. *Levinson; not in* Q.   OSD. CASHIER] *This ed.;* Casher *Q.*
2. SH.] *This ed.;* Cash. *Q.*

---

72 SH. Simpson correctly assigns this speech to Harbert, rather than *Q*'s *Ham.*
79. *backed*] mounted (*OED v* 10); cf. 1 *Henry IV*, 'That roan shall be my throne /
Well, I will back him straight' (2.4.70–1).

Scene 5] The action occurs at Sir Thomas Curtis's house.

Curtis. Upon my life some creditors of his,
  That hearing of his matching with my daughter,
  Come to demand some money which he owes them.
  It is even so. They know he hath received
  His marriage money; they perceive he's flush,   10
  And mean to share with him ere all be gone.
  I'll see the sequel: here he comes himself,
  And with him–O the body of me–
  Half the tradesmen in the town, I think.

> *Enter* STUKELEY *with bags of money. After him thronging*
> *Arthur* CROSS *the mercer, John* SPARING *the vintner,*
> *William* SHARP, [BLUNT *the buckler-maker, George* HAZARD
> *the*] *tennis-keeper, Henry* CRACK *the fencer, and Geoffrey*
> BLURT, *Bailiff of Finsbury, with written notes in their hands.*

Stukeley. Now, ye slaves, a man can no sooner step   15
  Into a little wealth, but presently
  You'll have the scent of him, you'll visit him.
  Here's bills enough; had I now as many
  Shot and pikes, I would with a valiant band
  Of mine own subjects march among the Irish.   20
  But let me see. Deliver your petition,
  I'll prove an honest man a'the Chancery.
                                    CROSS *delivers his bill.*
Curtis. Little law, I fear, and lesser conscience.
Stukeley. The gross sum of your debt, sir?
Cross. Two hundred pound.   25
Stukeley. For what?
Cross. For silks and velvets, sir.
Stukeley. Your name?
Cross. Arthur Cross, the mercer.

---

14. SD. BLUNT *the buckler-maker, George* HAZARD *the*] *This ed.*; Tho, Thump, Geo, haz, *Q*; Tho. Thump, Geo. Hazard *Simpson.*

14 SD. BLUNT] the buckler-maker's name changes here to Thomas Thump in *Q*, but I have retained the Scene 3 name (see n. 3.27 SD). Thump, like Blunt, is apt for the profession, and appears to be traditional–in *2 Henry VI*, Shakespeare names an armourer's apprentice Peter Thump, although he is John David in Hall and Holinshed (see n. 2.92).
  BLURT] An onomatopoeic word, the Elizabethan equivalent of the 'raspberry'. 'Blurt' was associated with constables, as shown by the title character of Dekker's (or Middleton's) *Blurt, Master Constable* (1601), and Hilts's protestations to Constable Tobie Turfe in Jonson's *Tale of a Tub*, 'You'll clap a dog of waxe as soone, Old Blurt. / Come, spare not me, Sir; I am no mans wife' (2.2.62–3).
  22. *Chancery*] one of England's three principal courts, presided over by the Lord Chancellor, where cases of equity were heard.

Stukeley. Well Master Cross, the first syllable of your name might have   30
   spared ye this labour. But all is one, there's your money.
                                                            [*Exit* CROSS.]
Curtis. Two hundred pounds? So there's an end of that.
   I will be sworn I got it not so soon.
Stukeley. Your title to my purse?
Sparing. Thirty pounds, sir.   35
Stukeley. For what?
Sparing. For tavern suppers, and for quarts of wine.
Stukeley. O, at the Greyhound in Fleet Street.
Sparing. Ay, sir, the same.
Stukeley. Your name is Sparing?   40
Sparing. John Sparing, sir, the vintner.
Curtis. You spared not him when you did score so much.
Stukeley. There, Master Sparing, would I were your scholar
   That I might learn to spare as well as you.
                                                      Exit SPARING.
Curtis. That will ne'er be until it be too late.   45
Stukeley. Now, sir, to you.
Sharp. Your servant sir, William Sharp, for bilboes, foxes and Toledo
   blades.
Stukeley. What?
Sharp. Forty marks.   50
Stukeley. You cut somewhat deep, Master Sharp, but there's a preser-
   vative for a green wound.
                                                         [*Exit* SHARP.]
Curtis. Beshrew me, but it wounds me; what preservative have I for
   that?
Stukeley. Of whence are you?   55
Blunt. Thomas Blunt, sir, the buckler-maker of Saint Giles.
Stukeley. The sum thereunto belonging?
Blunt. Fifteen pound, sir, for broad-lined bucklers, beside steel pikes.

---

31. SD.] *This ed.; not in* Q.   52. SD] *This ed.; not in* Q.   56. SH.] *This ed.;* Thu.
Q *(Sc. 5).*   Thomas Blunt] *This ed.;* Tho Thumpe Q; Thomas Thump *Simpson.*

---

31. SD.] Q has no exit for Cross here, but, as Sparing, Blunt and Blurt exit after
being paid, the other creditors are obviously meant to do likewise.
   42. score] write up a bill or tally (*OED v* 10a); cf. *1 Henry IV,* 'Score a pint of
bastard in the Half-moon' (2.5.26–7).
   46–7. *Toledo blades*] the best weapons came from Bilbao (see n. 2.92) and Toledo;
cf. Brainworm selling a sword in *Every Man in His Humour,* ''tis a most pure Toledo'
(F, 2.4.80–1); see also Edelman, *Military,* pp. 328–30.
   52. *green*] new, unhealed (*OED a* 10).
   56. *Saint Giles*] a poor area of London at the time, south of what is now New
Oxford Street (Sugden).

Curtis. Body of me, half the money would arm five tall fellows for the
    wars.   60

Stukeley. Blunt, I will not answer you with the like violence, for if I
    should, the broadest buckler that e'er you made would not defend
    you from being bankrupt.

Blunt. I thank your worship.

                                             Exit [BLUNT].

Stukeley. Are you sick of the yellows too?   65

Hazard. Not so sick, sir, but I hope to have a child's part by your last
    will and testament.

Curtis. There's a knave. He thinks after they are paid he means to go
    and hang himself. What's his legacy?

Stukeley. For tennis balls when the French ambassador was here,   70
    thirteen pound! Is it so much?

Hazard. Just so much with the fouling of fair linen when you were hot.

Curtis. Fair linen? Hoy day! your fair linen wipes him of a good deal
    of money.

Stukeley. George Hazard, I take it that's your name?   75

Hazard. My name is so, sir.

Stukeley. George, you have hit the hazard.

                    Gives him money. [*Exit* HAZARD.]

Curtis. It was a hazard whether he would have hit or no, but for my
    money.

Stukeley. What else?   80

---

61. Blunt] *This ed.;* Thumpe *Q;* Thump *Simpson.* 63. bankrupt] *This ed.;* banker-
out *Q.* 64. SD. BLUNT] *This ed.;* Thumpe *Q;* Thump *Simpson.* 77. SD. *Exit*
HAZARD] *This ed.; not in Q.*

---

    65. *yellows*] lit. jaundice, but usually applied to livestock; fig. jealousy (*OED*). Its
relevance to Hazard wanting payment is not clear, unless Stukeley is commenting on
Hazard's appearance.

    70–3. *French . . . linen*] Tennis originated in France, and was known as a French
game. Fashionable young men were expected to keep an extra shirt (of 'fair linen') at
the court, so as to be able to change out of their sweat-stained clothes, as advised by
Dekker in *The Gull's Hornbook*: 'Discourse . . . how often you have sweat in the
tennis-court with that great lord – for indeed sweating together in France (I mean the
society of tennis!) is an argument of most dear affection even between noblemen and
peasants' (p. 94). Cf. Prince Hal to Poins, 'Or to bear the inventory of thy shirts as one
for superfluity, and another for use. But that the tennis-court keeper knows better than
I, for it is a low ebb of linen with thee when thou keepest not racket there' (*2H4*,
2.2.16–20).

    77. *hazard*] A hazard was an opening in the inner wall of a tennis court; one means
of scoring was to hit the ball through it; cf. *Henry V*, 'We will in France, by God's
grace, play a set / Shall strike his father's crown into the hazard' (1.2.262–3); see also
Shakespeare's England: An Account of the Life & Manners of His Age, v. 2, Oxford,
1916, pp. 459–63.

Crack. I hope, sir, your worship hath not forgot Harry Crack the fencer,
    for forfeits and veneys given upon a wager at the ninth button of
    your doublet, thirty crowns.
Curtis. Crack his crown and that makes one and thirty.
Stukeley. Well, Crack, I have no way to defend your thrust, but by this   85
    downright blow.
                                                            Gives him money.
Crack. I take it double, sir, an't please you.
Stukeley. Let it suffice. You're valiant, and my choler past.
    More clients yet? Your name?
                                                            [*Exit* CRACK.]
Blurt. Geoffrey Blurt, sir, Bailiff of Finsbury, for frays and bloodshed   90
    in the theatre fields, five marks.
Curtis. Body of me, ne'er a surgeon in this town would have asked
    more.
Stukeley. Blurt, I have no reason to pay thee whole.
Blurt. Why so, an't please you?   95
Stukeley. Jack Dudley and I were halves in that action. Take part of him.
Blurt. Alas sir, he's in Finsbury jail for hurting a man behind the wind-
    mills last Saturday.
Stukeley. Why then belike you have good pawn for your money.   100
Blurt. I would we had, sir.
Stukeley. Well, I see your dogged natures; a good sword-and-buckler
    man is of no reckoning amongst ye. But let the sheriff think, when
    he hath lost Jack Dudley, he loseth twenty mark a year as good fee

---

82. veneys] *This ed.;* vennyes *Q.*   87. an't] *This ed.;* and *Q;* an' 't *Simpson (& l. 95).*
89. SD.] *This ed.; not in Q.*   104. loseth] *Simpson;* looseth *Q.*

---

82. *veneys*] fencing bouts, from the French *venue* (veny *OED sb² 2*); cf. *Merry
Wives,* 'I bruised my shin th' other day, with playing at sword and dagger with a master
of fence, three veneys for a dish of stewed prunes' (1.1.263–6).
    90–1. *Finsbury . . . theatre fields*] The London district of Finsbury, north of Crip-
plegate and Moorgate, was an open field in Elizabethan times, a favourite walk for
citizens and their wives and the site of many a fray. The Theatre and the Curtain
stood nearby.
    98–9. *behind the windmills*] In Chapman's *Sir Giles Goosecap* (1602), Giles
remarks, 'I love daylight well, I thought it went away faster than it heeded, and run
after it into Finsbury to see the windmills go' (3.2.259–61).
    102–3. *sword-and-buckler man*] Fencing with sword and buckler was associated
with ruffians and the lower classes, those prone to frequent brawling; hence Hotspur's
dismissal of Prince Hal as a 'sword-and-buckler Prince of Wales' (*1H4,* 1.3.228); cf.
John Florio's Italian–English phrase book, *His Firste Fruites* (London, 1578, sig. E1v),
'What weapon is that buckler? A clownish dastardly weapon, not for a Gentleman';
see also Edelman, *Military,* pp. 61–2.
    104–5. *fee simple*] Fee simple, in law, is total ownership, able to be passed on to
one's heirs. Dudley, Stukeley's habitual opponent, will not be doing any more fighting,
so the sheriff is losing a permanent source of income in fines.

simple as e'er a baron in England holds. There's your amercia-   105
ments, and give Jack Dudley this from me to pay his fees.
Blurt. I thank ye, sir.

Exit BLURT.

Curtis. I would he had broke his pate ere he went, in earnest of a new
reckoning. Ah son, son, thou hast deceived my opinion, my daugh-
ter cast away, and I have bequeathed my money to a prodigal.   110
Stukeley. Father, why so, shall I not pay my debts?
Curtis. Not with my money, son, not with my money.
Stukeley. It is mine own, and Stukeley of his own
Will be as frank as shall the emperor.
I scorn this trash, betrayer of men's souls;   115
I'll spurn it with my foot, and with my hand
Rain showers of plenty on this barren land.
Were it my fortune could exceed the clouds,
Yet would I bear a mind surmounting that.
Father, you have enough for you, and for your store,   120
When mine is gone you must provide me more.

Exit [STUKELEY].

Curtis. Is it even so? The captain's words are true:
He is a spendthrift, but I'll keep him short.
He gets not a denier more than he hath.

Enter LADY CURTIS *and* OLD STUKELEY.

Lady Curtis. Husband, you are sent for in all the haste   125
To the Guildhall, about the soldiers
That are to be dispatched for Ireland.
Curtis. I may be sent for, wife, whither I will,
And 'tis no matter greatly where I go.
Lady Curtis. Why so, I pray?   130
Curtis. Would you e'er have thought
That taverns, fencers, bailiffs and such like,
Should by the fruits of my late sitting up
And early rising have maintained their state?
Old Stukeley. What mean ye, brother Curtis?   135
Curtis. Ah, brother Stukeley,
My meaning, had you been but here even now,
You might have scanned without my utterance.

---

112. SH.] *Simpson*; Stuk. *Q.*   117. showers] *Simpson*; shewers *Q.*   120. enough
for you] *This ed.*; enough for your *Q.*   121. SD.] *This ed.*; Exit *Q.*

---

105. *amerciaments*] fines or penalties set according to the 'mercy' of the aggrieved
party (*OED sb* 1).

124. *denier*] a French coin worth one-twelfth of a sou (*OED sb³*); cf. *Taming of the
Shrew*, 'You will not pay for the glasses you have burst? No, not a denier' (Ind.1.6–7).

Here was item, upon item, such a crew
As I ne'er saw one man indebted to.   140
[Exeunt]

Scene 6

Enter [STUKELEY'S LIEUTENANT,] ENSIGN, *Drum and soldiers.*

Stukeley's Lieutenant. Here stay we, soldiers, till the hour be come
Our captain did appoint to meet with us–
The valiant Stukeley–we shall have a guide,
There's not a better in the regiment.
It is not one will say unto his men,   5
'Give you assault upon the enemy',
But 'follow me', and so himself will be
The foremost man that shall begin the fight.
Nor will he nicely creep into the town
When we are lodged within the dampish field,   10
But voluntarily partake your toil
And of his private purse relieve your wants.
Ensign. Lieutenant, he's a gallant gentleman.
We know it well, and he that is not willing
To venture life with him, I would for my part   15
He might end his days worser than the pestilence.
Stukeley's Lieutenant. Nay if you look but on his mind,
Much more occasion shall ye find to love him.
He's liberal, and goes not to the wars
To make a gain of his poor soldiers' spoil,   20
But spoil the foe to make his soldiers gain.
And here he comes: stand all in good array!

Enter STUKELEY *and his wife* [NELL].

Stukeley. I prithee, wife, importune me no more.
Might tears persuade or words prevail with me,
Thy tears and words ere this had won me straight.   25
But, 'tis not thou nor any power but his

---

140. SD.] *This ed. not in Q.*
Scene 6] *This ed.;* Sc. vi. *Levinson; not in Q.*   OSD. STUKELEY'S LIEUTENANT]
Simpson; Stukely, Lieft. *Q.*   1. SH.] *This ed.;* Lief., Lieu. *Q;* Lieu., Lieut. *Simpson.*
7. But 'follow me'] *Simpson;* follow me *Q.*   25. straight] *Simpson;* state *Q.*

Scene 6] The action continues in London. According to Nell (6.30) it is three days
since the wedding, but off-stage time is rarely consistent in plays of this type. How and
when law-student Stukeley became a captain is not specified.

     That has that power to take away my life
     That can abridge my purpose. I will go.
Nell. Shall then my joys have an end e'er they begin?
     And shall the term of three days being wife,   30
     For ever after cause a widowhood?
     We scarce are joined together and must part,
     We scarce are warm within our nuptial bed,
     And you forsake me there to freeze alone;
     O do not so, and if you ever loved,   35
     Or if you never loved, yet in regard
     Of my affection, leave me not so soon.
Stukeley. Good Lord, that thou wilt still importune me!
     Have I not said I undertake this task,
     Only to make thee great?
Nell.   But I desire   40
     To be no more than what I am already,
     So by your absence I be made no less.
Stukeley. But that contents not me. It is not chambering,
     Now I have beauty to be dallying with,
     Nor pampering of my self with belly cheer,
     Now I have got a little worldly pelf,   45
     That is the end or levels of my thought.
     I must have honour, honour is the thing
     Stukeley doth thirst for, and to climb the mount
     Where she is seated, gold shall be my footstool.   50
Nell. But there are many dangers by the way
     And hasty climbers quickly catch a fall.
Stukeley. He soonest loseth that despairs to win.
     But I have no such prejudicial fear,
     If there be any shall outlive the brunt   55
     Of raging war, or purchase dignity,
     I am persuaded to be one of those.
     If all miscarry, yet it will not grieve,
     Or grieve the less to die with company.
Nell. That name of death already martyrs me.   60
Stukeley. Tut, never fear, and if I chance to die,
     Thou being a lusty widow, there's enough
     Will gladly sue to be received of thee.
     The worst is, I confess, I leave thee poor,
     As taking with me all the jewels thou hast   65
     And all the coin was given me for thy dower.
     But I do leave thee with a wealthy father
     And one that will not see thee want, I know;

---

46. *pelf*] wealth, with the implication of 'ill-gotten gains' (*OED sb* 3).

Beside, thou hast a jointure of such lands,
As I am born unto, and therefore cease,   70
And let me seal thy lips up with this kiss.
Nell. Stay but a day or two and then depart.
Stukeley. Are not my soldiers ready? What a shame
Were it to send them forward and myself
Come lagging after, like to one that fears   75
Or went unwillingly unto the wars.
As thou respects me, talk no more to me.
Nell. Am I so odious that I may not speak?
Well I have listened when you talked ere now,
Or words had been the harvest of your hope.   80
But since to silence I am so enjoined,
I would my life might likewise have an end.
Stukeley. March hence away, or still there will be cast
Some let or other to detract our haste.

      As they are marching, enter CURTIS *and* OLD STUKELEY.

Curtis. Bones a dod, man, lay down thy tabor sticks   85
And hear me speak, or with my dudgeon dagger
I'll play a fit of mirth upon thy pate.
Why hear me, Tom, hear me son Stukeley, ha!
What, here today, and gone tomorrow? See,
Thy wife laments, canst thou behold her weep?   90
Stukeley. Sound drums, I say, I will not hear a word.
Old Stukeley. Wilt thou not hear thy father, graceless boy?
Stukeley. Father, unless you mean I shall be thought
A traitor to her majesty, a coward,
A sleepy dormouse and a carpet-squire,   95
Mix not my forward summer with sharp breath,
Nor intercept my purpose, being good.
Old Stukeley. I come not, wilful boy, as a reprover
Of any virtuous action thou intends,
But to reprove thy lack of husbandry   100

---

75. like to one] *Simpson*; like one *Q*.   76. unto the wars] *Simpson*; unto wars *Q*.
86. dudgeon] *This ed.*; Dudgen *Q*.

75. *like to one*] The verse in this scene is very regular, so *Q*'s unmetrical 'like one'
is probably a compositor's error.
77. *respects*] a common form of the second person singular (Abbot, p. 242; *Alcazar*,
n. 1.1.135).
86. *dudgeon dagger*] dudgeon (boxwood) was most favoured by turners for the
handles of knives and daggers (*OED sb¹* 2); cf. *Macbeth*, 'I see thee still / And on thy
blade and dudgeon gouts of blood' (2.1.45–6).
95. *carpet-squire*] a phoney squire, one more at home in a (carpeted) lady's boudoir
(carpet *OED sb6* a).

And the unthrifty courses thou hast used.
Learn to be sober, and not rashly thus
To rush into affairs of such great moment.
Stukeley. Father, I know not what you term rashness,
But any time since I was of the skill   105
Or strength to wield a sword, I vowed in heart
To be a soldier, and the time now serves
And now my vow shall be accomplishèd.
For any thing betwixt my wife and me,
We are agreed, however sour cheer   110
Do at our parting show the contrary.
If you as well as she can be persuaded,
Why so. If not, sound drums, I will not hear no more.
Curtis. Nay Tom, son Tom, thou art deceived in me.
I am not grieved that thou shouldst serve thy prince   115
Nor do I take exceptions at thy mind,
So long as honour is thy object, Tom.
But that without our knowledge thou departs
And on the sudden, body of me, 'tis that
That strikes a discontentment in us all.   120
Stukeley. I cannot help it, sir. With all my heart
And in all reverend duty of a son
I take my farewell, fathers, of you both,
Thus much entreating: if I ne'er return,
Ye would have both a care unto my wife.   125
                    [*Exeunt* STUKELEY *and soldiers.*
            Manent OLD STUKELEY, CURTIS, NELL.]
Old Stukeley. Well, brother Curtis, hope the best of him,
He may return a comfort to us all.
And were a not my son, I would commend
His resolution, 'tis heroical.
Curtis. There's no remedy now but patience,   130
But were the bargain to begin again
I would be twice advised ere I'd bestow
My daughter so. Iwis, so large a sum
Is more than I had thought should fly with wings

---

125. SD.] *This ed.;* Exit Q.   131. to begin] *Simpson;* to be begin Q.

---

109. *For*] regardless of.

113. *will not hear no more*] see n. 1.8.

118. *departs*] See n. 6.77.

128. *a not*] he not, a common construction; cf. *Much Ado*, 'Is a not approved in the height a villain' (4.1.302), and Ophelia's song in *Hamlet*, 'And will a not come again' (4.5.188).

133. *Iwis*] certainly, from Old English; cf. *Taming of the Shrew*, 'Iwis it is not half-way to her heart' (1.1.62).

Of vain expenses into Ireland.   135
But all is one. Come, daughter, never mourn,
I will not see thee want whilst I do live.
Old Stukeley. I hope she hath the like conceit of me.
Then comfort, girl, fear no extremity.

                                                          Exeunt.

                              Scene 7

        Enter O'NEILL, O'HANLON *and* MACKENER [*softly as by night*].

O'Neill. O'Hanlon.
O'Hanlon.   Ow.
O'Neill.   Tread softly on the stones,
The water tells us we are near the town.
Neil Mackener, come on, fix all our eyes
Upon the walls of this bewitchèd town
That harbours such a sort of English churls,   5
To see if any signal be set out
Where we shall enter to surprise Dundalk.
Mackener. O'Neill, speak softly, we are near the walls.

Scene 7] *This ed.*; Sc. vii a. *Levinson; not in Q.* OSD.] *subst. Q. softly as by night*]
Q (alt. Sc. 7). 1a. SH. *O'Neill*] *This ed.*; Oneale, One., Neale, Onele, On. *Q.*
1b. SH. *O'Hanlon*] *This ed.*; O Hamlon, Ham., Han. *Q*; Hanlon *Simpson.*

Scene 7] This is the first of six scenes set in Ireland; the locale is by the walls of
Dundalk. In *Q* it is followed by an alternative version, written in 'stage-Irish' dialect;
see p. 34 and Appendix III.
    OSD. O'NEILL] Those who managed to work out the Moroccan names in *The
Battle of Alcazar* have a new treat in store for them: the range of names given to the
same person by chroniclers and modern historians of Ireland is just as confusing.
Although *Q* is consistent with 'O'Neale', I follow the majority of modern texts in using
'O'Neill' for the famed Ulster rebel.
    O'HANLON] a south Ulster chieftain, whose lands Shane O'Neill plundered after he
returned from England in 1567 (Jonathan Bardon, *A History of Ulster*, Dundonald,
1992, p. 78); he would not have been fighting alongside O'Neill at Dundalk. In naming
O'Neill's confederates, the dramatist appears to have chosen Irish families that had
some association with him, regardless of actual significance. The English traveller Fynes
Moryson, who served as chief secretary to the Lord Deputy of Ireland Sir Charles Blount
from 1600 to 1603, writes in his *Itinerary*, 'Shane (or John) Oneale succeeding his
father, by killing his brother Matthew, and vexing his father to death, was cruell and
barbarous, and tyrannically challenged the neighbour lords to be his subjects' (sig.
Cc1v). Amongst the names then listed are 'O Hanlon, O Cahan . . . [and] O Quin' (see
n. 7.15).
    MACKENER] In his *Historie of Ireland* (p. 129), Campion writes of 'Secretary Neale
Mac Connor'; the Act of Attainder passed by the Irish parliament after Shane's death
names 'a barbarous clerk, named Neyll Mac Kever, whom hee [Shane] had in most reputation, and used for his secretory' (*Statutes*, p. 327).

The English sentinels do keep good watch.
If they descry us all our labour's lost.   10
O'Hanlon. Our labour's lost, for we can see no sign
Of any white that hangeth o'er the wall
Where we shall enter by our spies within.
O'Neill. A plague upon the drowsy drunken slaves,
Brian MacPhelim, and that Neil O'Quin,   15
Who being drunk or sleeping with his drabs,
Forget the business that they have in hand.
Mackener. O'Neill, be patient and suspect the worst.
They may unto the English be betrayed,
Or else perceiving strong watch everywhere,   20
Dare not approach the walls or gates for fear.
O'Hanlon. O'Neill, thy secretary says very true.
The English, knowing all the power so near,
Will be more watchful than their custom is,
So both our spies and friends dare not assay   25
To hang out signal, nor come near the port.
O'Neill. Why so it is. I know within Dundalk
I have ten friends to one the English have
(I mean of townsmen), but sure policy
Cannot by might attain our entrance in   30
That we might cut off all the English heads
Of theirs that watch, and theirs that sleep in beds.
Let us withdraw unto our troops again –
Tomorrow comes O'Cahan with galloglass

---

11. labour's] *conj. Levinson;* labors *Q.*   15. O'Quin] *This ed.;* O Quyme *Q.*
34. O'Cahan] *This ed.;* O Kane *Q;* O'Kane *Simpson.* galloglass] *This ed.;*
Gallinglasse *Q.*

---

15. *Brian MacPhelim*] Brian MacPhelim *Baccagh* [the lame] O'Neill would hardly
have been one of Shane O'Neill's spies inside Dundalk. This lord, of the Clandeboy
O'Neills (see n. 12.25), was one of Shane's major Ulster antagonists, and was knighted
by Queen Elizabeth, who, upon Shane's death, did 'wryt our letters of thanks' to him
and some other Irish lords (*SP Ire.* v. 21, 6 Jul. 1567). However, MacPhelim strongly
opposed English plans for the plantation of Ulster, and was hanged in 1574 (Connolly,
pp. 413–14).
    Neil O'Quin] Q's 'Neale O Quyme' must be a compositor's guess, and one cannot
say what name was intended; the most likely candidate is 'O'Quin', a family long associated with the Glens of Antrim (Edward MacLysaght, *Irish Families: Their Names,
Arms & Origins*, Dublin, 1957, p. 251). O'Quin appears in Moryson's list of those
whom Shane had oppressed (see n. 7.OSD).
    34. *O'Cahan*] The O'Cahans 'were closely allied to Macdonnells of the Glens of
Antrim' (Connolly, p. 399); hence it makes sense for their name to be used here (see
next n.).
    galloglass] John Dymmok, who is thought to have accompanied Essex to Ireland in
1599, writes, 'the Galloglass ar pycked and scelected [*sic*] men of great and mightie

And Teague Magennis with his lightfoot kern.   35
Then will we not come miching thus by night
But charge the town and win it by daylight.
O'Hanlon, captain Harbert shall be thine,
And Gainsford's ransom shall be Mackener's.
O'Hanlon. Thanks, great O'Neill.
Mackener.   Be whist! I hear one stir!   40
                              One coughs within.
O'Neill. Some English soldier that hath got the cough.
I'll ease that grief by cutting off his head.
Mackener. These English churls die if they lack their bed
And bread and beer, porridge, and powdered beef.

---

35. Teague Magennis] *This ed.*; Teage Magennies *Q;* Teague Magennies *Simpson.*
kern] *This ed.*; kerne *Q.*

---

bodies, crewell without compassion. The greatest force of the battell consisteth in them,
chosing rather to dye than to yeelde, so that when yt cometh to handy blowes they are
quickly slayne or win the feilde. They are armed with a shert of maile, a skull, and a
skeine: the weapon they most use is a batle axe, or halberd, six foote longe, the blade
whereof is somewhat like a shomakers knyfe, and without pyke, the stroke whereof is
deadly where yt lighteth' (Dymmok, p. 7). These fierce warriors were originally more
Scottish than Irish; the greatest of the galloglass families was the Macdonnells, 'the Irish
offshoot of the Scottish Highland family of MacDonald', with lands in both Kintyre
and County Antrim (Connolly, p. 335). Shakespeare correctly names them in *Macbeth*,
'the merciless Macdonald . . . from the Western Isles' (1.2.9–12); see also Edelman, *Military*, pp. 145–6.
     35. *Teague Magennis*] Another major Ulster family that 'craved succour of Henrie
Sidney Lord Deputy in the yeere 1565' in opposing Shane O'Neill (Moryson, sig.
Cc1v). Why he is called Teague, i.e. *Tadhg* or 'poet', is unclear, since the prominent
Magennis names were Art and Hugh (O'Hart, 1: 311–12). In Sir Robert Howard's
The Committee (1662), Teague became 'the prototype of many comic Irish servants'
(J. O. Bartley, 'The Development of a Stock Character', *MLR* 37 (1942): 442).
     lightfoot kern] Dymmok's *Treatice* (pp. 7–8) reads, 'the kerne is a kind of footeman,
sleightly armed with a sworde, a targett of woode, or a bow and sheafe of arrows with
barbed heades, or els 3 dartes, which they cast with a wonderfull facillity and nearnes,
a weapon more noysom to the enemy, especially horsemen, then yt is deadly'. Shakespeare alludes to the kern's 'lightfootedness', his ability to move quickly over wet and
marshy ground, when Macbeth compels 'these skipping kerns to trust their heels'
(1.2.30); see also Edelman, *Military*, pp. 186–8.
     36. *miching*] sneaking, lurking; cf. Hamlet's famous 'this is miching mallecho'
(3.2.131).
     40. *whist*] quiet.
     44. *powdered*] salted, preserved (*OED ppl.* 2). Gibes about the English soldier's
inability to fight without having plenty of his favourite food and drink are common in
Elizabethan drama, e.g. *1 Henry VI*, 'They want their porage and their fat bull beeves'
(1.2.9); see also Edelman, *Military*, pp. 47–9.

O'Hanlon. O marafastot! Shamrocks are no meat,   45
  Nor bonny clabbo, nor green water cresses,
  Nor our strong butter, nor our swelled oatmeal
  And drinking water brings them to the flux.
O'Neill. It is their niceness, silly puling fools!
Mackener. There be of them can fare as hard as we,   50
  And harder too, but drunkards and suchlike
  As spend their time in ale house surfeiting,
  And brothel houses quickly catch their bane.
O'Neill. One coughs again, let's slip aside unseen.
  Tomorrow we will ease them of their spleen.   55

                                              [*Exeunt.*]

Scene 8

Enter HARBERT *at one door with* [*his* LIEUTENANT *and*]
SOLDIERS, *and* VERNON *at another.*

Harbert. Good morrow, Master Vernon.
Vernon. Good morrow, Captain Harbert.
Harbert. Is it your use to be so early up?
  Such vigilance doth fit us soldiers best,
  To search our garrisons for fear of spies.   5
Vernon. And travellers, that use to walk the round
  Of every country to survey the world,
  Must not be friend with sleep and idleness.
  But in plain terms, I do prevent mine hour

---

48. flux] *n. Simpson;* Flixe *Q.*   55. SD.] *This ed.; not in Q.*

Scene 8] *This ed.;* Sc. viii. *Levinson; not in Q.*   OSD. *his* LIEUTENANT] *This ed.; not in Q.*   1. Good morrow] *Simpson;* God morrow *Q (& l .2).*   5. To search] *conj. Simpson;* And search *Q.*

---

45. *marafastot*] *marbhfhaisc ort,* 'shrouding (i.e. death) on you' (Bartley, *Teague,* p. 272).

Shamrocks are no meat] cf. Dekker's *Whore of Babylon,* 'One of those shamrock-eaters at one break fast / Slit fourescore wezand-pipes of ours' (5.6.98–9).

46. *bonny clabbo*] *bainne clabair,* buttermilk (Bartley, *Teague,* p. 272).

48. *flux*] a common term for dysentery (*OED sb* 1a).

Scene 8] The action continues at Dundalk.

4. *vigilance*] here simply being awake, rather than watchful for danger; although *OED*'s earliest citation (sb 2) is 1748.

5. *To search*] *Q* has 'and search'; the 'and' was probably brought forward from the next line.

6. *And travellers*] i.e. And [also, we] travellers . . .

9. *prevent*] anticipate (*OED v* 1).

By reason of a gentleman's report   10
That is a soldier and did walk the round,
Who coming in this morning to his rest,
Said the enemy was about the town tonight.
Harbert's Lieutenant. So said this soldier that stood sentinel,
    Now this last watch at dawning of the day,   15
    That he did hear hard by the water side,
    Near the north gate that opens toward the Fewes,
    Some trampling on the gravel up and down.
    He did but cough and thought to call to them
    And they were gone.   20
Harbert. Soldier, was it so?
Soldier. Yes, governor, I know 'twas Shane O'Neill,
    They were so whist whilst they were near the walls;
    Pray God they have no spies within the town.
Harbert. Thou pray'st too late, the townsmen all are spies   25
    And help and store them with provision,
    And love them better than us Englishmen.
Vernon. It behooves you therefore to be circumspect.
Harbert's Lieutenant. Fear not you that. I'll search the town myself,
    And place a double guard at every gate.   30
    How stands the wind?
Vernon.   From England, very fair.
Harbert. We look for fresh supplies to come from thence
    To strength our garrison, for it is but weak,
    And we must bear the brunt of all the north.
Vernon. Your men are healthful?
Harbert.   There's no soldier sick   35
    But he that drinks or spends his thrift at dice.
                                     Sound a drum afar off.
    What drum is this?
Vernon.   A drum without the town.
Harbert. Some band of men from England new arrived
    Or else some company of the English pale.
    Bid Captain Gainsford guard the southern port   40

---

14. SH. *Harbert's Lieutenant*] *This ed.*; Lieu. *Q*; Lieut. *Simpson* (& l. 29). 21. SH.]
This ed.; no new speaker Q. 24. they] *Simpson;* the *Q.* 25. townsmen all are]
Simpson; townsmen are *Q.* 36. spends] *Simpson;* spende *Q.*

---

13. *tonight*] see n. 3.25.
17. *Fewes*] the name of a district near Dundalk, an anglicised plural of the Gaelic
feadh, a wood or forest (Bartley, *Teague*, p. 272).
21 SH.] *Q* has this as part of the Lieutenant's line, but the soldier replies to the 'governor', who is Harbert (see 9.41).
33. *strength*] See *Alcazar*, n. 2.3.97.

Toward Tredaghe, and take that company in;
I'll see our troops in readiness this day,
For I expect the Irish soon at night.
Vernon. What will you do?
Harbert.   I'll to the southern port
To see what captain leads this band of men.   45
I make ye lieutenant governor for the time.

Exeunt.

Scene 9

Enter STUKELEY, *his* LIEUTENANT, ENSIGN, *drum,*
soldiers and company.

Stukeley. I muse what lord is governor of this town,
That comes not forth to welcome Stukeley in.
Stukeley's Lieutenant. The town's so long he cannot hear our drum,
And if he did he knows not whose it is.
Stukeley. Drum, thump thy tapskins hard about the pate,   5
And make the ram-heads hear that are within.

Drum sounds.

Enter VERNON, GAINSFORD *and soldiers.*

Zounds, who is that? Vernon with a partisan?
Is he a soldier? Then the enemy's dead.

44b. SH.] *conj. Levinson; before l. 46 Q.*   46. SD.] *Rt mgn prev. l. Q.*

Scene 9] *This ed.; Sc. ix. Levinson; not in Q.*   OSD. ENSIGN] *This ed.; Ancient Q.*
6. SD.] *follows prev. l. Q.*

----

41. *Tredaghe*] a village south of Dundalk in County Louth (Sugden).

44b. SH.] Q gives only the last line to Harbert, but Levinson's suggestion that his
speech begins here must be correct. 'Master' Vernon has no authority to decide on these
matters, and, if Harbert is not going anywhere, he need not appoint anyone as lieutenant governor.

Scene 9] The action is outside the walls of Dundalk.
OSD. ENSIGN] Stukeley's ensign of Scene 6 in Q is an 'ancient' in the Irish sequence,
perhaps an indication that a different author provided these scenes.
5. *tapskins*] drumsticks (*OED sb*, only cit.).
6. *ram-heads*] dolts or blockheads, with an implication of cuckoldry (*OED sb* 1).
6 SD.] As the drummer is told to 'thump . . . hard', he would not start until after
the second line of Stukeley's command, which would otherwise not be heard. Stukeley
probably signals a stop before 'Zounds'.
7–12.] One cannot be sure if Stukeley's and Vernon's lines are intended to be asides,
or directed to each other.
7. *partisan*] a long staff with a two-edged, triangular shaped blade; cf. *Hamlet*, 'Shall
I strike at it with my partisan?' (1.1.121).

Vernon. Is Stukeley come, whom I desire to shun?
And must he needs to Ireland follow me?   10
I will not draw that air wherein he breathes,
One kingdom shall not hold us if I can.
Gainsford. Is not this lusty Stukeley with his men?
Vernon. Yes, Captain Gainsford, this is lusty Tom.
Stukeley. These gallants are grown ceremonious,   15
They stand at gaze as if they knew me not,
Or else they strain a further compliment
To see if I will vail my bonnet first.
I'll eat my feather ere I move my hat
Before I see their crowns uncoverèd.   20
Stukeley's Lieutenant. Cherish that humour, it becomes your port.
Vernon. He doth expect we should salute him first.
Gainsford. 'Tis fit we should, for he's but new arrived.
Vernon. You're welcome into Ireland, Captain Stukeley.
Stukeley. Gramercies, Master Vernon, and well met,   25
I did not dream that you professèd arms.
Vernon. It is not my profession but my pleasure;
The governor being busy in the town,
Makes me lieutenant governor for the time.
Gainsford. Brave Captain Stukeley, welcome to Dundalk.   30
Stukeley. Thanks, Captain Gainsford, even with all my heart.
          STUKELEY'S LIEUTENANT *delivers a letter to* VERNON.
Vernon. To me, Lieutenant? From whom, I pray ye?
Stukeley's Lieutenant. From an old friend.
Vernon.   I'll see what friend it is.
Stukeley. What enemy lies there near about this town?
Gainsford. The rebel Shane O'Neill and all his power.   35
Stukeley. Why do ye not beat them home into their dens?
Gainsford. We have enough ado to keep the town.
Stukeley. To keep the town? Dare they beleaguer it?
Gainsford. Ay, and assault it.
Stukeley.   Hang them, savage slaves,
Belike they know you dare not issue out.   40
Who is governor here?
Gainsford.   That's Captain Harbert, sir.

---

15. ceremonious] *Simpson;* ceremonies *Q.*   29. Makes me] *Simpson;* makes we *Q.*

18. *vail*] doff (*OED v* 2).
21. *port*] rank, deportment; cf. *Henry V*, 'Then should the warlike Harry, like
himself / Assume the port of Mars' (Prol.5–6).
25. *Gramercies*] thanks, from the Old French *grant merci*; cf. *Taming of the Shrew*,
'Gramercies, Tranio, well thou dost advise' (1.1.41).

Stukeley. (*Aside alone*) 'Sdeath, I am bewitched – mine enemy
    governor.
  Well 'tis no matter, I'll about without him
  So soon as e'er I see him by this light.
  'Tis marvel he'll endure their proud approach;   45
  Harbert is valiant but the slaves are poor,
  And have no boot to fetch worth following them.
Gainsford. Yes, Captain Stukeley, they have gallant horse;
  The best in Ireland are of Ulster's breed.
  They have a prey of garrans, cows and sheep   50
  Well worth a brace of thousand pounds at least.
Stukeley. Hang cows and sheep, but have among their horse,
  I'll lose this head but I'll have hobbies from them.
  (*To Vernon*) What news from England that ye read so long?
Vernon. The largest news concerns yourself.
Stukeley.   Wherein?
                                   55
Vernon. Will Mallery writes, ye do not love your wife,
  You are unkind, you make not much of her.
Stukeley. Writes he I have not made much of my wife?
  (*To Gainsford*) I'll tell ye, captain, how much I have made,
  I have made away her portion and her plate,   60
  Her borders, bracelets, chains and all her rings
  And all the clothes belonging to her back,
  Save one poor gown, and he that can make more
  Of one poor wife, let him take her for me.
Vernon. Well, had I known you would have made so much,   65
  You should not have been troubled with my love.
Stukeley. Come, strike up drum, let's march into the town.
                      Exeunt all but VERNON.
Vernon. Well, go thy ways, a kingdom is too small
  For his expense that hath no mean at all.
  Doubtless if ever man was misbegot   70
  It is this Stukeley: of a boundless mind,

---

42. SD.] *rt mgn l.* 43 Q.   46. poor] *conj. Simpson;* proud Q.   53. lose] *Simpson;*
loose Q.   54. SD.] *rt mgn* Q.   56. Mallery] *This ed.;* Mallerye Q.   59. SD.] *rt mgn*
Q.   69. no mean] *Simpson;* ny mean Q.

46. *poor*] Simpson's emendation is probably correct, as Q's 'proud' is also in the
previous line.

50. *garrans*] a small and inferior kind of horse bred and used chiefly in Ireland and
Scotland (*OED sb¹*).

53. *hobbies*] small or middle-sized horses, bred in Ireland (*OED sb¹* 1); cf. Dekker,
Gull's Hornbook, where a young gallant is left 'five hundred a year only to keep an
Irish hobby, an Irish horse-boy, and himself like a gentleman' (p. 88).

Undaunted spirit, and uncontrolled spleen,
Lavish as is the liquid ocean
That drops his crowns e'en as the clouds drop rain.
Yet once I loved him better than myself, 75
When, like myself, too prodigal in love,
I gave my love to such a prodigal,
For which I hate the climate where he lives
As if his breath infected all the air.
And therefore Ireland now farewell to thee, 80
For though thy soil no venom will sustain,
There treads a monster on thy fruitful breast.
If any shipping be for Spain or France,
Aboard will I, and seek some further chance.

                                       [*Exit.*]

Scene 10

Enter HARBERT *in a shirt of mail and booted,*
and his Page *with him.*

Harbert. Boy, bid the sergeant major shut the gates
And see them guarded with a double ward.
That done, bid him command the companies
To man the walls; then bid the messenger
Haste with these letters to the Deputy. 5

                             Exit Page.

Enter STUKELEY.

Come, Captain Stukeley, where's your company?
Draw them with speed unto the water port.
Stukeley. Is there for every one a tankard there?
Harbert. How do you mean a tankard?
Stukeley.   Sir, in brief,
I made a vow, you know it well enough, 10

74. e'en] *This ed.;* even *Q.* 84. SD.] *This ed.; not in Q.*

Scene 10] *This ed.;* Sc. x. *Levinson; not in Q.* 7. Draw them] *Simpson;* draw
then *Q.*

76. *like myself*] Simpson suggests 'like himself', but the line makes sense as it stands.
81.] a reference to the legend of St Patrick ridding Ireland of its snakes.
Scene 10] The action is outside the walls of Dundalk.
5. *Deputy*] the Lord Deputy, the Queen's chief administrator in Ireland; see n. 12.79.
8. *tankard*] a large open tub-like vessel, usually used for carrying water (*OED sb* 1), or a drinking cup, akin to a beer mug (*OED sb* 2). The point of Stukeley's rejoinder, and how it relates to the quarrel with Harbert, is not clear.

For your kind speeches to my wife's old dad,
Sir Thomas Curtis, that wheresoever we met
I would fight with you. Therefore your tools!

He draws.

Harbert. What were my speeches?
Stukeley. That the old knight had cast away his daughter   15
When ye perceived she was bestowed on me.
Harbert. I spake those words and thou hast proved them true.
Stukeley. And for those words, Harbert, I'll fight with you.
Harbert. Rash hare-brained Stukeley, know'st thou what thou dost
To quarrel in a town of garrison   20
And draw thy weapon on the governor?
Stukeley. Zounds, have ye logic to defend your skin?
Lay by your tricks and take you to your tools.
Think ye your governor's title's rapier proof?
Harbert. Come, come, untruss, put off those coward shifts.   25
Stukeley, thou know'st I am a soldier
And hate the name of carpet-coward to death;
I tell thee but the discipline of war.
Stukeley. Gods, you may hang us then by the law!
By law of manhood here I challenge thee,   30
Lay by thy terms and answer like a man.
Harbert. Thou seest the public enemy is at hand
And we shall fight about a private brawl?
Stukeley. Nor shall that shift, Tom Harbert, serve thy turn.
Harbert. Then give me leave but to disarm myself,   35
Thou know'st I scorn t'have odds of any man.
Stukeley. Disarm of what? Of schoolboys' haberdines
Such as they cast at points in every street?
No, arm thy legs, put splinters in thy boots,

---

33. we shall] *Q; shall we conj. Adams.*

   13. *tools*] weapons; cf. *Romeo and Juliet*, 'Draw thy tool, here comes of the house of Montagues' (1.1.31).
   20. *quarrel . . . garrison*] For soldiers to quarrel while on active duty was a serious breach of discipline, as shown by Othello's reaction to the brawl between Cassio and Montano (2.3.206–9); see Edelman, *Military*, pp. 276–7.
   27. *carpet-coward*] as with 'carpet-squire' (6.95), a common expression for one who would prefer to avoid danger.
   29. *Gods*] Perhaps this should be 'God's', as a shortened form of 'God's bones' or 'God's wounds'.
   37. *haberdines*] obviously a game, as in *A Chaste Made in Cheapside* (4.1.56). D. L. Frost notes, 'haberdines are dried salt cod, but this game is unknown; probably it was like the modern children's game "kippers", in which fish cut out of paper are fanned along a confined course, the first "kipper" wafted across the line being the winner' (*Selected Plays of Thomas Middleton*, Cambridge, 1978, p. 152).
   39. *splinters*] variant of splints, overlapping metal plates or strips used in some parts of armour (splint *OED sb* 1a).

Casque on thy head, and gauntlets on thy hands.   40
Would thou wert armed in pistol-proof complete
And nothing bare but even thy very lips,
I hold my head I'll hurt thee in thy mouth.
Lay by thy scarecrow name of Governor
And arm thee else unto a finger's breadth.   45
Harbert. Braving braggart, since thou dost seek thy death,
Look to thyself. I'll speed thee if I can.
                                                    They fight.
Stukeley. Sir, your teeth bleeds. This picktooth is too keen.
                                        Drum soundeth and a bagpipe.
Harbert. Hark, the enemy's charges! We must to the walls.
Another time I'll pick your teeth as well.   50
Stukeley. Even when ye can, I said I would hit your mouth.
                                                    Exeunt.

Scene 11

Alarum is sounded, divers excursions, STUKELEY *pursues Shane*
O'NEILL *and Neil* MACKENER, *and after a good pretty fight his*
LIEUTENANT *and* ENSIGN *rescue* STUKELEY, *and chase the Irish out.*
Then an excursion betwixt HARBERT *and* O'HANLON, *and so*
a retreat sounded. Enter HARBERT, GAINSFORD *and some*
soldiers on the walls.

Harbert. Are all the gates and posterns closed again?
Gainsford. Ay, every one, and strong guards at them all.
Harbert. Who would have thought these naked savages,
These northern Irish durst have been so bold,
T'have given assault unto a warlike town?   5
Gainsford. Our suff'rance and remissness gives them heart.

40. gauntlets] *This ed.*; gantles Q.   51. SD.] *This ed.*; Exeunt Ambo Q.

Scene 11] *This ed.*; Sc. xi. *Levinson; not in Q.*   OSD. ENSIGN] *This ed.*; Auntient Q;
Ancient *Simpson.*

40. *casque*] helmet; cf. Chorus in *Henry V*, 'the very casques / That did affright the
air at Agincourt' (1.Pr. 13–14).
41. *pistol-proof*] with the introduction of firearms, armour was tested for strength
by firing a pistol at it from close range (Edelman, *Military*, pp. 270–2); cf. 2 *Henry IV*,
'She is pistol-proof, sir, you shall not hardly offend her' (2.4.113–14).
48. *bleeds*] The singular verb following a plural subject is common in early modern
usage (Abbott, pp. 235–7).
49. *charges*] drum and trumpet (here drum and bagpipe) signals for a charge,
not the attack itself; cf. *Richard II*, 'a charge sounded' (1.3.117 SD); see Edelman,
Military, p. 84.

Scene 11] In this scene, the upper gallery would represent the walls of Dundalk where
Harbert and Gainsford enter after the fighting.
OSD. ENSIGN] see n. 9 OSD.

We make them proud by mewing up ourselves
In wallèd towns, whilst they triumph abroad
And revel in the country as they please.
Harbert. Well, Sergeant Major, we will stir abroad.   10
This sudden sally was performed as men;
It cut three hundred rebels' throats at least
And did discomfit and disperse them all.
Gainsford. Had we pursued we had ta'en a lusty prey.
Harbert. Ye see 'tis night, and time we should retire   15
To guard the town. But hark, what drum is this?
Are any of our company without?
Gainsford. 'Tis lusty Stukeley, if any be abroad,
He is so eager to pursue the foe
And flesh his soldiers that are new arrived,   20
That he forgot or heard not the retreat.
At which gate shall he enter, Governor?
Harbert. He shall not enter. Give me all the keys,
I'll teach him duty and true discipline.

> *Enter [below]* STUKELEY, *his* LIEUTENANT, ENSIGN,
> *drum and soldiers. A noise within of driving beasts.*

Stukeley. Are the gates shut already? Open! How!   25
Harbert. Who knocks so boldly?
Stukeley.   Ha? Who's that above?
Harbert. Harbert the governor. Who is that below?
Stukeley. Stukeley the captain knocks to be let in.
Harbert. Stukeley the captain comes not in tonight.
Stukeley. How? Not tonight? I am sure ye do but jest.   30
Harbert. I do not use to jest in these affairs.
Stukeley. Ye do not jest and I must stay without,
I trust you'll let my company come in.
Harbert. Nor company, nor captain comes in here
Until the morning that the gates be ope.   35
Stukeley. We humbly thank ye, honourable sir!
What if the Irish should make head again
And set upon us? Would ye rescue us?
Harbert. No! Why retired ye not at the retreat,
As did myself and all the other troops?   40
Stukeley. Because I meant not to come empty home,
But bring some booty to enrich my men.
Besides, in prosecution we have slain
Two hundred Irish since you left the chase

---

24. SD. *Enter...*ENSIGN] *This   ed.;*   Enter   Stukly   Lieftenant: Auncient   *Q.*
25. Open! How!] *Simpson;* open how *Q.*   33. come in] *Simpson;* come in in *Q.*
34. SH.] *Simpson; no new speaker Q.*   36. humbly] *Simpson;* humble *Q.*

And brought a prey, six hundred cows at least,   45
Forty chief horse, a hundred hackney jades
And yet the governor will not let us in.
Harbert. No sir, I will not, and will answer it.
If all your throats be cut you are well served,
To teach ye know the discipline of war.   50
There is a time to fight, a time to cease,
A time to watch, a time to take your rest,
A time to open and to shut the ports,
And at this time, Stukeley, the gates are shut
And till a full time shall not be oped.   55
Stukeley. Solomon says with words mild,
'Spare the rod and spill the child':
Wholesome instruction, goodly discipline.
This is a simple piece of small revenge,
But this I vow: who shut me out by night   60
Shall never see me enter here by day.
Will ye, sir, let the prey taken in
For fear the Irish rescue it again?
Gainsford. 'Twere pity, sir, to lose so good a prey,
And greater pity but to lose one man.   65
Harbert. You may let in the prey. But keep them out.
Stukeley. Stay, Sergeant Major. O white-livered lout,
Dost thou respect a bullock or a jade
More than a man to God's own likeness made?
Harbert, thou get'st not one cow to thy share,   70
Nor a cow's tail, unless, as Cacus did,
I by the tail could draw one from the herd
And cast her at thy head the horns and all.
Harbert. Go make your cabin underneath the wall
And so good night.
Stukeley.   Farewell, go pick your teeth.   75
Exeunt HARBERT *and* GAINSFORD.

---

60. out by] *This ed.*; out of by *Q*; out at *Simpson*.   75. SD.] *subst. Q.*

---

45. *six hundred cows*] Cattle raiding was one of the chief forms of warfare in Ireland at this time (Seán 'O Domhnaill, 'Warfare in Sixteenth-century Ireland', *Irish Historical Studies* 5, no. 17 (1946): 29–54).
57. *spill the child*] 'He that spareth his rod hateth his own son' Proverbs, 13.24. 'Spill', in its original sense of 'kill' or 'injure' (*OED v* 3c), was common usage at the time; we hear 'spoil the child' today, but *OED*'s first citation for 'spoil' (*v* 13a), in the sense of damaging a child's character through overindulgence, is from 1694.
71. *Cacus*] While Hercules was driving cattle through hills that would one day be the site of Rome, the thief Cacus took some and drew them into his cave, leading them by the tail so as to leave a false trail. Hercules discovered the theft when the lowing of his beasts was answered by those in the cave (Harvey, p. 83).

How glad am I my trunks are yet aboard.
Lieutenant, Ensign, fellow soldiers all,
I would we might not part but needs we must,
Tom Stukeley cannot brook the least disgrace.
Tonight I'll bide such venture as you shall;   80
Let's man the bridge, the water flows apace,
If the enemy come he dare not pass the flood,
So on this side we with our prey are safe.
How many cows shall fall unto my share?
Stukeley's Lieutenant. All, if ye please, your valour compassed all.   85
Stukeley. Shall all the cows be mine? I'll not have one!
Thirty chief horse, if you will let me have,
To ship from hence to seek a better coast.
                              [*Hands them*] *his purse.*
Share that amongst ye, there's a hundred pound,
And two months' pay that's due unto myself   90
I give you frankly, drink it for my sake.
Stukeley's Lieutenant. But Captain, will you leave this land indeed?
Stukeley. Before the sun the morning doth salute
I'll see my hobbies safely sent aboard,
Then follow I that scorn to be controlled   95
Of any man that's meaner than a king.
Farewell O'Neill, if Stukeley here had stayed,
Thy head for treason, soon thou shouldst have paid.
                                        Exeunt.

Scene 12

Enter O'NEILL *with a halter about his neck,
and Neil* MACKENER *after him.*

Mackener. O what intends the great O'Neill by this?
O'Neill. Neil Mackener, I do not wear this cord
    As doubting or foredooming such a death,
    But thou, who art my secretary, know'st

77. Ensign] *This ed.;* Antient *Q;* Ancient *Simpson.*   88. SD. *Hands them*] *This ed.; not in Q.*

Scene 12.] *This ed.;* Sc. xii. *Levinson; not in Q.*

Scene 12] Simpson's note, 'The materials for this scene are in Holingshed', is very misleading. O'Neill's being dissuaded from surrendering to the English with a halter around his neck, his subsequent decision to go north and seek a new alliance with his traditional enemies, the Macdonnells, and his death at their hands, was a series of events that occurred over several months, and in several different places. What is most surprising about the scene as we have it is the failure to make use of one of the most dramatic stories from this period of Irish history: O'Neill's arrival at Clandeboy and his murder at a drunken feast is lamely portrayed.

That my unkind rebellions merit more.   5
Therefore I bear this hateful cord in sign
Of true repentance of my treasons past,
And at the Deputy's feet on humble knees
Will sue for pardon from her majesty
Whose clemency I grieve to have abused.   10
What sayest thou? Is't not my safest course?
Mackener. Can I believe that mighty Shane O'Neill
Is so deject in courage as he seems,
Or that his dauntless dragon-wingèd thoughts
Can humble them at any prince's feet?   15
O'Neill. What can I do? My forces are dispersed,
My kindred slain, my horses made a prey,
O'Cahan, O'Hanlon and Magennis killed.
If the Queen's power pursue I am but dead,
If I submit she is merciful,   20
Her Deputy will grant me life in her behalf.
Mackener. Thou canst not tell. The state offended stands
And thou condemned in every subject's eye,
And I am censured for my practices.
Rather retire thee into Clandeboy   25
Where Alexander and MacGilliam Buske

---

14. thoughts] *Simpson;* thoght *Q.*   18. O'Cahan] *This ed.;* Ocane *Q;* O'Kane
Simpson.   25. Clandeboy] *This ed.;* Clamgeboy *Q;* Clamgaboy *Simpson.*
26. MacGilliam Buske] *Simpson;* Mack Gilliam Buske *Q.*

5. *unkind*] unnatural; cf. *1 Henry VI*, 'But more when envy breeds unkind division'
(4.1.193).

13. *deject*] dejected; cf. Ophelia in *Hamlet*, 'And I, of ladies most deject and
wretched' (3.1.158).

25. *Clandeboy*] One of the three districts of County Antrim (the others being the
Glynns and the Route), taking its name from 'Clan-Hugh-Boy', i.e. Clan *Aodh Buidhe*
O'Neill. *Buidhe*, pronounced *Buie*, means 'yellow-haired'; see Samuel Lewis, *A Topo-
graphical Dictionary of Ireland*, London, 1837, p. 30, and n. following.

26. *Alexander*] In 1565, Shane O'Neill attacked the Macdonnells in their strong-
hold of Ballycastle. James, the eldest surviving son of Alexander Macdonnell, was
wounded and 'left to die in O'Neill's dungeon' (Hill, p. 139); his brother Angus was
slain (see n. 12.40), and the seventh of Alexander's eight sons, Sorley Buidhe, was taken
prisoner. The remaining Macdonnell forces were under the control of Alexander Oge
[*óg*, 'the younger'] Macdonnell.

MacGilliam Buske] Of all the Irish names in the play, this is the most intriguing. He
is 'Mac Gilly Asspuke' in the *Statutes* (p. 327), 'Mac Gillye Aspucke' in Campion
(p. 129), 'Mac-Gillispik' in Camden (2.105) and 'Mac Guillie' in Holinshed (6:337);
nineteenth-century historian Hill uses 'MacGillaspick' (p. 131). Whatever his name, his
father's sister was the wife of James Macdonnell (see previous n.), hence he is related
by marriage to Alexander Oge, and is avenging the death of his and Oge's 'dear cousin'
Angus (see n. 12.40; see also Hill, p. 142; Brady, p. 118).

May join their Scots unto thy scattered troops,
And re-enforce the English with fresh power.
If not, at least thy life is safe with them
Until thy friends may reunite themselves.   30
O'Neill. I would embrace thy counsel, but I fear
The wrongs that I have done unto the Scots
Sticks in the breast of Alexander Oge,
And he will take occasion of revenge.

Enter ALEXANDER OGE *and MacGilliam* BUSKE, *two Scots*

Mackener. Put it in proof, for here comes he and Buske.   35
Cast off thy cord, let not them see thy shame.
Alexander Oge. Gilliam, the news are true of great O'Neill:
Dundalk hath dashed his pride and quelled his power.
Buske. Occasion offers us a fair revenge
For our dear cousin young MacAngus' death.   40
Alexander Oge. Who'll take revenge on weakness that's depressed?
Buske. Who'll let his kinsman's blood unwreakèd rest?
O'Neill. Do they not see us – or disdain to see us?
Mackener. Salute them kindly.
O'Neill.   Gentlemen, good day.
Alexander MacSorley and Master Gilliam Buske,   45
Fortune hath frowned upon your friend O'Neill;
My troops are beaten by the English power.
If therefore you will join your Scottish aid,
With the remainder of my followers,
Your means may make recovery of my loss   50

---

28. re-enforce] *This ed.;* réenforce *Q,* reenforce *Simpson.*   34. SD. *MacGilliam*
BUSKE] *This ed.;* maister Gillian Buske *Q;* Master Gilliam Buske *Simpson.*   35. SH.]
Simpson; no new speaker Q.   37. Gilliam] *This ed.;* Gillam *Q.*   40. MacAngus]
Simpson; Mack Agnus *Q (& l. 59).*   45. MacSorley] *This ed.;* Mack Surlo *Q;* Mac
Surlo *Simpson.*

---

28. *re-enforce*] Simpson's gloss of 'renew the attack upon' seems demanded by the
context, but *OED* has no examples of 'reinforce' or 'reenforce' with this meaning.
Perhaps the line should read 're-enforce the Irish'.

33. *Oge*] see n. 12.26.

34 SD. *two Scots*] see n. 7.39.

40. *MacAngus*] i.e. Angus, the brother of James Macdonnell, killed fighting Shane
O'Neill; see n. 12.26.

42. *unwreakèd*] unavenged; cf. *Alcazar,* n. 1.1.109.

45. *Alexander MacSorley*] another name for Alexander Oge, the patronym deriving
from *Somhairle* MacDonnell, whom King Malcolm IV of Scotland made Thane of
Ireland in the twelfth century. This Sorley's descendants were styled 'lords of the Isles
or Hebrides, and the lords of Cantyre' (O'Hart, 1: 527); see also n. 12.26.

And you shall bind O'Neill to quite your love.
Alexander Oge. How can a rebel or a traitor hope
  Of good success against his sovereign?
  Awhile perhaps he may disturb the state
  And damn himself, but at the last he falls.   55
Mackener. I thought thou hadst despised the English churls.
Buske. Admit he did, how can he love O'Neill,
  But chiefly thee, that was the counsellor
  To cut off young MacAngus our dear cousin?
Mackener. Not my advice, but his too saucy braves   60
  To great O'Neill did cause his cutting off.
Buske. Speak such another word I'll cut thy throat,
  Thou trait'rous rebel Mackener.
O'Neill. MacGilliam Buske, upbraid not Neil Mackener.
  I did the deed and hold it was well done,   65
  Because he braved me in my own command.
Alexander Oge. As thou dost us now in our own command,
  For justifying of so foul a fact,
  Here is revenge. Traitors, have at you both!
            They draw and fight, O'NEILL *flies.*
  Fliest thou, thou traitorous coward Shane O'Neill?   70
  I am too light a'foot to let thee 'scape.
                    Exit after O'Neill.
Buske. I'll stop your flight, you shall not follow him.

---

51. quite] *subst. Simpson;* quit Q.   69. SD.] *This ed.*; They Draw and fight, Oneale
Flies, Alexander pursues him out: Busk and Mackener fight and Mack. is slaine Q.

---

51. *quite*] repay, requite (*OED v* 10).
62.] The play's reason for the quarrel, Mackener's comments about MacAngus, is
not nearly as exciting as the version accepted by all authorities at the time. As is
recorded in the *Statute* (pp. 327–8), the Scots and their visitors 'fell to quaffing and
drinking of wine'. At some point 'the said Gillaspuke demaunded of the secretorie,
whether hee had bruted abroad, that the ladie his aunt, wife unto James Mac Conill,
did offer to come out of Scotland into Ireland to marrie with Oneile; the secretorie
affirmed himselfe to bee the author of that report, and said withall, that if his aunt
were Queen of Scotland, shee might bee well contented to match herselfe with Oneyle
. . . [who] giving eare to the talke, began to maintayne his secretorics quarrell, and there-
upon Gillaspuke withdrew himselfe out of the tent, and came abroad amongst his men,
who forthwith raised a fray . . . and thrust into the tent, where the said Oneile was, and
there with their slaughter knives hewed him to pieces, slew his secretorie and all those
that were with him, except a verie few which escaped by their horses'. See also Brady,
passim.
  69 SD] This direction is followed, in Q, by '*Alexander pursues him out: Buske and
Mackener fight and Mack. is slain,* which is unusual in that (*a*) Alexander Oge speaks
two more lines and has another exit, and (*b*) five lines after Buske kills Mackener, Mackener gets up so Buske can kill him again.

Mackener. I meant it not, proud overweening Scot.
Buske. Have at thee then, rebellious Irishman.
                    They fight. MACKENER *is slain.*
    Enter ALEXANDER [OGE], *with O'Neill's head.*

Alexander Oge. I see we are victors both, MacGilliam Buske,   75
    Here is the head of traitorous Shane O'Neill.
Buske. And here's his bloody secretary dead.
Alexander Oge. No force, this head for present will I send,
    To that most noble English Deputy,
    That ministers justice as he were a god   80
    And guerdons virtue like a liberal king.
    This grateful present may procure our peace,
    And so the English fight and our fear may cease.
Buske. And may all Irish that with treason deal,
    Come to like end or worse than Shane O'Neill.   85
                                        Exeunt.

                        Scene 13

        Enter Hernando [GOVERNOR *of Cales*], *with* STUKELEY
        brought in with bills and halberds [*and* ATTENDANTS].

Stukeley. Had I known thus much, Governor, I would have burnt my
    ships in the haven before thy face, and have fed haddocks with my
    horses.
Governor. Is thou and all thou hast at my dispose, and dost deny me

---

Scene 13] *This ed.;* Sc. xiii. *Levinson; not in* Q.   OSD.] *This ed.;* Enter Hernand with
stuklie brought in with Bils. and halberds to them the Governors wife *Q*.

78. *No force*] no matter (force *OED sb¹* 20); cf. Peele, *Edward I*, 'no force no harme'
(l. 1136).
79. *Deputy*] A tribute either to Sir Henry Sidney, Lord Deputy at the time of Shane's
death, or to Sir William Russell, who served at the probable time of the play's
composition.
81. *guerdons*] rewards, cf. Costard in *Love's Labour's Lost*, 'O sweet guerdon!
better than remuneration' (3.1.165–6).
83. i.e. our fight against the English will be over, and our fear along with it.

Scene 13] The action takes place at the Governor's residence in 'Cales', i.e. Cadiz
(see n. 13.6). Stukeley actually landed at Vivero in Galicia, and all material in this part
of the play concerning Stukeley, Governor Hernando and his wife is fictional. This scene
bears the same irregularities in verse and prose as do the London scenes.
OSD.] As at 12.69 SD this direction is followed in *Q* by one that makes no sense:
'to them the Governor's wife'. She does not enter until l. 26.
4. *Is . . . hast*] See n. 10.48.

upon courtesy, what I may take whether thou wilt or no? Stuke-   5
ley, if thou be called so, I'll make thee know a governor of Cales.
Stukeley. Governor, will nothing but five of my horses serve your turn?
Sirrah, thou gets not one of them, and a hair would save thy life.
If I had as many horses as there be stones in the island, thou
shouldst not have one of them.   10
Governor. Know, Stukeley, too, it had been thy duty to have offered
them, and glad that I would grace thee to accept them. What is he
that dares thrust into this harbour, and not make tender of his
goods to me?
Stukeley. Why then know, Governor, here is once one that dares thrust   15
into this harbour, that will not make thee tender of a mite, nor
cares not of a hair how thou dost take it. I will not give one of my
hobbies for thy government.
Governor. I will be answerable to thee for thy horses.
Stukeley. Dost thou keep a toll booth? Zounds, dost thou make a   20
horse-courser of me?
Governor. Nay, sirrah, then I'll lay you by the heels, and I will have
them, every horse of them.
Stukeley. Thou get'st not so much as a nail of one of them, no, if thou
wouldst draw it with thy teeth. If you do, I'll clench it with your   25
scalp.

Enter GOVERNOR'S LADY.

Governor. Call me the Provost hither presently.

One goes.

Governor's Lady. (*To one of the attendants*) Sirrah, is this the English
gentleman which brought the horses?
Attendant. Madam, it is he, this is the man.   30

26. SD.] *This ed.;* Enter the Governor's wife *Q.* 28. SH.] *This ed.;* Lady *Q.* SD.] To
one of the attendants *divided over* 2 *ll. left mgn Q.* 30. SH.] *This ed.;* Ser. *Q (& at
l. 32).*

---

6. *Cales*] Cadiz. Cales was the usual form at the time (Sugden), although *Q* of
Alcazar has 'Cardis' (see *Alcazar*, n. 3.1.42). 'Cales' is retained here, since a one-
syllable word is required in four verse lines: 14.202, 14.229, 15.157, 17.26.
8. *thou gets*] See n. 6.77.
and . . . life] if your life depended on it; see n. l. 17.
9. *island*] Cadiz is on a peninsula, but is almost entirely surrounded by water.
17. *not of a hair*] a hair having no significance or value is proverbial (Tilley, H19).
19. *answerable*] *OED* offers no example of 'answerable' in the sense implied here,
that the Governor demands submission from Stukeley; perhaps an ironic question was
intended.
21. *horse-courser*] a horse-dealer; cf. the character Jordan Knockem, 'a hourse-
courser, and ranger o'Turnbull', in Jonson's *Bartholomew Fair.*
26. SD. GOVERNOR'S LADY] *Q* has 'Governor's Wife' in entry directions, but as
her speech heading is 'Lady', 'Governor's Lady' seems apt for the character's name.

Governor's Lady. How do they call him?

Attendant. His servants say his name is Signor Stukeley.

Governor's Lady. (*Aside*) Now by my troth and as I am a lady, I never
saw a fairer gentleman. I would it lay in my power to do him good.

Enter the PROVOST.

Governor. Sirrah, as I have seized your ships and horses, so I commit   35
your body unto prison until his highness' pleasure shall be known.
Provost, lay irons upon him and take him to your charge.

Governor's Lady. (*Aside*) Well, well, for all this, might I have my will,
in faith, his entertainment should be better.

Stukeley. You muddy slave, you may by your power do a little, but I'll   40
call you to a reckoning for this gear. And, sirrah, see a horse be
not lacking. If he be, I'll make thee on thy bare feet lead him in a
halter after me to the furthest part of Spain.

Governor. Go to, thou art a base pirate.

Stukeley. Sirrah muchacho – you that have eaten a horse and his tail   45
hangs out of your mouth – you lie. All that thou canst do shall not
get a horse. If Saint Jaques your saint want a horse, he should not
get one of them, he should go afoot else all the days of his life. By
this flesh and blood, I'll make thee repent it.

Governor. Away with him.   50

Exit STUKELEY [*guarded and* PROVOST].

Governor's Lady. Yet, good my lord, consider what you do.
Surely the confidence of this man's spirit
Shows that his blood is either great or noble,
Or that his fortune's at his own command.

Governor. I hold him rather to be some desp'rate pirate,   55
That thinks to domineer upon the land
As he is used amongst his mates at sea.

Governor's Lady. Besides, it's less disgrace to bear his braves
Here, where your power is absolute and free
And where he wholly stands at your dispose,   60
Than in a place indifferent to either
And where you both should stand in equal terms.

Governor. If I did prize his honour with mine own,
Then, wife, perhaps I might allow your reason.

Governor's Lady. Besides, perhaps they may be for a present   65
Which now his heat restrains him to disclose,
Which should they be to any prince of Spain,

33. SD. *Aside*] *rt mgn* Q.   38. SD. *Aside*] *left mgn, before l.* 39 Q.   43. part]
Simpson; pare Q.   50. SD. *guarded and* PROVOST] *This ed.; not in* Q.   58. SH.]
Simpson; *no new speaker* Q.

47. *Saint Jaques your saint*] Santiago or St James, the patron saint of Spain. As
Stukeley is being insulting, he may intend a pun on 'Jaques' and 'jakes', a privy.

How ill it may be taken at your hands.
Governor. This his committing gives some cause to doubt.
I care not were they sent unto the devil,   70
Where the commission of my government
Gives me as much as I demand of him.
Tomorrow I'll unto the court myself;
Today I have some business in the isle
And 'twill be evening ere I do return.   75
                                        Exit GOVERNOR.

                            Enter PROVOST.

Governor's Lady. Provost.
Provost. Madam.
Governor's Lady. Where have you yet bestowed this gentleman?
Provost. Madam, he's here within the palace yet,
Ready to go unto the marshalsea;   80
He had been gone, but that upon some business
I come to know his honour's pleasure in,
And he is gone.
Governor's Lady.   But Provost, since your prisoner
Is not departed, I pray thee bring him hither.   85
I'll see if by persuasion I can win him
To yield and to submit unto my lord.
Provost. Madam I will.   *He fetcheth* [STUKELEY] *in.*
Governor's Lady. I thank you, give us leave a little.
                                        [*Exit* PROVOST]
Fair gentleman, but that it is too late   90
To call back yesterday, I would have wished
That you had dealt more kindly with my lord.
Sir, it should seem you have been unacquainted
With the hot bloods and temper of our clime,
Or with a Spaniard's noble disposition,   95
Whereas your kind submission might have wrought
What your high spleen and courage cannot do.
Stukeley. Fair courteous lady, had your beauteous self
Asked any thing, a noble English heart

---

84. SH.] *Simpson; no new speaker Q.* 89. SD.] *This ed.; not in Q.*

69. *committing*] offending; 'commit' was sometimes used in a non-specific sense
(*OED v* 6c).
74. *business in the isle*] see n. 13.9.
80. *marshalsea*] here a palace court; in England, a court formerly held before the
steward and the knight marshal of the royal household (later before a barrister
appointed by the knight marshal). Originally it heard cases between the monarch's servants, subsequently having wider jurisdiction (*OED*). Most references in early modern
texts are to the Southwark prison, to which those found guilty by this court were sent.
83. *he is gone*] i.e. the Governor.

Had made you mistress of your own desires.   100
But to be threatened and subjected by him,
Zounds, first I'll fray him out on's government
And vex his very marrow in his bones.
Thinks he, because I am fallen into his hands,
I fear his power? 'Sblood, I'll stare his eyes out first.   105
He looks not on the sun I dare not brave,
I am Stukeley, let him know my name.
Governor's Lady. Brave gentleman, yet I could have wished
I had but been of counsel with your thoughts;
But without breach or touch of modesty,   110
Even for the love I bear unto your country,
Mine honour kept unstained, which I protest
I prize beyond the thing I hold the dearest,
Command what ever lieth in my power
To comfort you in this extremity.   115
Stukeley. Madam,
How much your noble Spanish courtesy hath power in me
A faithful English heart shall manifest,
And I will be the champion of your honour
Wherever I become in Christendom.   120
Governor's Lady. Yes, know a lady of Spain can be as kind
As any English woman of them all.
What is it, signor, I can help you with?
Stukeley. My liberty's the thing I most desire.
Governor's Lady. That presently I cannot warrant you,   125
But I will labour for it to my lord,
With all the means my wits can all devise.
Stukeley. Then this, madam: might I possibly obtain but to work some
means for me, by your best endeavours, that I may have but one
of my horses that I will choose, and but respite for one day to ride 130
a little way, upon some earnest business now, in the absence of
your husband? And as I am a soldier and a gentleman, and by the
honours of my nation, I will come back by the prefixed hour.
Governor's Lady. Sir, should I devise some means for the accomplish-
ment of your desire, and that it should come to my husband's ear 135
before your return, I should hearken for your coming back. Besides,
if by this means you should seek to escape, greater treasons might
be objected than I hope you are guilty of, and what danger both
my life and honour might incur I imagine you are not ignorant.
Stukeley. Madam, if all your wits can but hide it but from your 140

116–17. Madam, / How] *This ed.*; Madam: how Q.

---

102. *fray*] frighten (*OED v¹*).
120. *become*] arrive, come to be (*OED v* 1a).

husband, if he should come before I return, for the other I dare
pawn my soul to you, that I will hold my word.
Governor's Lady. Go to, mine honour and life is your bail.
Let your
return be six o'clock in the evening. I will once trust an Englishman on his word.   *Exeunt.*   145

Scene 14

Enter KING PHILIP, *with him* ALVA *and* SANCTO DAVILA,
with them [BOTELLIO] *the Portugal ambassador.*

King Philip. Speak, reverend intercessor for the state
Of young Sebastian, King of Portugal.

Scene 14] *This ed.;* Sc. xiv. *Levinson; not in* Q.   OSD. BOTELLIO] *This ed.; not in*
Q.   Portugal] *This ed.;* Portingall Q.   1. SH.] *This ed.;* Phil., Phill. *Q;* Phil. *Simpson.*
2. Portugal] *This ed.;* Portingall Q.

Scene 14] The action takes place at the court of Philip II, but is not localised in any
genuine sense. The idea of Stukeley going from Cadiz to Madrid and back in a day
would be absurd in a realistic play, but perfectly normal in Elizabethan dramaturgy,
where time and place are very fluid.

OSD. ALVA] Fernando Alvarez de Toledo, Duke of Alva (1508–83), was Philip II's
most trusted and distinguished general, whose last campaign was the invasion of Portugal to secure the crown for Philip after the battle of Alcazar. The *Uniting* (p. 300)
records, 'With him died (as a man may say) all the warlike discipline of Spaine, for
there remained not any one captaine equall unto him: He was of a goodly stature, of
visage leane and grave, hee had rare gifts of nature, and fortune, the which he augmented much by arte; he was of a noble minde; of a readie and subtill spirite, assured
in judgement, and peaceable.'

SANCTO DAVILA] Sancho de Avila (d. 1583) was the leader of the mutinous Spanish
troops responsible for the 'fury of Antwerp' in 1576, as depicted in *A Larum for London*
(c. 1599), where he is named Sancto Danila. He was 'stroke with a horse' while on the
Portuguese campaign, and died soon after his master Alva, 'the which caused the Castil-
lians to mourne: for although he were but marshall generall of the fielde, yet remaining, after the duke of Alva, of greatest knowledge amongst the Spaniards in the arte of
warre . . . He was a man without feare, and happie in warre, esteemed by the Duke of
Alva above all the soldiers of his time' (*Uniting*, p. 307); see also p. 16.

BOTELLIO] Diego Botelho, or 'Diego Boteglio the Elder' in the *Uniting*, was Don
Antonio's chief agent in his efforts to gain the Portuguese throne, a person well known
in England at the time of this play's first performance. He was with Antonio as the pretender, pursued by Sancho de Avila, and made several narrow escapes (see n. 26 OSD).
In July of 1581 Bernardino di Mendoza, Philip II's ambassador to London, reported
that a party of Portuguese had arrived in England, remarking 'the oldest man in the
company is tall and thin and wears glasses, and may therefore be Diego Botello'. *Del-
l'unione* and the *Uniting* have the Italian spelling 'Boteglio', but he is anonymous in
the anti-Spanish *Explanation*, referred to as 'the Kinges agent, whose name is purposely
concealed in this booke for a certaine consideration' (*CSP Spn.* (1580–86), p. 143;
Explanation, pp. 34–5; *Uniting*, p. 216).

2. *Portugal*] Q indiscriminately mixes 'Portugal' and 'Portingall', so I adopt the
modern form.

What craves our dear entire-beloved cousin,
Wherein we may befriend his majesty?
Botellio. First, sacred King: the sovereign of my faith   5
And Portugal's undoubted supreme head
Doth kindly greet your highness in all love.
Next, on behalf of your respective care
And the league-bond of natural amity,
Which he mistrusts not, but combines ye both   10
As being kinsmen, he entreats this boon:
That whereas lately from the King of Fez,
Muly Mahamet, to my royal master,
Hath honourable embassage been sent
And great entreaty made to crave his aid   15
Against Molocco, brother to that king,
Who now intrudes upon Mahamet's bounds,
And building on his privilege of age
And inequality of matchless strength,
Strives to deprive him of his diadem,   20
It would seem good unto your princely self,
As in the like we shall be ready still,
At Spain's entreaty to assist my lord
With some such necessary strength of war,
As in this action may conclude a peace   25
To Portugal's great profit and renown.
King Philip. Are then Molocco and his brother king
At civil mutiny among themselves?
Botellio. They are, my lord, and many woeful days
Th'afflicted Barbary hath suffered spoil   30
And been a prey unto her natural subjects.
King Philip. The right is in Molocco. Wherefore, then,
Would Prince Sebastian aid the other part?
Beside, Mahamet is an infidel,
From whose associate fellowship, in this   35
And all things else, we Christians must refrain.

---

5. SH.] *This ed.;* Bot. *Q.*   16. ff. Molocco] *This ed.;* Mullucco *Q.*   26. Portugal's]
This ed.; Portingalls *Q.*

---

12. *Fez*] see *Alcazar* n. 1.1.49.
  16. *Molocco, brother to that king*] i.e. Muly Molocco, or Abdelmelec, as in *Alcazar.*
Of course, he was Muly Mahamet's uncle, not brother; the author must have based
these lines, as he does later sequences, on the *Explanation* (p. 3), where the same
mistake occurs: 'Mulei Mahumet Kinge (as hee pretended) of Fez and Maroccos, who
by Mulei Maluco his brother was expelled and driven out of his kingdome'. The relationship is given correctly at 22.58.

Botellio. Grace but his reasons with your mild conceit
    Whereon he grounds his lawful resolution,
    And, mighty Philip, you shall quickly find
    This his intent to be most honourable.   40
    Not for regard of any supreme claim
    The stern Mahamet lays unto the crown,
    Nor any justice that in his behalf
    May be presumed upon, doth stout Sebastian
    List to this motion, but for honour's sake,   45
    For Portugal's chief good, and to advance
    The Christian true religion through those parts,
    Is he inclined to undertake this war.
King Philip. How can that be? Acquaint us with your meaning.
Botellio. This, worthy King: 'tis not unknown to you,   50
    That divers towns and cities situate
    Within the borders of rich Barbary,
    Which King Emanuel conquered by his sword
    And left appropriate still to be enjoyed
    Of such as should be kings in Portugal,   55
    Are but by this prevention like to fall
    And be confiscate to the Moor again.
    But by an army thither brought in time,
    Not only these great cities shall be kept,
    But raising this Mahamet to the crown   60
    And quite extinguishing his brother's claim
    When we have planted him; and that by us,
    The country is subdued and kept in awe,
    We shall not only still retain our own
    But for Mahamet to subscribe to us,   65
    And either he and his to change their faith,
    And worship that eternal God we do,
    Or disannulling, be deprived of life,
    And so assume the government ourselves.
King Philip. This tastes of honour and of policy.   70
    Might it with like success be brought to pass?
Botellio. With your assistance, there's no doubt, my lord,
    But what we have imagined shall ere long,
    Be truly and effectually performed.

---

56. Are] *Simpson;* Or *Q.*   61. extinguishing] *This ed.;* distinguishing *Q.*   66. his to change] *Simpson;* his change *Q.*   68. Or] *Simpson;* And *Q.*

53. *King Emanuel*] Manoel I of Portugal, reigned 1495–1521.
61. *extinguishing*] Simpson retains *Q*'s 'distinguishing', suggesting that it could mean 'extinguishing', but this sense is not in *OED*; a compositor's error is more likely.

King Philip. Ay, but Molocco's army doth consist   75
　　Of dreadless Turks and warlike Saracens.
　　Is much to be suspected in this case.
Botellio. What can they do, though great their number be,
　　When for their single force we come in strength
　　Of Spain, of Portugal and Barbary?   80
King Philip. Your reasons have prevailed. What power is it
　　Our loving cousin doth request of us?
Botellio. Of horse and foot indifferently commixed,
　　Only ten thousand will supply his want.
King Philip. Botellio, so I take it you are called,   85
　　Give place a while till with our faithful lords
　　We have advised us better on the cause,
　　And then you shall have answer presently.

　　　　　　　　　　　　　　　　Exit BOTELLIO.

　　Now, you supporters of our royal state,
　　Alva, and Sanct Davila, briefly show   90
　　What your opinion is touching the suit
　　Of neighbouring Portugal's fame-thirsty king.
Alva. That he attempts an enterprise, my liege,
　　Will sooner break his neck than make him great.
Davila. That hereby if occasion be laid hold on,   95
　　That Spain and Portugal shall be unite,
　　And you the sovereign ruler of them both.
King Philip. Express thy meaning, Davila, in that point.
Davila. It shall not need I stand on circumstance.
　　Your highness knows, Sebastian once removed,   100
　　The way is open solely for yourself,
　　Either by force or by corrupting gold,
　　To step into the throne. Now for a mean
　　To cut him off, what better way than this:

---

77. case] *Simpson;* casse *Q.* 80. Portugal] *This ed.;* Portingall *Q.* 86. lords]
Simpson; lord *Q.* 88. SD.] *rt mgn, l. 89 Q.* 90. ff. Davila] *This ed.;* Danulo *Q.*
92. Portugal's] *This ed.;* Portingals *Q.* 95. SH.] *This ed.;* Da. *Q.* 96. Portugal]
This ed.; Portingall Q; Portingale *Simpson (& l. 118).*

　76. *Saracens*] Originally, a name given to the nomadic people of the Syro-Arabian
desert (*OED sb* 1a); by this time a general term for Turk or other Moslem nation; cf.
Richard II, 'black pagans, Turks, and Saracens' (4.1.86).
　77. *Is much*] There is much. The dropping of a subject before 'is' was not uncom-
mon (Abbott, pp. 291–2).
　90. *Davila*] Q has 'Davila' for the entering SD, and 'Danulo' or 'Danula' in the dialogue. As there is no way of knowing which name was intended, I have kept the more
accurate Davila; see n. 14 OSD
　96. *unite*] a form of 'united' (*OED ppl*).

To sooth his purpose and to draw him on	105
With expectation of a strong supply.
But when he is set forth upon his way
And left his country, that without reproach
And scandal to his name he cannot retire,
Then to proclaim on pain of speedy death,	110
That not a Spaniard seem to join with him.
So landed once in desert Barbary,
His weakened soldiers and himself at once
Shall fall before Molocco's conquering sword.
Alva. Mean space, to colour your intent the better,	115
Muster your men as if you meant to aid him,
But with these men as soon as he is gone,
Approach the borders of fair Portugal,
That if it chance Sebastian do survive
The pagan's sword, yet in his absence we	120
May enter his dominions, sack his towns,
And take possession of the realm by force.
Davila. Withal dispatch ambassadors to Rome,
And forthwith to entreat the Pope's advice,
Who in no wise beforehand we are sure,	125
Will license any Christian potentate
To traffic or converse with heathen kings.
And so his prohibition may excuse
And serve to cloak your breach of promise with,
When 'tis perceived you do not aid Sebastian.	130
King Philip. You counsel well, and fitting our desire
That many years have wished that Portugal
And fruitful Castile, being one continent,
Had likewise been the subject of one sceptre.
Call forth th'ambassador as you have said,	135
So will we dally with our cousin's suit.

Enter BOTELLIO.

My lord Botellio, we have weighed the effect
Of your embassage, and in nature bound,
Beside the affection of near neighbourhood,
To do our kinsman and your noble king	140

---

132. Portugal] *This ed.; Portingall Q;* Portingal *Simpson.* 136. SD. BOTELLIO]
This ed.; Botella *(above l.) Q.* 138. embassage] *This ed.;* imbassage *Q.*

---

105. *sooth*] encourage, humour; cf. *The Wisdom of Doctor Dodypoll* (1600),
'Therefore (in any wise) prepare your selfe / To grace and sooth his great conceit of
him' (sig. B3r).

All offices of kindness that we can,
Tell him from us we only not commend
His haughty mind in this attempt of his,
But his discreet and politic proceeding,
And will therein, to further his intent,   145
Aid him with twice five thousand armèd soldiers
And fifty galleys all well furnishèd,
Which on the fourth of June near to the straits
Of Gibraltar, in a haven there
Called El Porto de Santa Maria,   150
Shall wait his coming on toward Africa
So wishing him a happy prosperous brother,
In all we may, we live to do him good.
Botellio. Thanks to the high and mighty King of Spain.
King Philip. Lord Sanct Davila, bring him on his way.   155
                    Exeunt BOTELLIO, DAVILA.
And, Alva, now what think ye of this plot?
Is it not too severe, ambitious,
And more deceitful than becomes a king?
Alva. A kingdom's thirst hath to dispense, my lord,
With any rigor or extremity,   160
And that which in mean men would seem a fault,
As leaning to ambition or suchlike,
Is in a king but well beseeming him.
Upon my life your grace hath well resolved
And howsoever vulgar wits repine,   165
Yet regal majesty must have his course.

                    Enter DAVILA.

King Philip. Davila, what news? You are so soon returned!
Davila. A gallant Englishman, my gracious lord,

---

149. Gibraltar] *This ed.;* Giberalter *Q.*   150. Santa] *This ed.;* Sancto *Q;* Sancta
Simpson.   151. Africa] *This ed.;* Apheryca *Q.*   155. Lord Sanct Davila] *This ed.;*
Lord Sancto Danulo *Q.*   155. SD.] *This ed.;* Exit Botel. Danulo. *Q.*

---

142. *only not*] Simpson substitutes 'not only', but *Q*'s construction appears elsewhere, e.g. Marston's *The Fawn* (1604), 'the only not beautiful, but very beauty of
women' (4.1.497–8).
    147. *fifty galleys*] See n. 19.15.
    149. *Gibraltar*] *Q*'s 'Giberalter' has the required four syllables, but with a pause
between 'Gibraltar' and 'in', the line scans reasonably well; see *Alcazar* n. 3.Prol.17.
    150. *Porto de Santa Maria*] Puerto di Santa Maria, a seaport on the south-west coast
of Spain, 60 miles north-west of Gibraltar (Sugden). This detail would have been taken
from the *Explanation* (p. 3).
    159–60. *dispense . . . with*] put up with (*OED v* 16).

Haughty in look and hasty in his business,
But now arrived at the court gate,   170
Earnestly craves admittance to your presence.
King Philip. An English gentleman! Let him draw near.

Enter STUKELEY.

Stukeley. Right high and mighty, if to kings installed
And sacredly anointed it belong
To minister true justice and relieve   175
The poor oppressèd stranger, then from thee,
Renownèd Philip, that by birth and place
Upholds the sceptre of a royal king,
Stukeley, a soldier and a gentleman,
But neither like a soldier nor a man   180
Of some of thy unworthy subjects handled,
Doth challenge justice at thy sacred hands,
And succour 'gainst oppression offered him.
King Philip. Oppression offered and by some of ours?
Stukeley. Yes, royal Philip, and in some respect   185
The vile abuse doth touch your majesty.
King Philip. Stand up and tell the manner of thy grief,
And on our royal name we promise thee
Th'offender shall be sharply punishèd.
Alva. A lusty man, believe me, of his limbs.   190
Davila. Ay, and as knightly in his talk, beside.
Stukeley. Thus, kingly Philip: having served of late
Under my prince's army in the field
Against the rude rebellious Irish, where
Upon desire to travel, and especially   195
Upon affection that I had to see
Your princely court so honourably famed,
As also to make tender of my love
And duteous service to your majesty,
Shipping myself with other private goods   200
Which I had purchased by my dint of sword,
I came to Cales, where landed with my prey,
In number thirty hobbies for the shore.
One Don Hernando there, your Governor,

---

177. birth and place] *This ed.;* birth of place *Q;* place of birth *conj. Simpson.*
204. Hernando] *This ed.;* Herando *Q (& l. 237).*

---

177. *birth and place*] Simpson's 'place of birth' cannot be correct, since Stukeley is
not referring to the city or country in which King Philip was born, but to both his
'birth' and his 'place', in the sense of 'high rank or position' (*OED sb¹* 9b); cf. *Histrio-
mastix,* 'Are you the men (for birth and place) admir'd?' (sig. A3v).

Attacheth both my ship and all therein,   205
And though I tell him that the hobbies were
A present for your grace and for that cause
I thither brought them, yet the uncivil lord,
Because he might not have one horse of them
To his own use, clapped irons on my heels,   210
And in a dungeon, like a gripple churl.
I think his purpose was to famish me,
But that by strange adventure and good hap,
I 'scaped his tyrant fingers, hoping here
If I might once get opportunity   215
To let your highness understand thereof,
I should find remedy against his wrong.
King Philip. Have we such base ignoble substitutes
That dare so heinously oppress a stranger,
And such a one as came to offer us   220
The bounty of his heart in friendly gifts?
Let there be sent a messenger forthwith
To bring the wretch to answer his abuse,
And, Stukeley, welcome to King Philip's court.
Repose thyself, thou shalt have right with me,   225
And favour too, again thine enemy.
Stukeley. I thank your majesty, but must entreat
You would vouchsafe to pardon me in this:
I needs must back again to Cales, my lord.
King Philip. Be not afraid thy goods shall be purloined;   230
There's not a mite but he shall bring it forth,
Or of his own purse make it good to thee.
Stukeley. It is not that, an't please your majesty,
But I have passed my word I will return
And Stukeley holds his promise as religion.   235
King Philip. Well then, my lord of Alva give in charge,
Some of our pensioners attend on him,
To bring Hernando hither safely guarded.
Alva. It shall be done, my lord.

                                        Exeunt.

---

206. him] *This ed.;* them *Q.*   227. entreat] *This ed.;* intreat *Q.*   233. an't] *This ed.;*
and *Q;* an' *Simpson.*   237. pensioners] *Simpson;* pentioners *Q.*

---

211. *gripple*] tight-fisted, griping (the sense of 'complaining' is restricted to
American slang). The 'gripple churl' is the Governor, not Stukeley; cf. *The Weakest
Goeth to the Wall* (c. 1595–1600), 'this gripple miser, uncivill wretch' (sig. D4r).
226. *again*] against (*OED prep* 6); cf. Middleton, *Your Five Gallants*, 'Go and
suborn my knave again me here' (2.3.176–7).
237. *pensioners*] in early use, paid or hired soldiers, mercenaries (*OED sb* 1a).

Scene 15

Enter PROVOST *and* GOVERNOR'S [LADY]

Provost. What shall we do? The time draws on,
　The English captain promised to return
　But yet he comes not. If my lord should miss him
　My life were lost, your credit thereby cracked.
Governor's Lady. Content thee, Provost. Such apparent signs　　　5
　Of manly disposition shine in him
　Of valour, gentry and what not beside,
　As I presume if he remain alive,
　He will return at his prefixèd hour;
　As yet the respite that was granted him　　　10
　Is not expired. I do not doubt ere then
　But he will rid us of the fear we are in.
Provost. Had we but, madam, known which way he went,
　Or had himself but told us of the place
　To which he purposèd to make his journey,　　　15
　There had been yet some comfort and some hope.
　But ignorant of both, how can we choose
　But be suspicious and almost despair?
Governor's Lady. Thou talk'st absurdly! Had we known the place,
　The cause which made him and which way he went,　　　20
　What thank were that to us to let him go,
　Where we were sure to find him out again?
　Or how should trial of his faith appear
　In matters of no weight or jeopardy?
　Now being so that of our free accord,　　　25
　Without the least respect but to his promise,
　He was dismissed, and that he clearly sees
　'Tis at his charge to stay on his return,
　And yet will unconstrainèd keep his vow,
　Approves him truly loyal, us truly loving.　　　30
Provost. If I be called in question for his absence,
　Madam, I must rely upon your wit.

Enter [GOVERNOR].

Governor's Lady. Be that thy refuge. Here Hernando comes.
Governor. Provost, I have bethought me at the last
　How to dispose of Stukeley and his goods:　　　35

Scene 15] *This ed.; Sc. xv. Levinson; not in Q.* OSD. LADY] *This ed.; wife Q.*
14. himself but told] *Simpson;* himselfe tolde *Q.* 32. SD. GOVERNOR.] *This ed.;*
Hcrando *Q.* 33. Hernando] *This ed.;* Herando *Q (Sc. 15, exc. l. 89* Hernando.*)*

Scene 15] The action returns to the Governor's residence in Cadiz.

Part of his horses I will give the king
And part I will bestow upon my friends.
To these conditions if he condescend,
I am content he shall have liberty,
And he, his ship and men be so discharged;   40
But otherwise I'll cause his ship be sunk
And he and his as pirates suffer death.
Therefore go fetch him to me presently,
I may be certain if he'll yield or no.
Provost. [*Aside*] Ah, madam, I am strucken dumb and dead!   45
    What shall I answer to my lord's demand?
Governor's Lady. [*Aside*] Be not so fearful lest thy guilty looks
    Argue suspicion of some treachery.
Governor. Dost hear me, Provost? Fetch me Stukeley forth.
Governor's Lady. [*Aside*] Make it as though thou understands
    him not.   50
Governor. Madam, what whispers he into your ear,
    That he neglects to do as I command?
Governor's Lady. He tells me, my lord, the English captain
    Is grown submiss and very tractable,
    And of himself is ready to resign   55
    As much as you require to have of him,
    And that even now after his counsel heard,
    How best he might crave pardon for his pride,
    His stiff resistance, and audacious words,
    Whereto he answered that his readiest way   60
    Was by petition to solicit you.
    And so he tells me, that he left him studying
    How to intend some quaint conceited method
    Might draw remorse from your displeasèd mind.
Governor. Is he, Provost, become flexible?   65
Provost. Exceeding mild and penitent, my lord.
Governor. I thought his stomach would come down at last.
    Go bid him save a labour with his pen
    And tell him we are here. Let it suffice
    If with his tongue he do recant his fault.   70
Governor's Lady. Nay, let him write, for writing will remain
    When words but spoken may be soon forgot.
    It makes the better on your side, my lord,
    That underneath his hand it shall appear
    By his consent and not by your constraint   75

---

45. SD. *Aside*] *This ed.; not in* Q.   47. SD. *Aside*] *This ed.; not in* Q.   50. SD.
Aside] *This ed.; not in* Q.

---

54. *submiss*] See *Alcazar*, n. 2.3.19.

He made surrender of his prize to you.
So shall the world, what after chance do fall,
Clear your extortion and abuse.
Governor. It cannot be but he hath done ere this.
I prithee see – much matter in few lines   80
Is quickly caught by one of meaner wit.
Governor's Lady. It were not good to trouble him so soon.
Governor. I will not subject my desire herein
And wait upon his leisure. Look, I say.
Governor's Lady. (*Aside*) Without some cunning shift we are undone.   85
Governor. Why stay'st thou, Provost, when I bid thee go?
Governor's Lady. [*Aside*] Withdraw thy self to satisfy his mind.
Provost. [*Aside*] Help my excuse, sweet madam, if I fail.
Governor's Lady. Let me alone. [*Exit* PROVOST.] My lord, how glad
   am I
There shall be now atonement of this strife,   90
And that this English gentleman is pleased
To yield obedience, and yourself as willing
To be appeased at his humility.
Governor. I tell thee, wife, he stooped in happy time
Or all submission else had come too late.   95

Enter PROVOST.

Where is he, Provost? Will he come to us?
Governor's Lady. [*Aside*] Is he not yet returned?
Provost (Aside)   Madam, not yet.
Governor's Lady. [*Aside*] Then do I fear our plot will be discovered.
Governor. Why speak'st not, man? Where is thy prisoner?
Provost. He hath not yet, my lord, set down his mind;   100
He doth entreat your honour stay awhile
And he will then have made an end of all.
Governor. I'll wait no longer on his mastership.
Give me the key, I'll fetch him forth myself.
Governor's Lady. What will you do? You fetch him forth yourself?   105
I would not that for all the wealth in Spain!
Will you so much annoy your vital powers

---

77. do fall] *This ed.; to fall Q.*   81. caught] *This ed.; cought Q; coughed Simpson.*
85. SD. *Aside] rt mgn Q.*   87. SD. *Aside] This ed.; not in Q.*   88. SD. *Aside] This
ed.; not in Q.*   89. SD.] *This ed.; not in Q.*   97a. SD. *Aside] This ed.; not in Q;
Simpson brackets ll. 97–8 with single Aside rt mgn.*   97b. SD. *Aside] rt mgn Q.*   98.
SD. *Aside] This ed.; not in Q.*

---

81. caught] Simpson proposes that the Stukeley's 'lines' are to be 'coughed', citing
Henry VIII, 'Tongues spit their duties out' (1.2.62), but it is hard to see how the image
might refer to writing, as distinct from speaking. More likely, Stukeley must have
'caught' the lines, i.e. 'apprehend[ed] by the senses or intellect' (*catch OED v* 35a).

As to oppress them with the prison stink?
You shall not, if you love me, come so near.
The place is mortally infected lately,   110
And as the Provost tells me, divers die
Of strange diseases, and no longer since
Than the last morning two were buried thence!
Ask him, my lord, if this be true or no.
Provost. It is most certain there are many sick,   115
And therefore, good my lord, refrain the place.
Governor. Unless thou bring him straight way to my sight,
Nor danger nor entreaty shall prevail
But I will enter at the door myself.
Governor's Lady. (*Aside*) See once again, it may be he's come.   120
Mean space I'll hold him with some other talk.
Provost. [*Aside*] Do, gentle madam.
Governor's Lady. [*Aside*]   If he be not come,
Protract the time as much as in thee lies.
Provost. [*Aside*] I'll tarry long enough, ne'er doubt of that.
Governor. Sirrah, before thou go: bring him forth   125
Or look to lie in irons as he doth.

                                        [*Exit* PROVOST]
Governor's Lady. I have not seen you often times, my lord,
So out of patience and so far from quiet.
You were not wont in things as great as this
But that you would be persuaded by my words.   130
Governor. I cannot tell how I may think of you,
Your busying of yourself so much herein
And speaking for this Englishman so oft,
Makes me suspect more than I thought to do.
Governor's Lady. Suspect as how, that I do favour him?   135
Or is't your meaning that I go about
To set him free? You're best accuse me flatly
That I have taught him here to break the prison.
Is this the recompense for my good will?
Have I this thank for being provident   140
And careful for your health? Go where you will,
Suspect thyself and me, cut short thy days,
Do any thing that may disparage you,
Hereafter I will learn to hold my tongue.
Governor. How now, my love, what, angry for a word?   145
Governor's Lady. Have I not reason when you grow suspicious
Of me that am yourself your bosom friend?

---

120. SD. *Aside*] *follows next l., rt mgn Q; Simpson brackets ll. 120–4 with single* Aside
rt mgn.   122. SD. *Aside*] *This ed.; not in Q (& next 2 speeches).*   126. SD.] *This
ed.; not in Q.*

Governor. I prithee be content, I meant no harm.
　I know thou wouldst not prejudice my state
　To be the empress of all Asia here.　　　　　　　　　　　150
　Now he comes.

　　　　Enter [PROVOST, *with*] STUKELEY *in gyves.*

Governor's Lady. [*Aside*] Then do I cast off fear,
　And whilst I live hereafter will I trust
　An Englishman the better for his sake.
Governor. Where's the submission that ye told me of?　　　155
　Call ye this repentance for his pride?
Stukeley. What craves the unjust Governor of Cales?
Governor. Obstinate captain, that thou lend thy knee
　And make surrender of what I require,
　Or thou and thine like pirates all shall die.　　　　　　160
Stukeley. I cannot hear, I would you would speak louder.
Governor. Dost thou deride me?
Stukeley.　　　　　　　　　　　Not deride you, sir,
　But for my hobbies I'll not spare a hair
　So much of their tails to pick your teeth.
Governor's Lady. Sweet captain, speak him fair at my entreaty.　　165
Stukeley. Madam, I owe my life to do you service,
　But for his threats I do not care a rush.
Governor. How have I been deluded by your words.
　He scorns me still! Knock off his iron gyves
　And let an executioner be sent for.　　　　　　　　　　170
　I will not stir until I see him dead.
Stukeley. Hernando, I do dare the worst thou canst.
Governor's Lady. O do not provoke him so.
Stukeley. Content you, madam, Stukeley bears a mind
　That will not melt at any tyrant's words.　　　　　　　175
Governor. Call'st thou me tyrant too? It is enough.

　　　　　　　Enter [VALDES].

150–1. Asia here. / Now he comes] *Simpson;* Now he comes *part of SD in Q.*　151.
SD. PROVOST, *with*] *This ed.; not in Q.*　152. SD. *Aside*] *This ed.; not in Q.*　176.
SD.] *This ed.;* Enter Marshall *Q.*

---

151. *Now he comes*] Q has this as a part of the ensuing stage direction, but it must
be the Governor's line.
　SD. *gyves*] See n. 3. 66.
　167. *rush*] straw, a common trope for something of no value (*OED sb*1 2).
　176. SD. VALDES] The 'Marshall' of this direction in Q is later identified as Valdes
at 16.43 SD. Like O'Neill, Alva and Sancho Davila, Don Pedro de Valdés was a famous

In sooth I'll try your patience for that word.
Valdes. Hernando, in his majesty's high name,
  I charge you presently prepare yourself
  To make appearance at the court this night   180
  And bring this gentleman your prisoner here,
  Together with such horses as you have
  Of his in your possession. Fail you not,
  As you will answer it unto your peril.
Governor. How knows the king he was my prisoner?   185
Valdes. What answer make ye? Will, you go with me?
Governor. With all my heart. [*Aside*] This Stukeley is some devil
  And with his sorcery hath incensed the King.
Stukeley. Hernando, if your lordship want a horse,
  One of my hobbies is at your command.   190
Governor. He flatters me, but I must dissemble with him.
  Brave Signor Stukeley, whatsoe'er hath passed
  Betwixt yourself and me, conceive the best:
  It was but trial of your fortitude,
  And now I see you are no less indeed   195
  Than what you seem, a valiant gentleman,
  I do embrace you with a brother's love.
  Come, let us go. I'll do you any grace
  Unto the King my honour extends unto.
Stukeley. When I do need it, I will thank ye, sir.   200
  But, madam, wherein may I quittance you,
  Whose kindness is the cause of all my good?
Governor's Lady. I crave not more for any thing I do
  But that you virtuously report of me,
  And in remembrance of me wear this scarf.   205
Stukeley. This on mine arm, yourself within my heart,
  Doth Stukeley vow perpetually to bear.

                          Exeunt.

---

178. SH.] *This ed.*; Marshall *Q.*   187. SD. *Aside*] *This ed.; not in Q.*

---

individual whose name is used without much reference to his historical role. As commander of the Andalusian fleet and captain of the *Nuestra Señora del Rosario* in the Armada of 1588, he was captured by Sir Francis Drake, who reported the taking of 'a man of greate estimacyon wyth the King of Spayne'. Valdés remained in England until 1593. See *SP Dom. Eliz.* v. 213 [31 July 1588]; *CSP Spn.* (1587–1603), p. 286; Edelman, *Military*, p. 261.

  201. *quittance*] repay; cf. Heywood, *2 Edward IV*, 'Jane Shoare or I may quittance you for this' (sig. X2v).

Scene 16

Enter VERNON *and a* MASTER OF A SHIP *with the* LANTADO
and two or three officers.

Vernon. Signor Lantado, by your patience,
It is no wrack, nor you by law can seize
Upon the ship or goods here cast away.
Lantado. Sir, sir, your negative is of no force.
You are part owner hap'ly of the ship   5
Or else cape-merchant ventured in the freight.
Your speech is partial to save ship and goods.
Vernon. Examine then the master of his oath.
Lantado. So we intend.
Ship's Master.   Sir, you have known me long,
And never knew me falsify my word,   10
Much less mine oath, which I will freely pawn
My life and all, to testify the truth.
Lantado. Whence was the ship?
Ship's Master.   Of London.
Lantado.   What her name?
Ship's Master. The Pelican.
Lantado.   What burden was she of?
Ship's Master. Two hundred ton.   15
Lantado. And what her lading?
Ship's Master.   Packs of English cloth.
This gentleman ought neither ship nor goods
But came from Britain as a passenger,
For at Saint Mallowes we had cause to touch

Scene 16] *This ed.*; Sc. xvi. *Levinson; not in Q.*   6. cape-merchant] *Simpson*; cape-marchant *Q.*   9. SH.] *This ed.*; Ship. M., Ship. Ma., M. Ship. *Q*; M. Ship. *Simpson.*

Scene 16] The setting is the court of Philip II.
OSD. LANTADO] *Adelantado*, a Spanish grandee, lord-lieutenant or governor of a province (*OED*); cf. *Alchemist*, 'What is he, Generall? An Adalantado, / A grandee, girl' (3.3.50–1).
2. *wrack*] shipwreck (*OED sb* 2). Legally, goods cast ashore belong to the finder.
6. *cape-merchant*] head-merchant, or head of traders; derived from 'capo' or similar word (*OED*).
8. *of his oath*] Adams (p. 129) suggests 'on his oath', but cf. *London Prodigal*, one of the 'added seven playes' to the Shakespeare *Third Folio* (1664), 'let him borrow of his oath / For of his word no body will trust him' (p. 2).
17. *ought*] owned (*OED v* 1).
18. *Britain*] i.e. Brittany.
19. *Saint Mallowes*] St Malo, a harbour on the north coast of Brittany. 'It stands on the rocky islet of Aron, and communicates with the mainland by a causeway called *Le Sillon*' (Sugden).

To take aboard a merchant's factor there,   20
And there we found this honest gentleman,
Very desirous to be shipped for Spain.
In luckless hour he brought his trunks aboard
And in more hapless time the same are lost.
Vernon. Small loss were that if all the rest were safe.   25
The men are lost, only we two survive,
Whom you by shows of pity have enforced
To come ashore and leave the crazèd ship.
And will ye now forget what you have sworn
And seek to make a wrack of that is none?   30
Set us aboard again and let us bide
The hazard of the tempest and the tide.
Lantado. Ye are ashore, and thank me for your lives,
Which said, why should you value ship or goods?
You swear you are but passenger; let pass,   35
Let the owners and the merchant wear the loss.
Ship's Master. What if he should? The master there am I,
And were I dead, if any did survive
And live aboard, you cannot make a wrack.
Vernon. No, I will kneel before the King of Spain   40
Before my countrymen such loss sustain.
Lantado. Proud Englishman, since thou art peremptory,
Thou shalt nor kneel nor see his majesty.
Away with them!

> *Trumpets sound. Enter* KING PHILIP *leaning on* STUKELEY'S
> *shoulder,* ALVA, DAVILA, VALDES *that was the messenger*
> [*to Governor*] *Hernando before, and, bare,* GOVERNOR
> *Hernando after, with other*[s].

King Philip. Heroic Stukeley, on our royal word,   45
We never did esteem a present more
Than those fair Irish horse of your frank gift.
Stukeley. Redoubted Philip, royal Catholic King,
It pleaseth so the bounty of your spirit
To reckon them that are of little worth;   50
But if your highness know my inward zeal
To do you service past the world's compare,

---

31. aboard] *Simpson;* abroad *Q.*   44. SD.] *subst. Q.*

---

28. *crazèd*] damaged (*OED ppl* 1); cf. *Jew of Malta,* 'They wondered how you durst
with so much wealth / Trust such a crazèd vessel, and so far' (1.1.79–80).
44. SD. bare] bareheaded.

You would esteem those thirty Irish jades
As thirty mites to all the Indian mines.
King Philip. How we esteem your present and yourself,   55
Our instant favours shall advertise you.
Alva and Sanct Davila shall declare
To gallant Stukeley what regard we bear.
Vernon. [*Aside*] Cross of all crosses, why should sea and wind
Spare me to live where double death's assigned?   60
Is't possible that Stukeley, so deject
In England, lives in Spain in such respect?
King Philip. Stay, what are these?
Vernon.   Poor suitors to your grace.
An English ship is split here in the race,
And this Lantado, the vice admiral,   65
Coming aboard and seeing us alive,
The sole remainder of a hundred souls,
Enticèd us by Christian promises
To come ashore as pitying our case.
Our feet no sooner touched this Spanish earth   70
Than he would make a wrack of ship and goods.
Lantado. Dread sovereign, true, the ship is split and sunk
And every billow over-rakes the hull.
This living couple, crept up to the poop
In dread of danger and of present death,   75
In charity I took to save their lives.
Ship's Master. With promise and proviso, gracious King,
That no advantage should be ta'en thereof,
Else had I stayed though he had gone ashore.
King Philip. Why, what are you?
Ship's Master.   The master of the ship.   80
King Philip. And he the owner or the venturer,
And would deceive us of our royalty?
Vernon. Upon my life, great King, I meant it not.
I am no owner, nor yet venturer.
I came but in her as a passenger,   85
But afore I saw the tide was at the highest
And ebbing water would have laid us dry,
The ship belonging to my place of birth,
I was resolved to bide the utmost brunt,

---

57. Sanct Davila] *This ed.;* Sancto Danula *Q.*   59. SD. Aside] *This ed.; not in Q.*

61. *deject*] dejected, as at 12.13. This is an odd thing for Vernon to say, since we do not see Stukeley 'deject' in any of the English scenes – perhaps an indication of collaborators not being consistent (see pp. 37–8).
86. *afore*] an obsolete form of 'for' (*OED prep*).

And save the ship and goods for th' English owners.   90
King Philip. Whereof you may be one.
Stukeley.   Hear me, great King.
    If you believe this breast have any spark
    Of honour or of vulgar honesty,
    Then credit me: this gentleman that speaks
    Was never owner of a ship in's life,   95
    Nor merchant-venturer, though both trades be good,
    But well derived of rich and gentle birth,
    Holds it his bliss to be a traveller.
King Philip. Your protestations have persuaded us.
    Lantado, leave them and discharge the ship,   100
    And gentleman and shipper stay without.
    This honourable countryman of yours
    Shall bring our further pleasure for your good.
Vernon. [*Aside*] If in the basilisk's forprising eye
    Be safety for the object it beholds,   105
    Then Stukeley may to Vernon comfort bring,
    Else men are safe at sea when sirens sing.
            [*Exeunt*] VERNON, SHIP'S MASTER *and* LANTADO.
King Philip. Now, gallant Stukeley, boast of Philip's grace
    By such employments as we have assigned:
    The King our cousin, Don Sebastian,   110
    Solicits us for aid to Africa
    In hope to conquer the Barbarians.
    The farther princes of that parchèd soil
    Are at contention who shall wear the crown,
    And the young King of Portugal believes,   115
    And so do we, their strife shall breed him peace;
    And for he stands engaged by royal oath
    To help the King of Fez against his foe,
    And craves assistance from us of his blood,

---

104. SD. *Aside*] *This ed.; not in Q.*   forprising] *This ed.;* fore-prizzing *Q.*   107. SD.
Exeunt] *This ed.;* Exit *Q.*   115. Portugal] *This ed.;* Portingall *Q.*   118. King of Fez]
Simpson; king Fez *Q.*

---

    93. *vulgar*] common, ordinary (*OED adj* 3), with no implication of coarseness or
bad taste.
    104. *basilisk's forprising eye*] *OED*'s definition of 'forprise', citing this line, as 'to
take into or include by anticipation' is not consistent with the basilisk's ability to kill
with a glance. Here, the word is more probably a compound of the prefix 'for' as implying harm or destruction (*OED pref.* 5), and 'prise' as 'to seize, capture' (*OED v²*); cf.
Hamlet, 'This is the very ecstasy of love / Whose violent property fordoes itself'
(2.1.103–4).
    112. *Barbarians*] Moors, from Barbary (*Alcazar*, 1.Prol.12); see also p. 38.
    119. *his blood*] his kinsmen (Simpson).

120

We have consented with condition
To give it him, if Rome doth hold it fit.
And you, brave Stukeley, are the man select
To carry to the Pope our embassy,
And we will furnish you for these affairs.
Do not admire the strangeness of our choice   125
In pointing you before our native nobles,
But think our love, our hope, or your desert,
Or all conjoined, advance you to this place.
Stukeley. Most sacred and most mighty King of Spain,
  Though many reasons might withstand belief   130
  That you would choose me your ambassador,
  Yet since your highness twice hath spoke the word
  I humbly credit and accept the charge.
King Philip. And to defray your charge in our affairs
  Our bounty shall exceed her usual bounds: 135
  First, for it is the time of Jubilee,
  Next, for you go from Philip King of Spain,
  And last for high regard we hold you in.
Stukeley. Which favour I will study to deserve.
King Philip. It is deserved. Valdes, deliver you   140
  Five thousand ducats to Don Stukeley's hands.
  Here are our letters and commission
  With such instruction as concern the cause.
  So much for that. Now for your countrymen,
  Whose ship miscarried here upon our coast: 145
  We do allow them all convenient help
  For your sake, to recover ship and goods,
  And that their loss may seem so much the less,
  We do acquit them of all custom fees.
  So, gallant Stukeley, carry them these news,   150
  And make you ready for these great affairs.
Stukeley. Ready to serve and follow your command.
Exit STUKELEY.
King Philip. Are not these English like their country fish
  Called gudgeons, that will bite at every bait?

---

129. and most mighty] *Simpson*; and mighty *Q*. 139. Which] *Simpson*; With *Q*.

121. *if . . . fit*] In fact, Philip II was doing everything he could to resist the Pope's demands that he support the invasion of Ireland, and was well aware that Gregory violently opposed involvement in Africa (see pp. 7–10).

136. *the time of Jubilee*] The Jubilee of the Counter-Reformation was in 1575. Stukeley was then in Rome, but this had nothing to do with any plan to invade Morocco.

154. *gudgeons*] small European fresh-water fish, proverbially a gullible person (*OED sb¹* 2).

How easily the credulous fools believe   155
The thing they fancy, or would wish of chance,
Using no precepts of art prospective
To see what end each project sorteth to.
Hernando, tell me what is thy conceit
Of our election and of Stukeley's worth?   160
Governor. Most gracious and dread sovereign, pardon me
To speak of Stukeley in particular,
Because your frown lies heavy on me yet,
For that I did and offered him at Cales.
But generally I censure th'English thus: 165
Hardy but rash, witty but overweening,
Else would this English hot-brain weigh th'intent
Your highness hath in thus employing him.
King Philip. Thou judgest rightly. It is not for love
We bear this nation that we grace him thus,   170
But use him as the agent of our guile.
For if the matter were of great import,
Or that we would keep touch with Portugal
And aid his voyage into Barbary,
Stukeley should have no hand in these affairs.   175
But now we deal as lords of vineyards use,
Stop with one bush two gaps into their ground:
One must we send to Rome to Jubilee,
And Stukeley for his gift must have reward;
One bounty gilded with employment's grace   180
Serves both the turns, and sends proud Stukeley hence.
Valdes, five thousand ducats, pay him that,
So are we rid of a fond Englishman.

                                                        [*Exeunt*]

Scene 17

Enter STUKELEY *with* VERNON *and the* SHIP'S MASTER

Stukeley. But is it certain that my wife is dead?
Ship's Master. Sure as I live I saw her burièd.

159. Hernando] *This ed.;* Hernandes Q.   173. Portugal] *This ed.;* Portingall Q.
183. SD.] *This ed.;* Exit Omnes Q.

Scene 17] *This ed.;* Sc. xvii. *Levinson; not in* Q.   OSD.] *subst.* Q.

---

156. *of chance*] by chance or fortune.
173. *keep touch*] keep faith (touch OED sb 24).
183. *fond*] foolish, silly (*OED a* 2).

Scene 17] The action continues at the court of Philip II.

First died the mother, then the daughter next,
Then old Sir Thomas Curtis lived not long
And died not rich, but what was left, he gave   5
Part to his brother, part to the hospital.
Stukeley. Then where's the part he left his son-in-law?
Ship's Master. Pardon me, sir, he left no part for you.
Vernon. Your part and grand part were consumed too soon
To have a portion left you at the last.   10
Stukeley. Friend Vernon, leave such discontenting speech.
Your melancholy overflows your spleen
Even as the billows over-rack your ship,
Whose loss the King for my sake will restore.
Then tax me not, good Vernon, with grand parts;   15
What's twenty thousand pound to a free heart,
Twenty weeks' charges for a gentleman?
A thousand pound a week's but fair expense.
Vernon. Your wife died not worth such a week's expense.
Stukeley. What remedy? Yet Stukeley will not want;   20
She's gone, and all her friends, their heads are laid.
Good resurrection have they at the last,
Then shall we meet again. In the mean space
Tom Stukeley lives, lusty Tom Stukeley,
Graced by the greatest King of Christendom.   25

Enter NUNCIO.

Nuncio. The Governor of Cales, Hernando, stays
To cry you mercy and to take his leave.
                                          Exit NUNCIO
Stukeley. There let him stay. I leave him to himself.
I love him not nor malice one so mean.

Enter VALDES.

Valdes. The King, Don Stukeley, prays to speak with you   30
But even a word; he will not stay you long.

---

25. SD.] *This ed;* Enter one of the K. men *Q.*   26. SH.] *Simpson;* Nuntio *Q.*
Hernando] *This ed.;* Hernandes *Q;* Hernandez *Simpson.*   27. SD. NUNCIO]
Simpson; Nuntio *Q.*   29. SD.] *Simpson;* Enter *part of SH in Q.*

5. *died not rich*] Cf. the comment recorded in the *State Papers* that Stukeley raided
his wife's ample inheritance (see p. 6).

25. SD. NUNCIO] usually a papal legate, here an ordinary messenger (*OED sb* 2);
cf. *Twelfth Night*, 'She will attend it better in thy youth / Than in a nuncio's of more
grave aspect' (1.4.27–8).

29. *malice*] to regard with malice (*OED v* 2), common in early modern usage; cf. *1
Tamburlaine*, 'In spite of them shall malice my estate' (1.1.159).

Stukeley. I shall attend his highness by and by.
                                              [*Exit*] VALDES.
    For old acquaintance and for country's sake,
    Vernon and Master, let me banquet you.
    It shall be no disgrace to feast with me   35
    Whom the King useth with so great respect.
Ship's Master. Pardon, sir, I must go see my ship,
    Whose owner shall be thankful for your favour.
Stukeley. What says Master Vernon?
Vernon.   I, some other time
    May trouble you, although it be not now.   40
Stukeley. As your occasions shall induce you, sir.
                                          Exit STUKELEY.
Vernon. Good Master, see if any thing of mine
    May from the ship be safely brought ashore,
    And I will see your pains considerèd.
Ship's Master. I do not doubt but all your stuff is safe,   45
    The hatches are as close as any chest;
    Nothing takes hurt but what is in the hold
    Because the keel is split upon the sands.
    I'll send your trunks ashore and then provide
    To seek our drowned men and to bury them.   50
                                  Exit [SHIP'S MASTER].
Vernon. Not all the drowned, but those are drowned and dead,
    For I am drowned in my conceit alive.
    Some sin of mine hath so offended heaven
    That heaven still sends offence unto mine eye.
    What should I think of Stukeley or myself?   55
    Either was he created for my scourge
    Or I was born the foil to his fair haps,
    Or in our birth our stars were retrograde.
    In Ireland there he braved his governor,
    In Spain he is companion to the King;   60
    His fortune mounts and mine stoops to the ground,
    He as the vine, I as the colewort grow,
    I live in every air but where he breathes;
    His eye is as the Gorgon's head to me
    And doth transform my senses into stone.   65

32. SD. Exit.] *This ed.*; Exeuut *Q.*   50. SD.] *This ed.*; Exir *Q.*   61. fortune] *This ed.*; fortunes *Q.*

57. *haps*] chance or fortune (good or bad) that falls to any one (hap OED sb¹ 1).
62. *colewort*] a type of cabbage; cf. Middleton's *Mad World My Masters*, 'Sir Aquitan Colewort, most welcome' (2.1.3–4).

Some hold Spain's climate to be very hot,
I feel my blood congealed to ice in Spain;
The leopard lives not near the elephant,
Nor I near Stukeley. Spain, farewell to thee,
Either I'll range this universe about   70
Or I will be where Stukeley hath no being.

                                                    Exit.

Scene 18

Enter STUKELEY, VALDES, *Stukeley's* PAGE,
and one bearing bags sealed.

Stukeley. How many ducats did the King assign?
Valdes. Five thousand.
Stukeley.   Are they all within these bags?
Valdes. Well near.
Stukeley.   How near?
Valdes.   Perhaps some twenty want.
                          The bags are set on the table.
Stukeley. Why should there want a marmady? a mite?
Doth the King know that any ducats lacks?   5
Valdes. He doth, and saw the bags would hold no more
And sealed them with his signet, as you see.
Stukeley. Valdes, return them. I will have none of them,
And tell thy master, the great King of Spain,
I honour him but scorn his niggardice   10
                          Cast the bags to the ground.
And spurn abridgèd bounty with my foot.
Abate base twenty from five thousand ducats,
I'll give five thousand ducats to my boy.
If I had promised Philip all the world
Or any kingdom, England sole except,   15
I would have perished or performed my word
And not reserved one cottage to myself,

Scene 18] *This ed.; Sc. xviii. Levinson; not in Q.*

68.] seemingly proverbial, but there is nothing in Aelian, Albertus Magnus or Topsell on this subject.

Scene 18] The action continues at Philip II's court.

4. *marmady*] presumably 'maravedi', at the time a copper coin of little value (*OED sb* 1).

5. *ducats lacks*] See n. 10.48.

Nor so much ground as would have made my grave.
Foutre for ducats if he take the tithe!
Tell him I'll do his business at Rome   20
Upon my proper cost; but for his crowns
Since they come curtailed, carry them again.
Come, boy, to horse, away! Spaniard, farewell.
Valdes. Stay sir, I pray ye, till I move the King.
Stukeley. Thou mov'st a mountain sooner than my mind.   25
                                        [*Exeunt*] STUKELEY *and his* PAGE.
Valdes. What a high spirit hath this Englishman.
He tunes his speeches to a kingly key,
Conquers the world, and casts it at his heels.

                    Enter KING PHILIP *and his lords.*

Here comes the King.
King Philip.   How now, is Stukeley gone?
Valdes. Gone, and will do your business at Rome,   30
Though he refused the ducats you assigned.
King Philip. How so?
Valdes.   Because that twenty ducats want.
King Philip. Amongst five thousand may not twenty lack?
Valdes. No, he supposeth you repent your gift
If you abridge your bounty but a mite.   35
King Philip. Not for the world shall Stukeley go without.
Go add a thousand ducats more to these
And post and pray him not to be displeased.
Tell him I did it but to try his mind
Which I commend above my treasury,   40
If England have but fifty thousand such
The power of Spain their coast shall never touch.
Come, lords, to horse, to Seville lies our way,
Valdes, I charge you to eschew delay.
                                                       Exeunt Omnes.

---

19. Foutre] *Simpson;* Footer *Q.*   25. SD. *Exeunt*] *This ed.;* Exit *Q.*   34. No, he]
Simpson; No no, he *Q.*   42. shall never touch] *Simpson;* shall touch *Q.*   43. Seville]
This ed.; Cyvilt *Q.*

19. *Foutre*] lit. 'fuck'; cf. Pistol in 2 *Henry IV*, 'A foutre [Q fowtre F footra] for
thine office!' (5.3.116).
43. *Seville*] *Q's* 'Cyvilt' is one of several early modern spellings. Emphasis was
always on the first syllable; e.g. *Jew of Malta*, 'Their voyage will be worth ten thousand crowns / In Florence, Venice, Antwerp, London, Seville' (4.1.70–1).

Scene 19

Enter SEBASTIAN, ANTONIO, *the* CARDINAL [*Henry*] *and* BOTELLIO.

Sebastian. The great and honoured promise thou return'st us
From our brave kinsman, Philip King of Spain,
My dear Botello, adds a second life
Unto the action that we have in hand.
The joyful breath that issues from thy lips   5
Comes like a lusty gale to stuff our sails,
Curling the smooth brows of the Afric deep.
O let me hear thy tongue sound once again
The cheerful promise of our new supplies.
Botellio. Why thus: imperial Spain bade me return   10
Unto the great puissant Portugal
Ten thousand foot of gallant Spanish blood,
Men born in honour and exploits in war
And not on Indian or base bastard Moor;
Fifty his galleys of the proudest vessels   15
That to this day yet ever bare an oar,
To meet you at the Port de Sant Maria
The fourth of June.
Sebastian. The fourth of June, at Port de Sant Maria:
Ten thousand foot, and fifty of his galleys   20
By land and sea and at a certain time!
O what a gallant harmony is here;
Methinks that I could stand and still repeat them
A month together, they so please my soul.
Ha Antonio, O what an army's here!   25

Turning to [*Antonio*]

Scene 19] *This ed.*; Sc. xix. *Levinson; not in Q.*   OSD.] *This ed.*; Enter Sebastian,
Antonia, Herando, the Cardnall and Botellio *Q.*   1. SH] *This ed.*; Seba., Sebast. *Q.*
11. Portugal] *This ed.*; Portingall *Q.*   25. SD.] *This ed.*; Turning to the king of
Portingall *Q.*

Scene 19] The action moves to the court of King Sebastian, Lisbon.
OSD. CARDINAL Henry] King Sebastian's great-uncle, who ruled Portugal for a
short time after Sebastian's death. Q's 'Herando' is probably a misreading of 'Hen.',
the compositor confusing him with the Governor; he is 'Henry' in the *Explanation* (see
pp. 15–16).
11. *puissant*] Here pronounced with three syllables, as in *Henry V*, 'And make
imaginary puissance' (Prol.25).
15. *Fifty his galleys*] This and subsequent details of what Philip promised Sebastian
are taken from the *Explanation* (p. 3).
16. *bare*] common as past tense of 'bear' at the time; cf. *Romeo and Juliet*, 'Who
bare my letter then to Romeo?' (5.2.13).
25 SD.] Adams (p. 109) takes Q's very strange direction, '*Turning to the king of
Portingall*', as evidence that the scene comes from the 'lost' play he calls *Sebastian and*

I tell thee, cousin, never Christian king
Came with so proud a power to Africa.
Antonio. And yet the greatness of your royal spirit
  Makes all this nothing, so your glory shines
  Above the power of Spain and Portugal.   30
Sebastian. Cousin Antonio, to pay Botellio back
  The interest of his Spanish embassy,
  As you have taken muster of our powers,
  Report the number what our army is.
Antonio. Unto your number of ten thousand Spaniards   35
  In the King's army, add to this, Botellio:
  Three thousand mercenary Spanish Moors,
  Of voluntary valiant Portugals
  Three thousand three score special men of arms;
  The garrison of Tangier; and light horsemen   40
  Five thousand and four hundred;
  Five thousand Germans and Italians;
  My power three thousand; and the Duke Avero's
  Doubles my number, if fully more,
  Besides the power that we do expect from Rome.   45
  Thirty-seven thousand we are now complete.
Sebastian. Our army joined with that Mahamet brings,
  His Barbarians and his mountain Moors
  Brought from the deserts of burnt Africa,
  His valiant Turks, trained up in spoil of war,   50
  His soldiers of Morocco and of Sirus,
  To fifty thousand as his promise is.
  Ha, brave Antonio, there will be a power
  To affright the very walls of Fez

---

30. Portugal] *This ed.;* Portingall *Q.* 38. Portugals] *This ed.;* Portingals *Q;* Portingalls *Simpson.* 40. Tangier] *n. Simpson;* Taieer *Q.* 54. Fez] *Simpson;* Fes *Q.*

Antonio: 'this error may be due to the fact that the latter part of the play represented [Antonio] as king'. More likely, it is another careless error deriving from the author's dependence upon the *Explanation*, a work written to justify Antonio's claim, and where he is referred to as 'King' Anthony or 'the King Don Antonio' from p. 26 onwards (see pp. 34–7).

43. *Duke Avero's*] See *Alcazar,* n. 2.4.54.

50. *valiant Turks*] Abdelmelec's 'dreadless Turks' (14.76), led by Calsepius Bashaw in *Alcazar,* appear to have changed sides temporarily. *Henry V* has a similar inconsistency – Henry fears a Scottish invasion if he goes to France (1.2.136–9), yet Captain Jamy's Scots fight alongside him at Agincourt.

51. *Sirus*] possibly Syrtis, two bays on the north coast of Africa; Syrtis Major is the present Gulf of Sidra, Syrtis Minor the Gulf of Cabes (Sugden).

54. *Fez*] Q has 'Fes' here, and 'Fesse' thereafter, but 'Fez' in the earlier Spanish scenes, perhaps another indication that the Spanish and African sequences had different authors.

And make stout Afric tremble at the sight,   55
Where we shall brave her on the sunburned plains
And with our cannons crush her wanton head.
O, my Antonio, how I long to see
How Spanish blood and Turkish will agree.
Antonio. How shall it please your sacred majesty   60
To appoint the sev'ral charges of this war?
Sebastian. Cousin Antonio, in this heat of war,
For the safety of our royal kingdom,
Let us yet speak of things concern our peace,
Although but brief. First, our dearest cousin,   65
For your princely self:
Your right unto the crown of Portugal
As first and nearest of our royal blood,
That should we fail, the next in our succession
'Tis you and yours to sit upon our throne,   70
Which is our pleasure to be publishèd.
Antonio. Long may my liege and sovereign lord, Sebastian,
Sit on the royal throne of Portugal.
Sebastian. We thank you, princely cousin.
Our dear and reverend uncle Cardinal,   75
Unto ourself commit our wars in Africa.
For the great trust we repose in you,
We do bequeath our kingdom's government,
As one whose wisdom and nobility
Deserves the great protection of our realm.   80
Cardinal. The most unworthy of that royal place,
Whose many years and imbecility
Are but too weak to underprop the burden;
But may the remnant of my age be spent
To Portugal's relief and your content.   85
Sebastian. Now, Antony, unto our several charges:
Yourself will share the fortunes in these wars;
We do commit a garrison of Tangier

---

55. sight] *Simpson;* fight *Q.*   67. Portugal] *This ed.;* Portingall *Q.*   73. Portugal]
This ed.; portingall *Q;* Portingall *Simpson.*   81. SH.] *This ed.;* Card. *Q.*
85. Portugal's] *This ed.;* Portngals *Q;* Portingals *Simpson.*   88. Tangier] *This ed.;*
Tanieers *Q.*

67.] Sebastian's naming Antonio as his successor has no historical basis, although
the merits, or lack thereof, of Antonio's claim are the subject of both the *Explanation*
(for) and the *Uniting* (against); see pp. 26–7.

82. *many years and imbecility*] age and physical weakness – 'imbecility' as 'stupid-
ity' came into use in the nineteenth century. Cardinal Henry was only sixty-seven, but
was 'deaf, half-blind, toothless, senile and racked by tuberculosis' (Henry Kamen, *Philip
of Spain*, New Haven, 1997, p. 170).

Unto the leading of Alvares Peres,
Our voluntary Portugals to Lodovico Caesar,   90
The mercenary Spaniards to Alonso,
Meneses lieutenant general of our forces,
Tavora for the German colonel.
And now set forward, let our ensigns fly,
Either victorious or if conquered die.   95

                                                  [Exeunt.]

Scene 20

Enter CHORUS.

Chorus. Thus far through patience of your gentle ears
    Hath Stukeley's life in comic history
    Been new revived, that long ago lay wracked
    In dust of Afric with his body there.
    Thus far upon the steps of high promotion   5
    His happy stars advanced him. Now at highest,
    As clearest summer days have darkest nights
    And every thing must finish, so in him,
    His state declining draws unto an end.
    For by the Pope created as you heard   10
    Marquess of Ireland, with that new honour
    Embarked and victualled, think him on the sea,
    And that the time Sebastian had set down
    To meet with Philip's promised aid is past.
    Toward Afric he, toward Ireland the other,   15
    Are both addressed upon the boisterous waves,
    But, meeting, what strange accident befell.

---

90. Portugals] *This ed.;* Portingalls Q.   92. Meneses] *This ed.;* Mereneces Q.   93.
Tavora] *This ed.;* Tanara Q.   95. SD.] *This ed.; not in* Q.

Scene 20] *This ed.;* Sc. xx. Levinson; *not in* Q.

---

  89. *Alvares Peres*] Alvaro Peres de Tavora; see *Alcazar*, n. 4.1.30.
  90. *Lodovico Caesar*] See *Alcazar*, n. 3.4.72.
  90–2. The author has done no better than Peele at writing troop lists in blank verse
(see *Alcazar*, 4.1.38–42).
  91. *mercenary Spaniards to Alonso*] see *Alcazar*, n. 4.1.35.
  92. *Meneses lieutenant general*] Duarte Meneses, Governor of Tangier, see *Alcazar*,
n. 3.3 OSD.
  93. *Tavora*] Christophero de Tavora, see *Alcazar*, n. 2.4.75.

  10–11. *as you heard / Marquess of Ireland*] an apparent reference to a scene or
scenes, missing from Q, showing Stukeley's adventures in Rome, but see pp. 44–5.

How he was altered from his first intent
And he, deluded by the hope he had
To be ascribèd by the Castile King,　　　　　　　　　　20
Regard this show and plainly see the thing.

Enter at one door PHILIP *King of Spain,* ALVA *and soldiers. They*
take their stand. Then enter another way, SEBASTIAN, *Don*
ANTONIO, AVERO, *with drums and ensigns. They likewise take their*
stand. After some pause ANTONIO *is sent forth to Philip, who, with*
obeisance done, approaching away again very disdainfully; and as the
Spanish soldiers are about to follow Antonio, PHILIP *with his drawn*
sword stops them and so departs. Whereat SEBASTIAN *makes show*
of great displeasure, but whispering with his lords, each encouraging
[the] other as they are about to depart. Enter STUKELEY *and his*
Italian band, who, keeping aloof, SEBASTIAN *sends Antonio to him,*
with whom STUKELEY *draws near toward the King, and having*
awhile conferred at last retires to his soldiers, to whom he makes
show of persuading them to join with the Portuguese. At first they
seem to mislike, but [at] last they yield. And so both armies meeting,
[they] embrace, when with a sudden thunder-clap the sky is on fire
and the blazing star appears, which they, prognosticating to be
fortunate, depart very joyfully.

So far was Philip, as you have beheld,
From lending aid unto the Portuguese,
He, not content to undergo the blot
Of breach of promise, but with naked sword　　　　　25
Of unavoided justice threatens such
As should but offer to depart the land.
Whereby the prince, though very much disturbed
Yet not dismayed, so haughty was his mind,
Resolveth still to prosecute his journey.　　　　　　30
And whilst they are debating on the cause,
Stukeley by weather is driven in to them,
Who, being known what countryman he was,
What ships he had and what Italian bands

---

21. SD. *on fire*] *Simpson;* one fire *Q.*　24. He, not] *This ed.; Is* not *Q.*

20. *ascribèd*] presumably 'promoted' or 'advanced', although the closest *OED* definition for 'ascribe' is the rare 'to appoint to a vacancy' (*v* 4).
  21. *Regard this show*] The action of the following dumb show is taken directly from
the *Explanation* (see *Alcazar,* n. 3.3.39).
  24. *He, not*] 'He', or similar, needs to replace *Q*'s 'Is' here, otherwise the sentence
has no subject. The sense is that Philip not only withheld aid but actively forbade
volunteers from helping Sebastian.
  26. *unavoided*] unavoidable.

212 CAPTAIN THOMAS STUKELEY [SC. 21

And whereto he was bound, th'offence thereof,   35
The great dishonour and impiety
Laid open by Sebastian, straight recants
And moves his soldiers, which with much ado
At last are won to make for Barbary.
No sooner was this fellowship contrived   40
And they had joined their armies both in one,
But heaven, displeased with their rash enterprise,
Sent such a fatal comet in the air,
Which they misconst'ring shone successfully,
Do haste the faster, furrowing through the deep.   45
And now suppose (but woe the wretched hour,
And woe that damned Mahamet, whose guile
This tender and unskilled yet valiant king
Was thus allured unto a timeless death),
That in Arzil, a town in Barbary,   50
They all are landed and not far from thence
Do meet that straggling fugitive, the Moor,
With some small forces. What doth then ensue
We may discourse, but Christendom shall rue.

Exit.

Scene 21

Enter MULY MAHAMET *with* CALIPOLIS, *drawn in their chariot,
with them a* MESSENGER *from Sebastian.*

Muly Mahamet. Go let ten thousand of our guard be sent
To entertain the great Sebastian,
And welcome, Christian, to the King of Fez,
And tell the Portugal, thy royal master,

50. Arzil] *This ed.;* Tyrill *Q.*

Scene 21] *This ed.;* Sc. xxi. *Levinson; not in Q.* 1. SH.] *This ed.;* sebast. *Q;* Maham. *Simpson.* 3. ff. Fez] *Simpson;* Fesse *Q.* 4. Portugal] *This ed.;* portingall *Q,*

35-7. th'offence thereof ... Sebastian] This idea appears to draw on *Alcazar*, 2.4.98–136.
43. *fatal comet*] See *Alcazar*, n. 1.1.42.
44. *shone successfully*] i.e. augured their success.
50. *Arzil*] *Q*'s 'Tyrill' must be a misreading (Sugden); see *Alcazar*, n. 4.1.3.

Scene 21] None of the dialogue in the scene suggests a precise locale; in *Alcazar* the first meeting of Muly Mahamet and Sebastian occurs at Tangier.
OSD. chariot] The Rose's chariot, used in *Tamburlaine* and in *Alcazar*, is put into action again (see *Alcazar*, n. 1.2 OSD; p. 28).

That Afric makes obeisance to his feet   5
And stoops her proud head lower than his knee.
Tell him mine eyes are thirsty for his presence.
Messenger. I will return to tell your highness' pleasure.
Muly Mahamet. Do so, begone.
                                        [*Exit* MESSENGER.]
And let our chariot be drawn softly forward,   10
Where I and my Calipolis will sit
To grace the entrance of great Portugal.
Now, fair Calipolis, rouse thy proud beauty,
And strike their eyes with verdure of thyself.

            He leaps from his chariot.
    Enter SEBASTIAN, [ANTONIO *and* STUKELEY]
            at the sound of trumpets.

Dismount thee, Muly, from thy chariot wheels   15
To entertain the mighty Christian king.
Welcome, Sebastian, King of Portugal.
Sebastian. Thanks to the mighty and imperial Fez.
Why thus alights the mighty emperor?
Muly Mahamet. That I will do great Portugal the grace   20
To set thee by Calipolis my queen.
Sebastian. Let mighty Muly's self supply that place
And give me leave to attend upon your love.
Muly Mahamet. Mount thee, Sebastian, Muly doth command,
It is my pleasure, I will have it so.   25
Mount thee, brave lord, and sit thee on her side
And say, Sebastian, that the son of Phoebus
Upon his father's fiery burnished car
Ne'er sat so glorious as the Portugal.
Jove would exchange his sceptre for thy seat   30
And would abandon Juno's godlike bed,
Might he enjoy my fair Calipolis.
Welcome Sebastian, love, to Africa.

9. SH.] *This ed.;* Maha., Muly, Muli. *Q.* 9. SD.] *This ed.; not in Q.* 12. Portugal]
This ed.; Portingale *Q.* 14. verdure] *This ed.;* verder *Q.* 14. SD. ANTONIO
and STUKELEY] *This ed.; not in Q.* 17. Portugal] *This ed.;* portingale *Q.*
20. Portugal] *This ed.;* portingall *Q.* 29. Portugal] *This ed.;* portingall *Q;* Portingale
Simpson.

14. *verdure*] unless Calipolis is intended to turn bright green, the word must be
taken figuratively as her 'fresh or flourishing condition' (*OED sb* 6).
27–8.] In the *Metamorphoses,* Ovid tells the story of Phoebus Apollo granting his
son Phaethon's wish to drive the sun chariot. Unable to control the 'four swift horses
of the sun' (2.153), Phaethon took the chariot far too close to Africa, hence 'the
Aethiops then turned black, so men believe' (2.236); cf. *Alcazar,* n. 2.1.39.

Calipolis. All welcome that Calipolis can give
   To the renownèd mighty Portuguese.   35
   Here sit, sweet prince, and rest thee after toil.
   I'll wipe thy brows with leaves more sweet and soft
   Than is the down of Cytherea's doves,
   I'll fan thy face with the delicious plumes
   Of that sweet wonder of Arabia.   40
   With precious waters I'll refresh thy curls,
   Whose very savour shall make panthers wild
   And lonely smell of those delicious sweets,
   And with such glorious liquors please thy taste
   As Helen's goblet never did contain,   45
   Nor never graced the banquets of the gods.
Muly Mahamet. Then speak, the comfort of great Muly's life.
   Her teeth more white than Caucas' frosty clots,
   Where she unlocks the portals of her lips,

---

35. Portuguese] *This ed.;* Portinguyse *Q.*   38. doves] *This ed.;* fans *Q;* swans *conj. Adams.*   40. Arabia. / With] *This ed.;* Arabia, / With *Q.*   43. lonely] *This ed.;* lively *Q.*

---

38. *Cytherea's doves*] Cytherea is another name for Venus – one of the several legends associated with her birth has her emerging from the sea by the shores of the island of Cythera. *Q* has 'Cithereas fans', but 'fans' is obviously taken from the succeeding line – Venus's bird was the dove, as in the *Metamorphoses*: 'Juno's fine bird whose tail bright stars adorn / Jove's weapon bearer, Cytherea's doves / And the whole tribe of birds' (15.385–7).

40. *sweet wonder of Arabia*] the Phoenix, cf. *Selimus,* 'The sacred Phoenix of Arabia / Loadeth his wings with pretious perfumes' (sig. H3r).

41. *precious waters*] frankincense. The image derives from the same passage in *Metamorphoses* used for 'Cytherea's doves': Ovid next describes the Phoenix, which feeds on 'oils / Of balsam and the tears of frankincense [*turis lacrimis*]' (15.393–4). According to Calipolis, such tears, or 'precious waters', make an excellent hair conditioner.

42–3. *panthers wild / And lonely*] *Q* has 'wild / And lively', but 'lonely' seems more apt, even though *OED*'s earliest citation is Coriolanus' 'I go alone / Like to a lonely dragon' (4.1.30–1). The sense seems to be that 'wild and lonely' panthers would come to smell the 'delicious sweets' of Sebastian's frankincense-rinsed curls. Topsell, in *The Historie of Foure-Footed Beasts* (London, 1607, pp. 575, 500), cites Albertus Magnus on the panther, 'commonly called a pardall, a leopard . . . so great is the love of this beast to all spices and aromaticall trees, that they come over the mountaine Taurus through Armenia and Silia, when the winds bring the savor of sweet gum unto them'.

48. *Caucas' frosty clots*] the snow on the Caucasus. A clot could be any lump or rounded mass (*OED sb* 1); cf. William Baldwin, *The Funeralles of King Edward the Sixt* (London, 1560, sig. A4r), 'In rockes and caves of snow and clottred yse'.

Beauty, a phoenix, burneth in her eye,   50
Which there still liveth as it still doth die.
Stukeley. Why here's a gallant, here's a king indeed!
He speaks all Mars! Tut, let me follow such a
Lad as this! This is pure fire,
Every look he casts flasheth like lightning,   55
There's mettle in this boy,
He brings a breath that sets our sails on fire.
Why now I see we shall have cuffs indeed.
Antonio. Now afore God, he is a gallant prince.
Muly Mahamet. What princes be these in your company?   60
Sebastian. That is our cousin Prince Antonio,
The other Stukeley, the brave Irish Marquess.
Muly Mahamet. Noble Antonio, and renownèd Marquess,
Ten thousand welcomes into Africa.
Antonio. Thanks to great Muly.
Stukeley.   To your mightiness.   65
Muly Mahamet. Next, now, the neighing of our warlike horse
Shall shake the palace of commanding Jove,
Our roaring cannons tear the highest clouds
And fright the sun out of his wonted course.
Afric, I'll dye thy tawny sands in blood   70
And set a purple on thy sunburnt face.
This is the day thy terror first began.
Before great Muly, King Sebastian,
Drive on, and I will lackey by thy side.
These Christian lords I trust will take no scorn   75
When Muly Hamet bears them company.
Away!

                                                   Exeunt.

---

73. King] *This ed.*; and *Q.*

52–8. Stukeley, in these seven lines, returns to the Stukeley of the first half of the
play, irreverent and dismissive of pretension. As this is the only passage that bears the
metrical irregularities of the early scenes, it seems likely that the author of the London
sequence provided it as a later revision (see p. 42).
  54. *Lad*] Stukeley is being particularly insulting by using 'lad' here and 'boy' at l.
56; cf. Coriolanus' indignant repeating of the word (5.6.112–17).
  71. *purple*] pustule, or bubo of the plague (*OED n* 4a).
  73. *King Sebastian*] *Q*'s 'and Sebastian' is nonsensical.
  74. *lackey*] to do service as a lackey (*OED v* 1); cf. Heywood, *Brazen Age* 'I'le lackey
by thee wheresoer'e thou goest' (sig. B4v).
  76. *Muly Hamet*] Muly Mahamet, the verse requiring four syllables.

Scene 22

Two trumpets sound at either end: Enter [at one door]
MULY HAMET, *and [at another door]* ANTONIO.

Antonio. Second thy sound, whate'er thou be'st that call'st,
  And with thy proud importance greet our ears.
Muly Hamet. What African or warlike Portugal
  Comes forth to answer?
Antonio.   Muly Hamet, aye?
Muly Hamet. Antonio?   5
Antonio. The same, proud Moor, that proud Portugal.
Muly Hamet. Where is Sebastian?
  He comes not forth himself to answer me?

Enter SEBASTIAN, [MULY] MAHAMET *and [their] train.*

Sebastian. Here, Muly Hamet, here, stout African.
  What wouldst thou, Hamet, with the Portuguese?   10
  Where's Abdelmelec, thy proud haughty brother?

Enter ABDELMELEC *and his train.*

Abdelmelec. Here, brave Sebastian, King of Portugal.
Sebastian. O art thou there? Thyself in presence then,
  What wouldst thou beg, proud Abdelmelec? Speak!
Abdelmelec. Beg? It is a word I never heard before,   15
  Yet understand I what thou mean'st thereby.
  There's not a child of manly Sharif's line
  But scorns to beg of Mahomet himself.
  We shall lead Fortune with us bound about
  And sell her bounty as we do our slaves.   20
  We mount her back, and manage her for war
  As we do use to serve Barbarian horse,
  And check her with the snaffle and the reins.

Scene 22] *This ed.;* Sc. xxii. *Levinson; not in* Q.   OSD.] *This ed.;* Two Trumpets
sound at either end: Enter Mully hamet and Antonio *Q.*   1. sound] *This ed.;* sonne
Q.   3. SH.] *This ed.;* Muly Ham., Muly, Hamet, Maha. *Q.* Portugal] *This ed.;*
Portingall *Q*; Portingale *Simpson.*   7–8. Sebastian? / he comes not forth himself] *This
ed.;* sebastian: he comes not forth / Himselfe *Q;* Sebastian? he comes not forth / Himself
Simpson.   8. SD.] *This ed.;* Enter Sebastian: Mahamet and the traine *Q.*   12. SH.]
This ed.; Abdel *Q.* Portugal] *This ed.;* Portingall *Q*; Portingal *Simpson.*   15. Beg?
It is] *This ed.;* Beg, it is *Q*; Beg, 'tis *Simpson.*   17. Sharif's] *This ed.;* Zariks *Q.*
23. reins] *Simpson;* razins *Q.*

  Scene 22] The action occurs near Alcazar.
  OSD.] MULY HAMET] i.e. Muly Mahamet Seth of *Alcazar*, Abdelmelec's brother
and successor (see fig. 1; pp. 31–3).
  17. Sharif's] See *Alcazar*, n. 1.1.50.

We bend her swelling crest, and stop and turn
As it best likes us, haughty Portugals.   25
Sebastian. We'll spur your jennet, lusty African,
And with our pistols we'll prick her pampered sides
Until with yerking she do break her girths,
And fling her gallant rider in the field,
And say, proud Moor, that so said Portugal.   30
Abdelmelec. Thy words do sound of honour, Christian King,
Which makes me therefore pity thee the more
And sorrow that thy valour should be sunk
In such a vasty unknown sea of arms,
Where thy high courage cannot bear that sail   35
That thy proud haughty spirit would gladly have.
Therefore, Sebastian, cast aside these arms
That thou unjustly bear'st against thy friend,
And leave that traitor that but trains thee on
Into the jaws of thy destruction.   40
Muly Mahamet. Brave young Sebastian, King of Portugal,
And Don Antonio, hear me, gallant lords:
Muly Mahamet, but you are in presence,
Would think himself damned everlastingly
But to hold crack with so base a slave,   45
Whose coward melting soul for very fear
Comes frighted up and down within his bosom
And fain would find a passage from his breast,
So daunted with the terror of our arms,
That he is mad his soldiers will not fly,   50
That with some colour he might turn his back.
Seest thou, the power of Afric's in my hand,

---

25. Portugals] *This ed.*; portingalls *Q*; Portingales *Simpson*.   28. yerking] *This ed.*; yarking *Q*.   30. Portugal] *This ed.*; Portingall *Q*.   35. high courage] *This ed.*; bid courage *Q*; old cordage *conj Simpson*.   38. bear'st] *This ed.*; beares *Q*; bears *Simpson*. 41. Portugal] *This ed.*; Portingall *Q*.   45. crack] *conj. Adams*; wrack *Q*.   48. passage] *conj. Adams*; message *Q*.

---

26. *jennet*] a small Spanish horse (*OED sb*[1]); cf. *Venus and Adonis*, 'A breeding jennet, lusty, young, and proud / Adonis' trampling courser doth espy' (ll. 260–1).
28. *yerking*] lashing out with hooves (*OED v* 5); cf. *Henry V*, 'our wounded steeds / Fret fetlock-deep in gore, and with wild rage / Yerk out their armèd heels at their dead masters' (4.7.76–8).
35. *high courage*] Levinson's suggestion (p. xvii) of 'hie' in place of *Q*'s 'hid' seems apt, the sense being 'your courage [alone] cannot bear the sail that your spirit deserves'.
45. *hold crack*] *Q*'s 'wrack' makes little sense; Adams's suggestion of 'crack' is consistent with 'loud talk, boast, brag' (*OED sb* 4). The line being short, some other (two-syllable) word might have been intended.

Like furious lightning in the hand of Jove,
To dash thy pride, and like a raging storm
To tear those Turkish flags that spread their silks   55
Upon the strands of peaceful Africa?
And quak'st not, slave, with terror of the same?
Muly Hamet. Dare but my brother's bastard and a slave,
That should have kneeled at Abdelmelec's feet,
Send these proud threats from his audacious lips?   60
Muly Mahamet. Down, dog, and crouch before the feet
Of great Morocco, of mighty Fez.
But why vouchsafe I language to this slave?
Hear me, Sebastian, thou brave Portuguese:
I, Muly Hamet, King of mighty Sus,   65
Whose country's bounds and limits do extend
From mighty Atlas, over all those lands
That stretch themselves to the Atlantic sea,
And look upon Canary's wealthy isles,
And on the west to Gibaltaras' straits,   70
Those fruitful forelands, and the famous towns,
Assure Sebastian, King of Portugal,
Most glorious and triumphant victory.
Abdelmelec. Hear me, Sebastian, hear me, youthful King,
And Abdelmelec will receive thee yet   75
And clip thee in the arms of gentle peace.
Forsake this tyrant and join hands with me,
And at thy pleasure quietly possess
The towns thou hold'st in Afric at this day,
Tangier, Zahara, Ceuta, Penon, Melilla,   80

---

72. Portugal] *This ed.;* portingall *Q;* Portingall *Simpson.*   80. Tangier] *This ed.;*
Aginer *Q.*   Zahara] *This ed.;* Zahanra *Q.*   Ceuta] *This ed.;* Seuta *Q.*

53. *lightning ... Jove*] Jove's bird, the eagle, is often depicted with lightning bolts
in its talons; cf. *Metamorphoses*, 'that bird whose talons bear the bolts / Of thunder,
favourite of heaven's king' (12.562–3).

55. *Turkish flags*] The Turks, who started on Abdelmelec's side, but were with Muly
Mahamet at 19.50, are now once again with Abdelmelec and Muly Mahamet Seth,
where they remain for the rest of the fight.

58. *my brother's bastard*] Cf. 14.16, where Muly Mahamet is said to be
Abdelmelec's brother.

65. *Sus*] Leo Africanus places the region of Sus as 'situate beyond Atlas, over against
the territorie of Hea, that is to say, the extreme part of Africa. Westward it beginneth
from the Ocean sea, and southward from the sandie deserts; on the north it is bounded
with the utmost town of Hea; on the east with that mighty river whereof the whole
region is named' (Brown, p. 248).

70. *Gibaltaras*] Q's metrical spelling is here retained; cf. 14.149.

80. *Tangier*] Q's 'Aginer' must be a misprint (Sugden); replacing it with Tangier
makes the line almost metrical.

Which Muly Mahamet will disposess thee of,
If by thy means he should obtain the day.
Sebastian. Say, Abdelmelec, tell me, wilt thou yet
Dismiss thy power, break these rebellious arms,
Which now thou bearest 'gainst the King of Fez?   85
And great Sebastian, King of Portugal,
Yet of Mahamet will obtain thy life.
Muly Hamet. Look on the power that Abdelmelec brings
Of brave resolvèd Turks and valiant Moors,
Approved Alarbes, puissant argolets   90
As numberless as be these Afric's sands,
And turn thee then and leave thy petty power,
The succour failing you expect from Spain,
And bow thy knees for mercy, Portugal.
Antonio. Our very slaves, our negroes, muleteers,   95
Able to give you battle in the field,
Then think of those that you must cope withal:
The Portugal and his approvèd power,

---

86. Portugal] *This ed.*; Portingall *Q*; Portingale *Simpson.*   90. Alarbes] *This ed.*;
Alarkes *Q*.   94. Portugal] *This ed.*; Portingall *Q (& l. 98).*

Zahara] Assuming 'Aginer' is Tangier, Abdelmelec's list of towns moves east along
the Barbary coast. Polemon's 'Zahara' (sig. R4r), which I adopt for *Q*'s 'Zahanra', is
an approximation of 'El-Ksar es Saghir'. Leo Africanus writes, 'Of the towne called
Casar Ezzaghir, that is, the little palace: this towne was built by Mansor the King and
Patriarke of Maroco upon the ocean seas shore, about twelve from Tangia and from
Septa eighteene miles . . . the King of Portugall toke [it] by a sudden surprise . . . in the
yeere of the Heigeira 863 [1458]' (Brown, p. 508).

Ceuta] the Spanish name for the ancient port of Septum, in Leo Africanus 'the great
citie of Septa . . . called by the Latines *Civitas*, and by the Portugals *Seupta*, was (according to our most approved authors) built by the Romanes upon the streits of Gibraltar,
being in olde time the head citie of all Mauritania, wherefore the Romanes made great
account thereof' (Brown, p. 509).

Penon] Penon de Velez, on the north coast of Morocco, half-way between Ceuta and
Melilla (Sugden). In 1564 Sir Thomas Chaloner, England's ambassador to Spain (see p.
5), reported a Spanish action against 'Pennon de Velez, a hold of strong style in
Barbarie and of grete importaunce for this countrey, lyeing not farre from the Straightes'
(Castries, 1: 83–4).

Melilla] A Moroccan port, about 170 miles east of the Straits of Gibraltar (Sugden).
Leo Africanus notes, 'this great and ancient towne built by the Africans upon a certaine bay or haven of the Mediterran sea . . . was called Mellela, which word in their
language signifieth honie' (Brown, p. 533).

90. *Alarbes*] Arabs, from the medieval Spanish *alárabe* or *alárave*; 'Alarbes' in
Polemon (sig. U1v), often seen as 'Alarves' or 'Larbies' in English texts.

argolets] See *Alcazar*, n. 1.2.2.

Muly Mahamet and his valiant Moors,
The Irish Marquess Stukeley and his troops   100
Of warlike Germans and Italians,
Alvares, Caesar, Meneses and Avero.
Proud Abdelmelec, kneel and beg for grace.
Abdelmelec. Then, proud Sebastian, I deny all means.
Muly Hamet. Therefore, Mahamet and Sebastian, farewell.   105

[*Exeunt.*]

Scene 23

Excursions. [Then] enter SEBASTIAN, ANTONIO, AVERO *and*
STUKELEY *in counsel together.*

Sebastian. Advise us, lords, if we this present night
Shall pass the river of Mucazen here,
Upon whose sandy banks our tents are pitched,
Or stay the morning fresh approaching sun.
Avero. In my opinion let us not remove.   5
The night is dark, the river passing deep
And we ourselves and all my troops, my lord,
Exceeding weary with the last day's march.
Antonio. My lord Avero counsels well, methinks.
Sebastian. What's your opinion, Marquess of Ireland?   10
Stukeley. My lord, might I persuade, neither tonight
Nor in the morning should ye cross the river.
Our men are weak, the enemy is strong,
Our men are feeble, they in perfect health.
Beside, 'tis better discipline, I judge,   15
To let them seek us here, than we them there,
Considering what advantage may be had
'Gainst them that first attempt to pass the river.

---

102. Meneses] *This ed.;* Menesis *Q.*   105. SD.] *This ed.; not in Q.*

Scene 23] *This ed.;* Sc. xxiii. *Levinson; not in Q.*   OSD.] *subst. Q.*   2. Mucazen]
This ed.; Mezaga *Q.*   3. sandy] *Simpson;* sundry *Q.*   15. Beside, 'tis] *This ed.;*
Beside tis *Q;* Beside his *Simpson.*

---

102. *Alvares, Caesar, Meneses and Avero*] See 19.89–93.

Scene 23] The setting is the Portuguese camp, near Alcazar.
    2. *Mucazen*] Alcazar is near the confluence of three rivers, so the site of the
Portuguese camp is a matter of some confusion. *Q*'s 'Mezaga' must be an attempt at
the *Uniting*'s 'Mucazen', i.e. the Wad el Mekhazen: 'the same day the Portugals had
passed Mucazen, and come to their fifth lodging, they were in doubt whether to
encampe on this side or on the other side of a small river, which begins in the marshes
of Alcasarquivir, part of the armie having passed the water, they turned head, resolv-
ing to lodge on this side' (p. 38).

Again, on this side whatsoever fall
We have Larissa and Morocco both,   20
Strong towns of succour to retire unto.
Sebastian. Retire unto? Talks Stukeley of retreat?
Are you invested with a marquess' name,
Graced with the title of a fiery spirit,
Renowned, and talkest so of fortitude,   25
And lurks there in your breast so mean a thought?
Can there issue from your lips a term,
So base and beggarly, as that of flight?
I rather thought that Stukeley would have said
'We bate here and are not swift enough   30
In seeking fit time to begin the fight'.
Stukeley. Conceit me not, Sebastian, at the worst.
You craved my counsel and in that respect
I speak my conscience. If you like it not
Condemn me not therefore of cowardice,   35
For what I said was as a faithful friend,
Careful we should embrace the safest course.
But as I am Tom Stukeley and a captain,
Never known yet to stand in fear of death,
Rise when you will, his foot that is the foremost,   40
His sword that's soonest drawn, my foot and sword
Shall be as forward and as quickly drawn.
Nay, do but follow and I'll lead the way,
I'll be the first shall wade up to the chin,
Or pass Mucazen's channel, and the first   45
Shall give assault unto the enemy,
So little do I fear th'extremest brunt
Or hardest fortune that attends on war.

                    Enter MULY [MAHAMET].

Muly Mahamet. To arms, brave King, to arms, courageous lords!
Bright crested victory doth waft us on,   50
And all advantages that may be had,
Offer to fill our hands with wishèd spoil
And cheer our hearts with endless happiness.
False Abdelmelec mortally is sick –

41. that's] *Simpson*; that *Q.* 45. Mucazen's] *This ed.*; Mezagas *Q.* 51. advan-
tages] *Simpson*; advantage *Q.*

---

30. *bate*] lit. 'beat our wings' (*OED* v^1 2a), the figurative sense is 'wait restlessly';
cf. *Romeo and Juliet*, 'my unmanned blood, bating in my cheeks' (3.2.14).
32 *Conceit*] imagine, think (*OED* v 2).
54. *Abdelmelec mortally is sick*] In *Alcazar* (4.2.36–60) Muly Mahamet does not
mention this.

For fear, I think, that we shall vanquish him.   55
His soldiers mutinise, and his best friends
Begin to waver and mistrust the cause,
Of which three thousand of his stout Alarbs,
Men very expert with the shield and lance,
This night are fled to us, who likewise tell   60
Of many thousands more that will revolt.
Were we but ordered once within the field,
I dare assure, ye had not crossed the river
(As now the daybreak calls us to labour),
So that there might be expeditious means   65
For such as do affect us to depart,
Half Abdelmelec's army would forsake him.
Sebastian. No longer, great Mahamet, will we linger.
We gave direction by our pioneers,
So soon as any beams of light appeared   70
Within the east, to settle to their work
And make our passage smoother through the ford,
And lest they loiter, we ourself in person
Will overlook them, that by ten o'clock,
Within yonder plain adjacent to Alcazar,   75
The lot of happy Fortune may be cast.
Come, lords, and each unto his several charges.
Muly Mahamet. Bravely resolved! Myself will follow you,
And so it happen that Mahamet speed,
I reck not who or Turk or Christian bleed.   *Exeunt.*   80

Scene 24

The trumpets sounding to the battle. Enter ABDELMELEC *and*
SEBASTIAN, *fighting; after them again,* MULY MAHAMET, *and*
MULY HAMET. *Then* ANTONIO, *with some other[s] passing away.*
Then they retire back, [leaving] ABDELMELEC *alone in the battle.*

Abdelmelec. Fetch me one drop of water, any man,
And I will give him Tangier's wealthy town.

58. Alarbs] *This ed.;* Alarks *Q.*   80. reck] *This ed.;* wreck *Q.*

Scene 24] *This ed.;* Sc. xxiv. *Levinson; not in Q.*   OSD.] *subst. Q.*   2. Tangier's]
This ed.; Taneers *Q.*

56–67. The idea, buried within a maze of subordinate clauses, is that, the moment
the Portuguese cross the river, Abdelmelec's army will desert him.
69. *pioneers*] See *Alcazar*, n. 4.1.8.
80. *reck*] care, give heed to; cf. *Hamlet*, 'and recks not his own rede' (1.3.51).

Scene 24] This and the remaining scenes occur on the field of battle.
OSD. Enter . . . fighting] This contradicts the information given at 23.54 that Abdelmelec is mortally ill; in *Alcazar* he is too sick to fight, entering 'in his chair' (5.1 OSD).
2. *Tangier's*] the only candidate for Q's 'Taneers', although it belonged to Portugal.

The sands of Afric are so parching hot
That when our blood doth light upon the earth,
The drops do seethe like cauldrons as they stand,   5
Till made like ink it cleave unto the hooves
Of our fierce jennets, which sink underneath us,
Overcome with heat. Some water, water, how!

> [*Enter*] SOLDIER, *running in haste.*

Soldier. My lord, you have been very lately sick
    And scarcely yet recovered your disease.   10
    Withdraw yourself out of the murdering press.
    Hazard not so the safety of us all.
Abdelmelec. Go, slave, and preach unto the droughty earth,
    Persuade it if thou canst to shun the rain;
    My soul to death is thirsty for revenge.   15
    Rush through the ranks, let the proud Christians know
    That Abdelmelec vows their overthrow.

> [*Exeunt*] *running.*

Scene 25

Enter SEBASTIAN.

Sebastian. The sun so heats our armour with his beams
    That it doth burn and sear our very flesh,
    That when we would stretch out our arms to strike,
    Our parchèd sinews crack like parchment's scrolls
    And fly in sunder, that our arms stands out   5
    Stiff as our lances, and our swords fall down
    And stick their envious points into the earth.

> [*Enter* MULY MAHAMET] *panting for breath.*

---

6. hooves] *This ed.;* hoove *Q.* 7. sink] *This ed.;* sunke *Q.* 8. SD.] *This ed.;*
Running in hast *below* Soldier SH. *Q.* 17. SD.] *This ed.;* Exit runing *Q.*

Scene 25] *This ed.;* Sc. xxv. *Levinson; not in Q.* 4. parchment's] *This ed.;* parchment
conj. Adams; parchments *Q.* 7. SD.] *This ed.; entry direction not in Q,* panting for
breath *below l. 6.*

---

7. *sink*] Q has 'sunk', but the sense seems to require the present tense.

5. *in sunder*] asunder, apart; cf. *White Devil,* 'like bones which broke in sunder'
(2.1.143).
    stands] See n. 10.48.
7 SD.] In dramatic manuscripts, stage directions are often written at the margin.
With Muly Mahamet's entry direction either absent or missed, the compositor placed

Muly Mahamet. There never yet was such a heat before
  Since Phaethon set this universe on fire,
  That the earth, fearing he had lived again   10
  And got into the chariot of the sun,
  Opens her wide mouth like a gaping hell.
Sebastian. (*Hastily*) Muly Mahamet, say, how stands the day?
Muly Mahamet. Fly, fly, Sebastian, for the foe prevails.
  Dughal, who led five thousand men of war,   15
  Is now revolted to the enemy.
  Farewell Sebastian, this our latest night
  I will assay to save myself by flight.

                              [*Exit* MULY MAHAMET.]

  Enter a company, set upon SEBASTIAN, *and kill him. They go out*
  [*carrying his body*]. *Enter a* soldier *bringing in* ABDELMELEC
        on his back, MULY HAMET *following.*

---

12. hell] *This ed.;* wall *Q.*   13. SD. *hastily*] *rt mgn, l.* 12 *Q.*   15. Dughal] *This ed.;*
Dugall *Q.*   18. SD. *Exit* MULY MAHAMET] *This ed.; not in Q.*   carrying his body]
This ed.; not in Q.   MULY HAMET] *This ed.;* muli-mahamet *Q.*

---

panting for breath one line too high. The placing of such directions is part of a major
textual crux at 27.13; see pp. 46–8.

  9. *Phaethon*] See n. 21.27–8.

  12. *hell*] *Q* reads 'wall', but all the imagery refers to the scorching heat of the day.
The words could easily be mistaken in Elizabethan handwriting; cf. *Alcazar*, n. 1.2.84.

  13 SD. *Hastily*] 'Hastily', at the right margin in *Q*, is more apt for an entry or exit
direction, but Muly Mahamet enters five lines earlier, and does not exit for another six;
cf. 25.7 SD.

  15. *Dughal*] The turning point of the battle of ar-Rukn (fought offstage in *Alcazar*,
1.2) was the defection of Said ad-Dughali, who commanded Muly Mahamet's Andalusian
regiment, to Abdelmelec (Cook, pp. 243–4). The author of this scene would have read of
this earlier battle in Polemon: 'the furious tempest continued so long, untill that
Mahamets armie being wearied both in heart and bodie, turned their backes. The fault of
that flight was ascribed to one Dugall, who being Captaine of the Andalousians, revolted
from Mahamet to Abdelmelec, with two thousande verie choice harquebuziers' (sig. S4r).

  17 *latest*] last, final; cf. Henry V at Harfleur, 'How yet resolves the Governor of the
town? / This is the latest parle we will admit' (3.3.84–5).

  18 SD.] Levinson marks the beginning of a new scene here, but the action would
have been continuous, without the stage ever clearing. From this point onwards my
scene division and numbering differs from Levinson's.

  carrying his body] In *Alcazar*, bodies are left on stage with no one to remove them
(see n. 5.1.57 SD). Here, we might assume that Sebastian's body is taken off, so it can
be brought on later – one did not kill a king in battle and leave the body for someone
else to claim the credit. Indeed, it is astonishing that Sebastian was slain at Alcazar,
rather than captured and held for what would have been, literally, a 'king's ransom'.
This would have been a contributing factor to the stories of various impostors claim-
ing to be the escaped king.

Muly Hamet. I ever feared that my courageous brother
  Would wade so far into this storm of war   20
  That he would be too lavish of his person.
Soldier. My lord, he died not by the dint of sword,
  But being overcome with toil and heat,
  Not well recovered of his dangerous sickness,
  Sunk down for faintness and gave up his soul.   25
Muly Hamet. In the secretest manner that thou canst devise,
  Convey his royal corse into our tent,
  For if his death should once be blown abroad,
  It were a means to overthrow the day.
                 Exit SOLDIER *carrying [the] body.*

         Enter a SOLDIER *running.*

  Speak, slave, who has th'advantage of the day?   30
Soldier. Our valiant Turks and Moors have got the field,
  Sebastian slain, Muly Mahamet fled,
  And Abdelmelec crowned with victory.
Muly Hamet. Shine, glorious sun, and bear unto the west
  News of our conquest, and fright those that dwell   35
  Under our feet with terror of our name.
  Rein in thy fiery palfreys yet awhile
  And trot them softly on those airy planks,
  To look upon the glory of the day.
                       [Exeunt.]

                   Scene 26

     Enter Don ANTONIO, *disguised like a priest,*
        fearfully looking about him.

Antonio. Ah, poor Antonio, which way canst thou take,
  But dreadful horror dogs thee at the heels?
  Sebastian slain, Muly Mahamet fled,

26. secretest] *Simpson;* secrets *Q.*   29. SD.] *This ed.; sentences in reverse order Q.*
39. SD.] *This ed.;* Exit *Q.*

Scene 26] *This ed.;* Sc. xxvii *Levinson; not in Q.*

OSD.] As amazing as it sounds, the story of Antonio's disguise seems to have been true; H. V. Livermore notes that Don Antonio 'managed to keep his identity concealed and was ransomed in the guise of a parish priest' (*A History of Portugal*, Cambridge, 1947, pp. 262–3). The episode is also recounted by Anthony Munday, *The Strangest Adventure that ever Happened*, London, 1601, sig. F2r; see also p. 37.

All Portugal's brave infantries slain
And not a man of mark or note alive.   5
Thou, glad to hide thee in a priest's disguise,
Thy chaplain that came with thee to the war
And in this battle likewise lost his life.
Heaven – be thou pleased – this yet may stand instead,
If not, thy will then be accomplishèd.   10

        Enter three or four Turkish SOLDIERS.

First Soldier. See, here's a priest yet left alive.
Sirrah, come hither, how hast thou escaped?
What, shall we kill him?
Second Soldier. No, kill him not, first let us ransack him.
What hast thou, sirrah, that may save thy life?   15
Antonio. All that I have, my friends, I'll give ye freely,
So it may please ye but to save my life,
Which to destroy will do ye little good.
Second Soldier. Come then, be brief. Let's see, what hast thou?
Antonio. This purse containeth all the coin I have.   20
These bracelets my dead lord bestowed on me,
That if I 'scaped, I might remember him
In my devotions and my daily prayers.
Second Soldier. Whose priest wast thou?
Antonio.   Ferdinand's, Duke of Avero's.
Second Soldier. Well listen, fellows, 'twill do us little good   25
To kill him when we may make benefit
By selling of him to be some man's slave.
And now I call to mind the wealthy Moor,
Amaleck that dwells here in Fez, he'll give
As much as any man. How say ye,   30
Shall it be so?
First Soldier.   No better counsel can be.
Antonio. Thy will, O God, be done, whate'er become of me.

                                     [*Exeunt.*]

---

4. Portugal's] *This ed.;* Portingalls *Q;* Portingales *Simpson.*   11. SH.] *This ed.;* 1.
Soul *Q;* 1 Sol. *Simpson.*   14. SH.] *This ed.;* 2. Soul *Q;* 2 Sol. *Simpson.*   29. here in
Fez, he'll give / As much] *This ed.;* in the Fesse, Heele give as much / as *Q.*   31b. SH.]
This ed.; 1. Sol. *Simpson;* 2. Soul *Q.*   32. SD.] *This ed.; not in Q.*

---

24. Ferdinand's] The Duke of Avero who died at Alcazar was Jorge de Lencastre
(see *Alcazar*, n. 2.4.54).
29. *here in Fez*] *Q*'s 'the Fesse', part of a run-on line, is very odd. Removing the
article makes the line somewhat more metrical, assuming 'Amaleck' is pronounced 'a-
MAL-ek'.

Scene 27

[*Enter*] CHORUS.

Chorus. Thus of Alcazar's battle in one day
Three kings at once did lose their hapless lives.
Your gentle favour must we needs entreat,
For rude presenting such a royal fight,
Which more imagination must supply   5
Than all our utmost strength can reach unto.
Suppose the soldiers, who you saw surprised
The poor dismayèd Prince Antonio,
Have sold him to the wealthy Moor they talked of,
And that such time as needs must be allowed,   10
Already he hath passed in servitude.
Sit now and see unto our story's end,
All those mishaps that this poor prince attend.
                                                     [*Exit.*]

Scene 28

Enter STUKELEY, *faint and weary being wounded, with him* VERNON.

Stukeley. Come, noble Vernon. That I meet you here,
Were the day far more bloody than it is,
Our hope more desperate and our lives beset
With greater peril than we can devise,
Yet should I laugh at death and think this field   5
But as an easy bed to sleep upon.
Vernon. O Master Stukeley, since there now remains
No way but one, and life must here have end,
Pardon my speech, if in a word or two,
Whilst here we breathe us, I discharge my soul: 10

Scene 27] *This ed.; not in Q or Levinson.*   OSD.] *This ed.;* Chorus *Q.*   1. SH.] *This
ed.; not in Q.*   11. passed] *Simpson;* past *Q.*   13. SD.] *This ed.;* After antonio's
going out / Enter Muly hamet with victorie *Q.*

Scene 28] *This ed.;* Sc. xxix *Levinson; not in Q.*

Scene 27] The exit of Antonio and his captors is one of many missing directions in
Q. The stage being clear, the entrance of the Chorus marks a new scene.
  12–13.] Antonio's further mishaps never appear (see p. 46).
  13 SD.] Q's direction at this point is 'After antonio's going out / Enter Muly hamet
with victorie'. For discussion of this matter see pp. 46–7.

Scene 28] This is the final scene in Q, inserted here to restore what is more likely to
have been the intended order (see p. 48).

I must confess, your presence I have shunned,
Not that I hate you, but because thereby
That grief which I did study to forget
Was still renewed, and therefore when we met,
In Ireland, Spain and at the last in Rome,   15
And that I saw I could no way direct
My course but always you were in my way,
I thought if Europe I forsook, that then
We should be far enough disjoined. But lo,
Even here in Afric we are met again   20
And now there is no parting but by death.
Stukeley. And then I hope that we shall meet in heaven.
Why, Master Vernon, in our birth we two
Were so ordained to be of one self heart,
To love one woman, breathe one country air,   25
And now at last, as we have sympathised
In our affections, led one kind of life,
So now we both shall die one kind of death,
In which let this our special comfort be,
That though this parchèd earth of Barbary   30
Drink no more English blood but of us twain,
Yet with this blood of ours the blood of kings
Shall be commixed, and with their fame our fame
Shall be eternised in the mouths of men.
Vernon. Forgive me then my former fond conceits   35
And ere we die let us embrace like friends.
Stukeley. Forgive me, rather, that must die before
I can requite the friendship you have shown.
                                        [They] embrace.
So this is all the will and testament
That we can make: our bodies we bequeath   40
To earth from whence they came, our souls to heaven,
But for a passing bell to toll our knell,
Ourselves will play the sextons and our swords
Shall ring our farewell on the burgonets
Of these bloodthirsty and uncivil Turks.   45

    Enter four or five Italian SOLDIERS. *They lay hands on him.*

Soldier. See where he is. Lay hands upon him, sirs.
Stukeley. Soldiers, what mean ye? Will you mutinise?

---

38. SD.] *This ed.;* Imbrace Q.   46. SH.] *This ed.; not in Q.*

---

   15. *at the last in Rome*] Whether or not the play as first performed had a Roman
sequence is discussed on pp. 44–5.

Vernon. He is your leader. Do you seek his life?
Soldier. [. . .] To lead us to destruction, but if he
   Had kept his oath he swore unto the Pope,   50
   We had been safe in Ireland, where now
   We perish here in Afric. But before
   We taste of death, we vow to see him dead.
   Then, brave Italians, stab him to the heart,
   That hath so wickedly behalved your lives.   55
Vernon. First, villains, you shall triumph in my death
   And either kill me too or set him free.
Stukeley. Hear me, you bloody villains.
Soldier.   Stab him, soldiers.
   VERNON *fights with some of them to save Stukeley and is*
     slain of them. In the mean while the rest stab Stukeley.
Stukeley. O have you slain my friend.
Soldier.   Yet doth he prate.
Stukeley. England, farewell. What fortune never yet   60
   Did cross Tom Stukeley in, to show her frown,
   By treason suffers him to be overthrown.
         Dies. [Exeunt SOLDIERS, *with bodies.]*

Scene 29

Enter MULY HAMET *with victory.*

Soldier. [. . .] The certain number that can yet be found.
   And of the Christian lords, the Duke of Avero

---

49. SH.] *This ed.;* 2 Q *(& ll. 58b, 59b).*   55. behalved] *This ed.;* behavide Q; bereaved *Simpson.*   62. SD. *Exeunt* SOLDIERS, *with bodies*] *This ed.; not in* Q.

Scene 29] *This ed.;* Sc. xxviii. *Levinson; not in* Q.   OSD]. *This ed.;* After antonio's going out / Enter Muly hamet with victorie Q.   2. lords, the] *This ed.;* lords / The Q. Avero / And] *This ed.;* averro: and Q.

---

49. *To lead us*] Some text is missing; the soldier's answer seems to start in the middle of a sentence.

55. *behalved*] the most likely reading for Q's 'behavide', a nonce word for 'shortened'.

Scene 29] This is the penultimate scene in Q, but placing it at the play's end resolves some textual problems. It also seems more likely that the play would close with a triumphant summing up by the victors, as do *Alcazar* and many other plays of the period (see pp. 45–8).

1. *certain number*] Clearly the number of enemy dead, but no one has asked the soldier for a report – a speech or speeches must have have been left out.

And the bishops of Coimbra and Oporto
The Irish marquess, Stukeley, Count Tavora,
Two hundred of the chief nobility of Portugal   5
And Muly Mahamet, passing of the ford
Of swift Larissa to escape by flight,
His horse and he both drownèd in the river.
Muly Hamet. See that the body of Sebastian,
Have Christian and kingly burial   10
After his country's manner, for in life
A braver spirit ne'er lived upon the same;
And let the Christian bodies be interred.
For Muly Mahamet, let his skin be flayed
From off the flesh from foot unto the head   15
And stuffed within, and so be borne about
Through all the parts of our dominions,
To terrify the like that shall pursue
To lift their swords against their sovereign.
And in memorial of this victory,   20
For ever after be this fourth of August
Kept holy to the service of our gods,
Through all our kingdoms and dominions.

                                          [*Exeunt.*]

                        Finis

3. bishops of Coimbra and Oporto] *n. Simpson*; bish. of Cambra, and Portua *Q*.   4.
Tavora] *This ed.*; Tanara *Q*.   5. Portugal] *This ed.*; Portingall *Q*; Portingale *Simpson*.
11. country's] *This ed.*; country *Q*.   23. SD. *Exeunt*] *This ed.*; *not in Q*.   Finis] *At
end prev. sc. Q*.

   3. *bishops of Coimbra and Oporto*] Polemon (sig. Y1ʳ) and the *Uniting* (p. 52)
report the death of the two bishops. *Q*'s 'Portua' for 'Oporto' comes from Polemon;
the *Uniting* has 'Porto'.
   7. See *Alcazar*, n. 4.2.42, 5.1.204.

APPENDIX I

THE BATTLE OF ALCAZAR:
PISANO, JONAS AND HERCULES

In naming Muly Mahamet's captain of horse Pisano (1.2.1), Peele set off a chain reaction of textual difficulties that all editors of this play have struggled to resolve. The name Pisano (i.e. 'the Pisan') comes from Captain Hercules de Pisa, as he is called in the *Uniting*,[1] and who was one of Stukeley's, not Muly Mahamet's, captains. Appointed by the Pope to lead the Italian troops, Pisano is described in Philip O'Sullevan's *Compendium* (1621) as 'a brave man and famed for his skill in military matters'.[2] He and Stukeley enjoyed a deep mutual hatred; upon arriving in Lisbon, Pisano sent a blistering report back to Rome, saying Stukeley's conduct 'is much which, indeed, it disgusts me to have to report', and accusing the Englishman of having no real interest in restoring the faith in Ireland, concluding, 'it seems that our Lord [the Pope] has been deceived'.[3]

Pisano's capture at Alcazar was noted by Bastiano San Giuseppe, the Pope's paymaster and commissary, who remained behind in Lisbon. After the battle he learned from some surviving Portuguese soldiers that the Italians

> thrice repulsed the furious onset of the foe; and the Portuguese themselves say that they verily died like Romans, for so they called them. Of a truth they may be deemed to have fought bravely, as no more than ten or fifteen at the most of those that were in the field were made slaves; among whom is Captain Hercole del Mastro da Pisa.[4]

The most likely reason for Peele's placing Pisano at the side of Muly Mahamet is that he wanted Muly's soldiers to be led by a renegade, when in fact it was Abdelmelec who placed Christians who had 'turned Turk' in command.[5]

Peele also departs from the historical record, and creates something of a mess, by making Stukeley's captains in 2.2 English instead of Italian: perhaps dramatically effective, but then he should not have named one of them 'Hercules', after the very same Pisano.[6] At the play's end, Stukeley is killed by his own soldiers, now Italians as they should have been all along, while retaining their English names in speech headings – Greg's surmise that this is the result of the same actors doubling the parts may be correct.[7]

In one sense, this is a problem only for readers: an audience in the theatre does not hear speech headings, and since 'Hercules' and 'Pisano' are not spoken together, Stukeley's assailants are simply Italian soldiers. But two completely new characters at this stage would be unlikely; in their short speeches the Italians sound like captains, not footsoldiers, and, even if they wore a different type of stage armour, spectators would have to wonder what happened to Jonas and Hercules. More likely, this is one of the many 'false starts' to be found in plays of this period, something that undoubtedly would have been resolved in performance, but not in the printer's copy. Unfortunately the document that would reveal all, the Plot, survives only for Acts 1–4.

NOTES

1 *Uniting*, p. 41; he is 'Capitano Hercole di Pisa' in *Dell'unione* (E4r).
2 Philip O'Sullevan, 'Compendium of the History of Catholic Ireland', in *Ireland under Elizabeth: Chapters towards a History of Ireland in the Reign of Elizabeth, being a portion of the History of Catholic Ireland*, trans. from the Latin by M. J. Byrne, Dublin, 1903, p. 20.
3 *CSP Rom.* (1572–78), pp. 443–4 (29 May 1578).
4 *CSP Rom.* (1572–78), p. 510 (29 Sept. 1578); see also pp. 8–10.
5 See n. 1.1.12.
6 'Jonas' appears to be fictional, unless he is *Giovanni* Rubiano, who shared command with Ercole da Pisa and who also complained bitterly about Stukeley; see *CSP Rom.* (1572–78) pp. 444–5 (29 May 1578). Giovanni, however, does not appear in the *Uniting*.
7 Greg, p. 118.

APPENDIX II

THE BATTLE OF ALCAZAR:
THE IRISH BISHOP

Commentators have searched for an historical counterpart for the Irish 'Bishop of Saint Asses' (2.2.49), a difficult task given that 'Asses' is an obvious pun on 'Saint Asaph', which is in Wales, not Ireland. More probably, the character is a composite of one English and several Irish clerics.

The pun on 'Asaph' must refer to Thomas Goldwell (d. 1585), who was elevated to the bishopric during the reign of Queen Mary; with the accession of Elizabeth, he became a leading member of the English Catholic community in Rome and, much to Elizabeth's annoyance, was a delegate to the Council of Trent in 1562. In *The English Romayne Life*, Anthony Munday describes the conversion sermons Rome's Jews were required to attend, noting that 'when any of them dooth chaunge his faith ... then is he there baptized by an English man, who is named Bishop Goldwell, sometime the Bishop of S. Asaph in Wales: he hath this office, maketh all the English priests in the colledge, and liveth there among the Theatines verye pontificallye'.[1] While Goldwell must have known Stukeley in Rome, there is no record of his accompanying him to Spain or Portugal.

Were it not for the pun, the best candidate would be Maurice Gibbon Fitzgibbon, Archbishop of Cashel, who represented the Earl of Desmond to both the Pope and Philip II. When Stukeley arrived in Spain, Cashel first urged Philip to make use of the Englishman, describing him as 'a very daring man, clever in war matters, in which he has been engaged most of his life',[2] but they soon became fierce rivals for Spanish and Papal favour. Cashel soon wrote again to Philip and to the Papal Nuncio, painting Stukeley's past in the worst possible colours (not hard to do), saying he had committed several murders, and that he 'had destroyed so many churches, monasteries, and images; and what favor could he promise to give, who was a native of England, who was so hated by his own people, and much more hated by the Irish, as well on account of the natural and common hatred the Irish bear against the English'.[3]

Cashel's failure to gain preferment from Philip led him in 1571 to Paris, where he began to play a double game, offering his services to Sir Francis Walsingham, and promising not only to reveal what he knew of Spanish

designs against England but to work for the English in Ireland if Elizabeth would restore him to his bishopric.[4] In April of that year Lord
Cobham wrote to Lord Burghley from Madrid that Cashel was 'a bastard
of the Geraldines', and was 'sent hence in displeasure of the King, for he
defaced Stuckley, and Stuckley discovered the bishop's dissolute life'.[5]

Stukeley's blaming his banishment from Spain on 'a blow [he] gave a
bishop's man' (5.1.151) does not appear to have any direct historical
source, although the Irish State Papers do record an incident that may
have suggested the line: 'the falling out of Stucley with the Bishop of
Cassell [sic] did rise upon this occasion that the Bishop did hide two Irishmen which were fled from Stucley; whereon Stucley came to the Bishop,
and finding his men in the Bishop's chamber threatened the Bishop'.[6]

Cashel was not in Lisbon at the time of Stukeley's arrival, and had no
part in trying to discourage him from diverting the expedition to Africa.
This task fell to the third and fourth bishops on our list, who were indeed
in Lisbon at the crucial moment. James Fagan and Leonard Sutton, two
English merchants, noticed the arrival of 'two Romishe Bishops ...
Conoghour O'Mulryan and Donough Oge O'Gallogher [sic]', with Stuke-
ley and his Italians.[7] The Franciscan friar and Bishop of Killaloe,
Conoghour O'Mulrian (often identified as Cornelius Ryan or Cornelius
O'Melrian), did not journey with Stukeley from Rome as Fagan and
Sutton appear to have thought. In November of 1577, on his way to
Ireland from Portugal, he was robbed by French pirates and had to return;
he was then sent to Madrid as Desmond's agent. Hearing of Stukeley's
landing in Portugal, O'Mulrian went immediately to Lisbon, reporting on
12 April 1578, 'we arrived in good health and spirits at Lisbon; the
Marquis was not there before us, nor to this day have we heard aught
from him'.[8] A month later, Robert Fontana, the Collector Apostolic in
Portugal, wrote to Cardinal Ptolomeo Galli, Secretary to Pope Gregory
XIII, that O'Mulrian was busy urging Stukeley to continue on to Ireland
with his Italian troops.[9]

Donough (or Donat) O'Gallogher, Bishop of Killala, was indeed one
of the clerics who accompanied Stukeley from Rome; his name comes to
light as a signatory to a letter written from Lisbon on 3 June 1578, telling
of Stukeley's generosity towards 'the Most Reverend Donat, Bishop of
Killala' and some other priests: 'We, the underwritten witnesses attest that
the most illustrious and Excellent Lord Thomas Stucley, Marquis of Lein-
ster, upon his arrival at this city of Lisbon, learning the penury of all the
Irishmen that by order of his Holiness accompanied him, convened them
all and offered each of them, according to his rank and the said Marquis's
resources, a daily stipend from his own purse'. Donat and two others
accepted; the rest refused 'the benevolence of the said most illustrious and

excellent Lord Marquis, asserting haughtily and obstinately that they were the subjects of no man, and would receive stipend from no man, save the Supreme Pontiff, or some King or great Prince'.[10] This document shows that Stukeley did not alienate every Irish Bishop he met – at least one, the Bishop of Killala, held him in some esteem.

NOTES

1 Anthony Munday, *The English Romayne Life*, ed. G. B. Harrison, New York, 1925, pp. 45–6.
2 Myles V. Ronan, *The Reformation in Ireland under Elizabeth: 1558–1580*, London, 1930, p. 335.
3 Patrick Francis Moran, *Spicilegium Ossoriense: being a collection of original letters and papers illustrative of the history of the Irish Church from the Reformation to the year 1800*, v. 1, Dublin, 1874, p. 68.
4 See Dudley Digges, *The Compleat Ambassador, or, Two Treaties of the Intended Marriage of Qu. Elizabeth of Glorious Memory*. London, 1655, pp. 58–75.
5 *CSP For.* (1569–71), p. 435 (27 Apr. 1571).
6 Quoted Ronan, p. 373.
7 *SP Ire.* v. 66 (30 Mar. 1579). Fagan and Sutton were deposed in Limerick some months after the events described.
8 *CSP Rom.* (1572–78), p. 402 (12 Apr. 1578).
9 *CSP Rom.* (1572–78), p. 429 (12 May 1578).
10 *CSP Rom.* (1572–78), pp. 449–50 (3 Jun 1578).

APPENDIX III

CAPTAIN THOMAS STUKELEY, SCENE 7:
'IRISH' VERSION

Perhaps the most curious anomaly in *Captain Thomas Stukeley* is the presence of this alternative Scene 7, in which O'Neill and his associates speak and act like 'stage Irishmen', employing many accurate Gaelic expressions. In this edition, names, stage directions and speech headings are regularised, otherwise *Q*'s spelling is retained (except for modernisation of u/v, i/j).

> *Enter* Shane O'NEILL, O'HANLON, *Neil* MACKENER *softly*
> *as by night.*

O'Neill. O'Hanlon.
O'Hanlon. Owe.
O'Neill. Fate is the token? Fate siegne that Brian Mack Phelem said he
    would hang oot?
O'Hanlon. I feate I kno not, ask the Shecretary.   5
O'Neill. Neale Mackener.
Mackener. Hest, Oneale, hest, pease! Too art at the vater seed.
O'Neill. Fate is the token bodeaugh breene? That I sall see ovare the
    valles of this toone of Dundalke.
Mackener. I'feat Oneale thoo art Saint Patrick his cushin and a great   10
    Lord, but thou art not weeze. The siegne is a paire of feete trouzes,
    or a feete shurt, or some feete blankead, to be hang oote ober the
    valles, fan we sall be let in at the lettle booygh dore by the abbay.
O'Neill. Esta clamper, thoo talkest to much the English upon the vall
    will heare the, lake, feagh bodeaugh. Dost thou see any thing feete?   15

OSD.] *subst. Q.* 1 SH.] *This ed.*; Onele, On, Oneale, One *Q.* 2 SH.] *This ed.*;
Humlon, Han. *Q.* 7 SH.] *This ed.*; Mack *Q.*

---

8. *bodeaugh breene*] *bodach bréan*, stinking lout (all definitions from J. O. Bartley, *Teague, Shenkin and Sawney: Being an Historical Account of the Earliest Irish, Welsh, and Scottish Characters in English Plays*, Cork, 1954, p. 272).
    13. *booygh*] *buidheach*, tiny.
    14. *Esta clamper*] *éist do chlampar*, stop your chatter.
    15. *feagh bodeaugh*] *féach bodach*, look you lout.

Mackener. No by this hand, Shan Oneal, we see no feat thing.
                                              One coughs within.
O'Hanlon. Cresh blesh us, fo ish tat ishe coughes?
Mackener. Saint Patrick blesh us, we be not betraid.
O'Neill. Mackener, mack deawle, marafastot art thou a feete liuerd
  kana: Tish some English churle in the toone that coughes, that is   20
  dree, some prood English souldior hees a dree cough, can drinke
  no vater. The English churle dees if he get not bread and porrage
  and a hose to lee in: but looke is the sieegne, oote, zeele cut his
  troate and help him of his cough fan I get into Dundalk.
Mackener. Bee this hand Oneale der is no siegne, zee am afaid Brian   25
  Mack Phelemy is wyd his streepo, and forgeats to hang a siegne or
  let us in.
O'Neill. No matter come, no noyse tis almost day, softly let us creepe
  aboote by the valles seed ane awan sone at night even at shuttene
  of the gates fan Ocane and Magennis come from Carlingford, we   30
  will enter lusttly the town Mackener O Hanlon, zee will giue you
  tree captaines to ransome.
O'Hanlon. Zee wil take tree prishoners and give thee too and take de
  turd my self.
O'Neill. Speake softly, O Hanlon, and gow make ready oore kerne and   35
  gallinglasse against night, and bid my bagpiper be ready to peep
  Ballootherie soon, for I will sleepe in Dundalke at night. Come go
  back into the Fewes again.
O'Hanlon. Slane haggat, Bryan Mac Phelemy.
Mackener. Slane lets, Rorie beg.   40
                                                          Exit.

39, 40 Slane] *This ed.*; Slaue *Q.*

19. *mac deawle*] *mac diabhal*, son of the devil.
marafastot] see n. 7.45.
20. *kana*] *cana*, whelp.
26. *streepo*] *striapach*, whore.
36–7. *peep Ballootherie*] perhaps *ballú*, gathering, or *bailiú tíre*, rallying the country.
The bagpiper is to 'peep' rallying music.
38. *Fewes*] See n. 8.17.
39. *Slane haggat*] *slán agat*, health at you (i.e. goodbye). Q's 'Slaue', here and in the
next line, must be a compositor's error.
40. *Slane lets, Rorie beg*] *slán leatsa Ruaire beag*, health with you (i.e. goodbye)
little Rory.

GLOSSARIAL INDEX TO
THE COMMENTARY

Commentary references for characters are given when the note includes some substantive point of discussion, e.g. Calipolis, or where material regarding the character's historical counterpart is included, e.g. Abdelmelec.

galloglass, *CTS* 7.34
gallows-clapper, *CTS* 2.103
garrans, *CTS* 9.50
German seas, *Alc* 2.4.126
Gibraltar, *CTS* 14.149
Gregory, Pope, *Alc* 2.4.139,
    5.1.156; *CTS* 16.121
gripple, *CTS* 14.211
God's blest, *CTS* 3.87
God's me, *CTS* 2.67
gramercies, *CTS* 9.25
green, *CTS* 5.52
Guadalupea, *Alc* 3.Prol.17
gudgeons, *CTS* 16.154
guerdons, *CTS* 12.81
gyved, *CTS* 3.66

haberdines, *CTS* 10.37
halter-sack, *CTS* 2.107
haps, *CTS* 17.57
harmless, *Alc* 2.3.48
harquebus, *Alc* 4.1.45
hazard, *CTS* 5.75
Henry, Cardinal, *CTS* 19.OSD,
    19.82
Hephaestion, *Alc* 2.4.76
Hercules, *Alc* 2.2.OSD;
    Appendix I
hilts, *CTS* 2.156
hobbies, *CTS* 9.53
holds, *Alc* 3.1.35, 3.2.18
horn-bucklers, *CTS* 2.92
horse and foot, *CTS* 2.183
horse-courser, *CTS* 13.21
hostage, *Alc* 3.4.34
huff, *Alc* 2.2.83
hugy, *Alc* 1.2.62

imagine, *Alc* 2.Prol.32
imbecility, *CTS* 19.82
imp, *Alc* 2.Prol.17–18
India, *Alc* 3.1.27
infortunate, *Alc* 5.1.85
Iris, *Alc* 5.Prol.9

iwis, *CTS* 6.133
Ixion's wheel, *Alc* 4.2.90

janissaries, *Alc* 1.1.32
jennet, *CTS* 22.26
John a-Nokes and John a-Styles,
    CTS 2.167
jointure, *CTS* 2.190
Jonas, *Alc* 2.2. OSD; Appendix I
Jubilee, *CTS* 16.136

kana, Appendix III
keep touch, *CTS* 16.173
kern, *CTS* 7.35
King of a mole-hill, *Alc* 2.2.81

lackey, *CTS* 21.74
Lantado, *CTS* 16.OSD
Larissa, *Alc* 4.2.42, 5.1.204
latest, *CTS* 25.17
laundresses, *Alc* 4.1.11
law French, *CTS* 2.168
leopard, *CTS* 17.68, *CTS* 21.42–3
let, *Alc* 4.2.44
Lethe, *Alc* 5.1.108
lieutenant general, *Alc* 5.1.160
lightfoot, *CTS* 7.35
lightning, *CTS* 22.53
Littleton, *CTS* 2.103–4.
Lodovic, Lord, *Alc* 3.4.72
lonely, *CTS* 21.42–3

MacAngus, *CTS* 12.40
mac deawle, Appendix III
Mackener, Neill, *CTS* 7.OSD
MacPhelim, Brian, *CTS* 7.15
MacSorley, Alexander, *CTS* 12.45
Magennis, Teague, *CTS* 7.35
malice, *CTS* 17.29
marafastot, *CTS* 7.45
marmady, *CTS* 18.4
Marquess, *Alc* 2.2.79
marshalea, *CTS* 13.80
Mazagan, *Alc* 3.4.73